THE DESTRUCTION OF DRESDEN

David Irving is the son of a Royal Navy commander. Educated at Imperial College of Science and Technology and at University College, London, he subsequently spent a year in Germany working in a steel mill and perfecting his fluency in the language. His best-known works include *The War Path: Hitler's Germany 1933–1939*, the two-volume *Hitler's War, The Trail of the Fox: The Life of Field-Marshal Erwin Rommel* (all available in Papermac), *Accident–The Death of General Sikorski* and *The Rise and Fall of the Luftwaffe*. He has translated *The Memoirs of Field-Marshal Keitel* and *The Memoirs of General Reinhard Gehlen*.

DAVID IRVING

THE
DESTRUCTION
OF DRESDEN

With a foreword by
Air Marshal Sir Robert Saundby
Deputy A.O.C-in-C. Bomber Command, 1943-1945

MACMILLAN

First published in Great Britain by William Kimber
& Co. Ltd 1963
Revised and updated 1971 and published by Corgi
Books Ltd

Published 1985 by
PAPERMAC
a division of Macmillan Publishers Limited
4 Little Essex Street London WC2R 3LF
and Basingstoke

Associated companies in Auckland, Delhi, Dublin,
Gaborone, Hamburg, Harare, Hong Kong,
Johannesburg, Kuala Lumpur, Lagos, Manzini,
Melbourne, Mexico City, Nairobi, New York, Singapore
and Tokyo

British Library Cataloguing in Publication Data
Irving, David
     The destruction of Dresden.
     1. World War, 1939-1945—Aerial operations
     2. Dresden (Germany)—Bombardment, 1945
     I. Title
     940.54'21   D785
     ISBN 0-333-40483-1

Printed in Finland by Werner Söderström Oy

FOREWORD

by

AIR MARSHAL SIR ROBERT SAUNDBY

K.C.B., K.B.E., M.C., D.F.C., A.F.C.

When the author of this book invited me to write a foreword to it, my first reaction was that I had been too closely concerned with the story. But though closely concerned I was not in any way responsible for the decision to make a full-scale air attack on Dresden. Nor was my Commander-in-Chief, Sir Arthur Harris. Our part was to carry out, to the best of our ability, the instructions we received from the Air Ministry. And, in this case, the Air Ministry was merely passing on instructions received from those responsible for the higher direction of the war.

This book is an impressive piece of work. The story is a highly dramatic and complex one, which still holds an element of mystery. I am still not satisfied that I fully understand why it happened. The author has, with immense industry and patience, gathered together all the evidence, separated fact from fiction, and given us a detailed account as near to the truth, perhaps, as we shall ever get.

That the bombing of Dresden was a great tragedy none can deny. That it was really a military necessity few, after reading this book, will believe. It was one of those terrible things that sometimes happen in wartime, brought about by an unfortunate combination of circumstances. Those who approved it were neither wicked nor cruel, though it may well be that they were too remote from the harsh realities of war to understand fully the appalling destructive power of air bombardment in the spring of 1945.

The advocates of nuclear disarmament seem to believe that, if they could achieve their aim, war would become tolerable and decent. They would do well to read this book and ponder the fate of Dresden, where 135,000 people died as the result of an air attack with conventional weapons. On the night of March 9th/10th, 1945, an air attack on Tokyo by American heavy bombers, using incendiary and high explosive bombs, caused the death of 83,793 people. The atom bomb dropped on Hiroshima killed 71,379 people.

Nuclear weapons are, of course, far more powerful nowadays, but it is a mistake to suppose that, if they were abolished, great cities could not be reduced to dust and ashes, and frightful massacres brought about, by aircraft using conventional weapons. And the removal of the fear of nuclear retaliation—which makes modern full-scale war amount to mutual annihilation—might once again make resort to war attractive to an aggressor.

It is not so much this or the other means of making war that is immoral or inhumane. What is immoral is war itself. Once full-scale war has broken out it can never be humanized or civilized, and if one side attempted to do so it would be most likely to be defeated. So long as we resort to war to settle differences between nations, so long will we have to endure the horrors, barbarities and excesses that war brings with it. That, to me, is the lesson of Dresden.

Nuclear power has at last brought us within sight of the end of full-scale war. It is now too violent to be a practicable means of solving anything. No war aim, no conceivable gain that war could bring, would be worth a straw when balanced against the fearful destruction and loss of life that would be suffered by both sides.

There has never been the slightest hope of abolishing war by agreement or disarmament, or for reasons of morality and humanity. If it disappears it will be because it has become so appallingly destructive that it can no longer serve any useful purpose.

This book tells, dispassionately and honestly, the story of a deeply tragic example, in time of war, of man's inhumanity to man. Let us hope that the horrors of Dresden and Tokyo, Hiroshima and Hamburg, may drive home to the whole human race the futility, savagery, and utter uselessness of modern warfare.

We must not make the fatal mistake, however, of believing that war can be avoided by unilateral disarmament, by resort to pacifism, or by striving for an unattainable neutrality. It is the balance of nuclear power that will keep the peace until mankind, as some day it must, comes to its senses.

PREFACE

IT is three years since I set out to gather the threads of the story behind the attack on Dresden, to unravel the tangled web of deceit and wartime enemy propaganda spun around the real nature of the target, and to analyse in detail the historical importance of the scheme of attacks during February 1945 in which the three major raids on Dresden found their place. I have tried to reconstruct the attack, minute by minute, throughout the fourteen hours and ten minutes of the triple blow which is estimated authoritatively to have killed more than 135,000 of the population of a city swollen to twice its peace-time size by a massive influx of refugees from the East, Allied and Russian prisoners of war, and thousands of forced labourers. There were, of course, for a variety of reasons, many servicemen in the city, quite apart from those in the military hospitals; the great barracks installations in Dresden-Neustadt alone provided accommodation for several thousands. But these barracks were not made the centre of the attack, and indeed they were undamaged until late April 1945. In the Dresden fire-storm casualties among military personnel were correspondingly light.

As I was warned when I commenced this project, my task was not as straightforward as if the attack on Dresden had been in the earlier years of the war.

For the early part of the war there are series of captured Luftwaffe documents in Washington and London, but the German operational War Diaries of 1945 were almost all destroyed during the days of the final collapse.

The greater part of my work has therefore devolved upon tracing the main personalities and airmen involved in the three raids on Dresden, and retrieving, if only temporarily, their 'souvenirs' for abstracting in this more permanent form. My thanks are due to the two hundred British airmen who readily provided me with the fragments of information I required. Similarly, some hundred American bomber and fighter-escort crews have provided me with details without which the chapter on the American attacks would have been impossible. The narrative account of the Luftwaffe side of the raids is of necessity more sketchy: the number of fighter pilots who not only took part in the defensive actions on the night that Dresden was the Main Force target, but who also survived the war, is indeed not great. I am indebted to the West German newspapers, and especially to the *Deutsches Fernsehen* for assisting me in my efforts to trace the surviving Luftwaffe personnel on whose statements the narrative description of the tragi-comic paralysis of the night fighters on the night of 13th–14th February 1945 is based.

．　　　．　　　．　　　．　　　．

The material for the description of the target, and of the effect of the attack on its inhabitants, comes from a wide variety of sources, not least from the two hundred former Dresden citizens, of whom space is found to identify only a handful in the list of references given at the end of this book; these citizens have provided me with statements on Dresden, and answered a set questionnaire on its industrial and military significance. At a risk of seriously limiting the volume and scope of eye-witness evidence, I have deemed it necessary to ensure that the material stems only from those now living in Western Germany or elsewhere in the free world; seventeen years of communist propaganda, especially on the Dresden tragedy, has not taught those still living in the city any respect for objectivity in their accounts, though I have of necessity consulted publications which have appeared in East Germany.

My gratitude for their assistance is due to Sir Arthur Harris, former Commander-in-Chief of Royal Air Force Bomber Command, and to Air Marshal Sir Robert Saundby, who has exercised his copious memory in recollecting the story behind the execution of the R.A.F. attacks, and who has patiently checked and criticised the text of this book.

In some chapters I have drawn extensively on the masterly official history *The Strategic Air Offensive against Germany 1939–1945* by Sir Charles Webster and Noble Frankland (H.M. Stationery Office, 4 Volumes, 1961). While recording my indebtedness to this work I wish to emphasize that in all passages where I either quote from it or draw on its information any conclusions (unless clearly indicated by quotation marks) are entirely my own. When I use the words 'the Official Historians' I am referring to its authors.

．　　　．　　　．　　　．　　　．

The narrative description of the execution of the attack would have been incomplete without the detailed statistics of the composition of the attacking and Pathfinder forces which were supplied by the Air Ministry's Historical Branch, and the full information provided by the Master Bombers for the two R.A.F. attacks on Dresden, who have also checked the finished manuscripts for flaws or incorrect emphasis in detail. In finding the surviving air personnel from these attacks, many newspapers such as the *Daily Telegraph, Guardian, The Scotsman, New York Times, Washington Post,* the R.A.F. Association's *Air Mail* magazine, and the U.S. Air Force magazine have all rendered indispensable assistance.

Undoubtedly there is much still to be written about the tragedy of Dresden. Some of the mysteries about the destruction of this city will probably always be mysteries. Many of them will certainly be cleared up when the American historian Joseph Warner Angell, Jr., of the U.S.A.F. Historical Division, is permitted to publish his own *Secret* study of the Dresden raids, written several years ago for the American Government. Mr. Angell is the only historian to have had access to a file containing personally signed papers and messages exchanged between Roosevelt, Churchill, Eisenhower, and the latter's Russian counterpart, together with back-up papers by working-level and higher-level staff officers. Both Mr. Angell and I have made repeated requests for the total declassification of this study, and our requests have been generously supported by General Spaatz and other high-ranking U.S.A.F. officers. These attempts have so far been successful in reducing it from its earlier *Top Secret* rating. Perhaps the twentieth anniversary of the event may see the publication of this document too.

Further acknowledgments are due to the Wiener Library, London, for the use of their extensive files of literature of National Socialist and allied countries, particularly for the chapter *The Reaction of the World* where the violent propaganda which countries sympathetic to Germany were able to generate is examined in close detail, particular reference being made to the wireless transmissions picked up by the B.B.C. Monitoring Posts throughout the world.

DAVID IRVING

AUTHOR'S NOTE

Figures for the final Dresden death-roll vary widely. The usual source of information about air raid casualties is the Report of the local Police President; however, neither the Dresden Police President, nor his Report—if indeed ever written—survived the end of the war. Unfortunately, too, the Reich Statistical Office ceased to collate air raid death statistics on 31st January 1945, some two weeks before the Dresden catastrophe.

Throughout this work, therefore, the author has relied on the figure supplied to him by the Dresden official in charge of the *Abteilung Tote* of the Bureau of Missing Persons, on whose final statistics the Police President himself would have relied. He estimated conservatively that 135,000 people were killed, including German and non-German people, and foreign labourers and prisoners of war. At the same time the author was informed by the Federal German Ministry of Statistics that soon after the raids the competent authority in Berlin for air-raid relief and welfare services accepted an estimate of between 120,000 and 150,000 killed in Dresden. The figure of 135,000 is higher than the generally accepted minimum of 35,000, and lower than the 200,000 and even higher figures quoted by American authorities.

The figure will shock many British people to whom it was hitherto unknown; but compassion for German civilians of February 1945 may be coupled with the reflection that for the suffering of civilians of neutral and Allied countries in the Second World War the Germans showed scant sympathy.

CONTENTS

Contents

PART ONE

DRESDEN: THE PRECEDENTS

CHAPTER I

THEY HAVE SOWN THE WIND

AIR historians trace the earliest roots of the area offensive against Germany to the events of 10th May 1940. Prior to this date, aerial attacks had been delivered by the Royal Air Force only against capital ships, bridges or gun installations. In the Nazi invasion of Poland in September 1939 the bombardment of Warsaw by the Luftwaffe which inflicted civilian casualties in that city before it surrendered created a precedent in the British view. It is to be observed that there is no international law specifically covering aerial warfare, though the Nuremberg International Military Tribunal accepted that certain articles of the Hague Convention were applicable to war in the air.

Warships in the Kiel Canal had been attacked as early as 4th September 1939, but it was not until the night of 19th–20th March 1940 that the first bombs were dropped on German soil, when a seaplane base on Sylt was bombed; three days earlier the Luftwaffe had raided the Orkney Islands, killing a British civilian.

The Royal Air Force had nevertheless continued to restrict its operations over Germany to 'nickelling'—dropping leaflets on the Reich, a pursuit which continued up to the evening of 10th May 1940, the day when the German invasion of France and the Low Countries began, but also the day on which Neville Chamberlain, a pronounced opponent of the use of the bomber as a weapon of terrorisation, was replaced by Winston Churchill.

At 3.59 p.m. on a warm but cloudy afternoon of 10th May 1940 in southern Germany, three twin-engined aircraft flying at an altitude around 5,000 feet appeared out of the cumulo-nimbus clouds over Freiburg-im-Breisgau; each dropped a stick of bombs and departed swiftly. The small but powerful 100-pounders exploded very wide of their original aiming point, the fighter airfield: only ten fell on the airfield, while thirty-one, including four failures, fell within the city limits to the west; six fell near the Gallwatz barracks and eleven fell on the Central Station. Two of the bombs fell on a children's playground in Kolmar-strasse. The Police

President reported a total of fifty-seven victims, including twenty-two children, thirteen women, eleven men, and eleven soldiers.

The German Propaganda Ministry's reaction was immediate, and the official D.N.B. News Agency stated that night: 'Three enemy aircraft today bombed the open town of Freiburg-im-Breisgau, which is completely outside the German Zone of Operations and has no military objectives', adding that the German Air Force would answer this 'illegal operation' in a like manner: 'From now on any further systematic enemy bombing of the German population will be returned by a five-fold number of German planes attacking a British or French town.'

A secret report by a Freiburg observation post that it had seen three German Heinkel bombers dropping sticks of bombs on the town only served to deepen the mystery.

The French, however, accused of having executed the attack, insisted that they were innocent, although a Potez 63 aircraft had been seen in the area; satisfied by this plea, the British Air Ministry published a clear warning that they regarded the German allegation as 'untrue and a further example of German mendacity'. They suspected an attempt at fabricating a preliminary justification for a Luftwaffe assault on Allied towns, and on the evening of 10th May the British Government made a formal declaration: while recalling that on 1st September 1939 they had given an assurance to the President of the still, nominally, neutral United States that the Royal Air Force had been given orders prohibiting the bombing of civilian populations—an assurance which it must be stated the British Prime Minister up to 10th May 1940 had rigidly observed—they now publicly proclaimed that they 'reserved the right to themselves of taking any action they considered appropriate' in the event of German air raids on civilian populations. Freiburg had, in fact, been bombed by German planes, though not apparently as part of a deep-laid conspiracy.

On the same day as the Freiburg incident Germany invaded Holland, Belgium and Luxembourg. Although in relation to other events on the same day the Freiburg incident was of minor significance, it was a further blow at the maintenance of humane principles in the conduct of aerial warfare.

·　　·　　·　　·　　·

Four days after the Freiburg affair, the Luftwaffe launched its most ill-famed raid of the whole war, during the battle for courageous Rotterdam. While, like the attack on Freiburg, this raid does not fall within the concept of an area attack, nevertheless any account of the prelude to the bombing war would be grossly incomplete without a description of the circumstances influencing British public opinion towards the later overwhelming attacks of the Royal Air Force on German towns.

The wartime Prime Minister himself afterwards referred to 'the long prepared treachery and brutality which culminated in the massacre of Rotterdam, where many thousands of Dutchmen were slaughtered'.

Theoretical excuses are possible, as a careful study of more recent records makes clear; although many of the most important Luftwaffe records were destroyed in an accidental fire at Potsdam on the night of 27th–28th February 1942, the origins and nature of the attack can be clearly outlined: by 13th May, the 22nd Airborne Division with 400 troops were in severe difficulties at the position where they had landed on 10th May, to the north-west of Rotterdam; 9th Panzer Division and *III./I.R.16* Infantry Regiment reinforcements had penetrated the city as far as the Maas bridge—captured on the very first day of the offensive by paratroops to prevent Dutch attempts to demolish it; the bridge was a Dutch defence keystone. At 4.00 p.m. on 13th May, Lieutenant Colonel von Cholchitz, Commander of the *III./I.R.16* troops, sent a deputation to the Dutch city Commandant demanding immediate surrender. The Commandant, Colonel Scharroo, refused to negotiate, and every indication was that during the night the Dutch would shell the German positions. The 22nd Airborne Division, beleaguered on the other side of Rotterdam, appealed for an air attack on the Dutch artillery before this bombardment could occur.

However, in spite of the urgent necessity for such a tactical attack, the eventual orders for the Rotterdam operation expressed a decidedly different intent:

> Resistance in Rotterdam is to be crushed with all means [General von Küchler, 18th Army Commander, ordered the XXXIXth Army Corps at 6.45 p.m. on 13th May]. If necessary the destruction of the city is to be threatened and carried out.

Luftflotte 2, Kesselring's Bomber Group, allocated bomber squadron *K.G.54* for the Rotterdam operation, and on the evening of 13th May a *K.G.54* liaison officer, Colonel Lackner, was dispatched to the 7th Air Division operations room to collect the target map 'on which the Dutch defensive zones which had to be destroyed by saturation bombing [*Bombenteppiche*] were drawn in', as General

Lackner later stated to Dr. Hans Jacobsen, the German author of the most definitive history of the Rotterdam affair; it should be said here that there is no documentary evidence to support Lackner's assertion that only these military defence zones were to be attacked. Even the Air Ministry Historical Branch's account of the Rotterdam attack, published in a volume of the Official History of the Second World War as an appendix, is erroneous in some respects.

The same evening, the 9th Panzer Division's interpreter was ordered to frame an ultimatum to the Dutch Commandant in the following terms:

> The resistance offered to the advancing German Army compels me to inform you that in the event that resistance is not ceased at once, the total destruction of the city will result. I request you, as a man of responsibility, to use your influence to avoid this. As a sign of good faith, I request you to send an intermediary. If within two hours I receive no answer, then I will be forced to employ the severest means of destruction.
> (Signed) SCHMIDT. O.C. German troops.

This was an obvious threat to the Dutch, but it was apparent that General Schmidt, the XXXIXth Army Corps Commander, hoped the Dutch would see reason and capitulate.

Not unnaturally, the Dutch saw no reason for such precipitate action; their communications with their C.-in-C. were intact and Northern Rotterdam was still securely in their hands.

. . . . .

Not until 1.40 p.m. on 14th May did the German intermediary return, the Dutch having held him in an attempt to win time; a British airborne landing with reinforcements was expected, but did not materialise. Nevertheless, Scharroo *had* mentioned that he would send a plenipotentiary at 2.00 p.m. to negotiate.

General Schmidt had no alternative but to postpone the air raid planned for 3.00 p.m. He radioed to the H.Q. of *Luftflotte 2*:

> The attack postponed on account of negotiations. Return the aircraft to Take-off Alert.

On the airfields at Quakenbrück, Delmenhorst and Hoya in Northern Germany some one hundred aircraft of *K.G.54* had already been briefed to attack the Rotterdam resistance zones, in two bomber-streams. The flying-time to Rotterdam would be about ninety-five to one hundred minutes; as early as noon the coded signal to attack had been given, after the intermediary's return was already long overdue; in the meantime, too, the 22nd Airborne Division had again radioed desperately for help.

K.G.54 was instructed to attack 'according to plan', unless red signal flares proclaimed the last-minute surrender of Rotterdam. At 1.25 p.m. the two formations took off, the right-hand bomber stream supplied by *II./K.G.54*, the left-hand one by *I./K.G.54*. At the same time, the Dutch, still playing for time, indicated that as General Schmidt's message 'was not signed and did not indicate your rank' they were not prepared to accept it; but the Dutch messenger, Captain Backer, was empowered to ascertain the German surrender conditions. Forty precious minutes passed while Generals Student, Schmidt and Hubicki (Commander of the 9th Panzer Division), formulated the conditions.

By then it was five minutes to the zero hour set for the postponed attack on Rotterdam. But it had not been possible to relay the recall-signal to the Heinkel bombers, as they had reeled in their trailing aerials on crossing the Dutch frontier, and were only in the very shortest radio range. General Speidel dispatched a swift fighter aircraft, piloted by Lieutenant Colonel Rieckhoff, to overtake and head off the bomber formations, but without success.

As soon as he heard the approaching bombers, Schmidt ordered the firing of red cartridges as pre-arranged, to signal that the attack was 'scrubbed'.

The Commander of the *I./K.G.54* bomber-stream attacking Rotterdam from the south reported:

> I was concentrating on looking out for any red lamps. My bomb-aimer dictated his readings on the clearly-identified aiming point over the radio. When he reported that he would have to release the bombs if they were not to overshoot the target—very important with German troops so close—I gave the order for their release, dead on three o'clock. Just then I saw two pitiful little red signal-cartridges arcing up, instead of the expected red signal-lamp. We could not hold back the bombs because the bomb release was fully automatic, nor could the two other aircraft in my leading flight. They dropped their bombs as soon as they saw mine go down. But my radio operator's signal got through just in time for the other aircraft.

Of the hundred He.111s, only forty heard the signal in time; the rest delivered a very concentrated attack on the designated aiming points.

Right at the start of the raid, the main water supply was cut off, and as earlier tactical air raids had largely drained the canal system, the weak local fire-service was unable to cope with the spreading fires, especially as one of the buildings most severely damaged was a margarine factory, from which streams of burning oil emerged. In fact, the Germans, in keeping with the nature of an air raid on gun positions, had used no incendiaries. Ninety-four tons of bombs had been dropped—1,150 hundred-pound and 158 five-hundred-pound bombs; by comparison, close to 9,000 tons of high explosive and incendiaries were dropped on the inland Ruhr port of Duisburg during the triple blow of 14th October 1944, for example.

At 3.30 p.m. Rotterdam capitulated, the Commandant protesting bitterly that the surrender negotiations were in hand before the attack had begun.

At 7.30 p.m. General Winkelmann, the Dutch C.-in-C., broadcast that

> Rotterdam, bombed this afternoon, suffered the fate of total war. Utrecht and other towns would soon have shared its fate. We have ceased to struggle.

As a tactical, close-support raid the assault had been overwhelming; as a strategic, 'terror-raid' the attack could not have attained its objective more dramatically. The German military leaders however insisted to the end that the raid had been purely tactical in its aims. "Was not your purpose to secure a strategic advantage by terrorising the people of Rotterdam?" questioned Sir David Maxwell-Fyfe of Field Marshal Kesselring at Nuremberg in 1946. "That I can deny with the clearest conscience," Kesselring replied. "We had only one task: to provide artillery support for Student's troops." As a German defence witness, he could hardly say anything else.

The German High Command's communiqué of 15th May 1940 announced with brazen effrontery that

> under the pressure of German dive-bombing attacks and the imminent tank assault on the city, Rotterdam has capitulated and thereby saved itself from destruction.

    •   •   •   •   •

By war-time standards, the casualties were not large: some 980 people had been killed, according to figures supplied (1962) by the

Rotterdam statistical authorities, mostly civilians, in fires which ravaged over 1·1 square miles of the most important part of the city; the conflagration was still burning in parts when the hastily organised German fire-fighting regiments under General Rumpf arrived some days later. Twenty thousand buildings were destroyed by the fires, and 78,000 people were made homeless.

With the fall of Rotterdam and the rest of Holland, apart from Zeeland province, it remained to the Allies only to gather what profit they could from the ruins. On 16th July the first shots in what was to develop into a virulent propaganda war-in-the-air were fired: the Royal Netherlands Legation in Washington issued a statement, on which the war-time British Prime Minister appears to have relied in his memoirs. The Dutch statement declared:

> When Rotterdam was bombed the Dutch Army's capitulation had already been handed to the German High Command. The crime against Rotterdam was a deliberate, fiendish assault on unarmed, undefended civilians. In the seven-and-a-half minutes that the planes were over the city, 30,000 people died—4,000 unoffending men, women and children per minute.

The Americans were horrified, and members of the British and American Air Force Film Units must have blushed when they read how 'the final ghoulish touch to this man-made inferno of death was that the Germans made aerial motion pictures of their handiwork.'

It should not have been necessary to have gone in such detail into the mounting and execution of the German air attack on Rotterdam in a book whose purpose is to describe the delivery of the triple-blow attack on Dresden five years later. Inevitably, one is tempted to rely on the contemporary stories of what the Germans did, especially in supporting the suggestion that in Dresden and the other major tragedies of the air offensive against Germany, the German people were only reaping the whirlwind their leaders had sown in 1940. Dramatic exaggerations die hard—not least those that are generated in the dire necessity of war-time morale-boosting. The objective historical researcher must, however, record only what really happened. Otherwise he performs disservice for posterity.

Waiving moral questions, whether it was a tactical operation or—as was claimed at Nuremberg—solely designed to terrorise the civilian population, bombardment was not illegal under the terms of Article 25 of the 1907 Hague Convention, to which both Britain and Germany were signatories: Rotterdam was not an undefended town.

But such considerations seem purely academic against the background of the Nazis' criminal seizure of neutral Holland.

．　　　．　　　．　　　．　　　．

The A.O.C.-in-C. of R.A.F. Fighter Command was convinced that the Luftwaffe could not be defeated over the Continent; the enemy bomber and fighter formations should somehow be enticed or provoked into daylight battle over the British Isles, within reach of the R.A.F.'s superior short-range fighter defences. With this requirement in mind, the first attacks were launched on targets east of the Rhine on the evening that the Rotterdam raid was announced to the world; less than twenty-five of the ninety-six bombers despatched even claimed to have found their targets. Not one enemy fighter was diverted from the operations supporting the German Battle for France. Only when France had fallen and the R.A.F. had repeatedly attacked the German mainland did the Führer decide to turn his attention to industrial targets in London.

On the night of 25th–26th August, 1940, the R.A.F.'s first attack on the Reich capital was launched, as a reprisal for the Luftwaffe raid of the night before in which for the first time bombs were dropped on Central London, damaging St. Giles, Cripplegate. The Battle of Britain by this time had been in progress for over six weeks. The first large-scale attack on the United Kingdom took place on July 10th, when 70 German aircraft raided the South Wales docks. Within a period of fifty-two days 1,333 civilians had been killed by air attacks throughout Britain. Attacks gained in intensity reaching a peak about the middle of August, aerodromes being the main target. Attacks on Portsmouth, Southampton, Hastings and Weymouth were followed within days by the heavy raids of the 15th, covering a wide area including Newcastle and Croydon, with a total loss of 76 German planes. The following day bombs fell for the first time on the suburbs of London. On the 18th the Few brought down 71 enemy planes; six days later, however, on the night of the 24th, the Luftwaffe again directed their attack over a wide range of target cities, including London, Birmingham and Liverpool.

In spite of the failure of the R.A.F. even on the nights following their first attack to inflict serious injury on the Reich capital, this new air assault provided the Führer, still fresh from the triumph of his western offensive, with the excuse of provocation he required. Speaking on 4th September at the Berlin Sport-palast he declared: "If they threaten to attack our cities, then we shall rub out theirs."

Undeterred, the R.A.F. launched yet further raids on Berlin, including a large one on the 6th.

On the afternoon of 7th September, three days after his threat, and two weeks after the first R.A.F. assault on Berlin, the Luftwaffe appeared in strength over London for the first time in a daylight raid: 247 bombers escorted by several hundred fighters pounded oil stores and dock installations along the lower reaches of the Thames with a total of 335 tons of high explosive and 440 incendiaries. This marks the end of the Battle of Britain; in the Blitz of London that followed, the Luftwaffe, between 7th September 1940 and 16th May 1941, claimed to have dropped 18,921 tons of bombs in 71 major attacks; by the end of 1940 the Blitz had cost 13,339 civilians their lives, and at one stage as many as 375,000 were estimated to be homeless.

. . . . .

Though doubts had been expressed about the effectiveness of the R.A.F. night bombing raids, neither the Air Ministry's nor Bomber Command's confidence in them appeared to wane during the summer and early autumn of 1940. Air Vice-Marshal Harris in a letter of 11th October to Sir Richard Peirse, who was then Commander in Chief of Bomber Command, spoke of the 'accuracy with which our aircraft hit military objectives as opposed to merely browning the towns'; and, although by late October Peirse had some reservations on the Command's capabilities, he had in September while he was Vice Chief of Air Staff in a letter to the Prime Minister firmly supported precision bombing of towns as opposed to indiscriminate bombing.

Nor in the light of evidence then available was this confidence misplaced. The Air Ministry's official channels of information, however contrary to American press reports, dovetailed in their accounts. Bomber Command's reports on the raids were detailed and unambiguous and contained few references to any difficulties encountered in locating targets. Nothing was done to dispel the impression of success given by these crew reports by the intelligence reports received from Germany and neutral countries. Many emphasised in particular the loss of morale caused by the raids; and one report of 10th October, noted in particular by Harris, estimated that the bombing had affected as much as 25 per cent of Germany's total productive capacity.

But a far different picture was being presented in the American press. *The Times* complained of the lack of publicity on the effects of the raids in the New York despatches of American correspondents still in Berlin. The headline in the *Herald Tribune* on 29th August read: 'No Trace of British raids in Berlin', and similar doubt had been cast by them on the alleged British success in Hamburg at the end of July. Nazi propagandists had been quick to take advantage of the presence of these neutral correspondents in Germany to parade them on tours of inspection of the damage claimed by the British.

Whether the Air Ministry saw these press reports or not, it not unnaturally based its support of the effectiveness of the bombing offensive on its own official sources of information. Reliance on the accuracy of the reports only began to diminish late in the autumn of 1940 when the prime importance of photographic evidence was acknowledged and a Photographic Reconnaissance Flight formed on 16th November. Previously, judgement of success had been based on theoretical assumptions on the accuracy of bomb aiming and navigation, assumptions that had been challenged only by a very few senior officers at High Wycombe, among them Sir Robert Saundby; he was profoundly sceptical of the claims made by bomber crews.

At Headquarters, Bomber Command, he has described, there was a map covered with red and black squares, the former being known oil plants in existence, the latter black squares being those that the R.A.F. had 'flattened'. On an inquiry from Saundby, the officer in charge of the map explained that as statistics had demonstrated that 100 tons of bombs would destroy half an oil plant, each of these plants marked in black, having received 200 tons, must have been destroyed; the officer knew that they *had* been hit, 'because those were the orders of the aircrews'. To this, Sir Robert Saundby is said to have replied caustically: 'You have not dropped 200 tons of bombs on these oil plants; you have *exported* 200 tons of bombs, and you must hope that some of them went near the target.' In these, the early days of Bomber Command, this remark must have deeply shocked the officer concerned; but it illustrates clearly the realistic attitude which Bomber Command's senior officers would have to adopt if the Command was to survive.

A typical 'black square' would have represented the Ilse Bergbau Synthetic Oil Refinery at Ruhland, close to Dresden, attacked by Bomber Command on the night of 10th–11th November, 1940:

> The great plant, identified by its six tall chimneys, was showered with incendiary bombs by the first arrivals, and the red glow of the many fires they started aided following raiders to pin-point their objectives. Direct hits with high-explosive bombs were scored among the

refinery buildings, and across the base of the chimney stacks, causing violent explosions, the force of which could be felt in the aircraft thousands of feet above. At the end of an hour's attack, great fires, giving off dense clouds of black smoke, were blazing in the refinery area and could be seen by the last of the raiders for twenty minutes after they turned on their 500 miles' flight back to England.

All this was in spite of cloud 'rising unbroken to more than 18,000 feet'. Dresden itself was 'also bombed for the first time', with large fires in the city's main railway junctions, and heavy damage to the gas, water and power installations, in 'an attack lasting from 9.15 until nearly 11 p.m'. Although Dresden's sirens sounded at 2.25 a.m., no bombs, in fact, fell. A previous 'first-ever' attack executed on Dresden on 22nd September, 1940, was reported in *Air Ministry Bulletin 1796*, when 'railway sidings were attacked and two hits were obtained on a goods train'. Once again the sirens did sound but no bombs were recorded as having fallen. Hansard's Parliamentary Report also correspondingly reported that two raids had been delivered on Dresden as early as 1940.

.   .   .   .   .

If the Air Ministry had been too optimistic about the ability of their rank-and-file airmen to navigate accurately by the stars to distant, pin-point targets, the Luftwaffe were more realistic: as early as March 1940 captured documents from crashed German bombers showed that the aircraft had been relying on *Knickebein* radio-beams for accurate navigation by night; when No. 80 Wing, an ad hoc Radio Counter-Measures organisation under Wing Commander E. B. Addison, discovered means of deflecting these beams, the Luftwaffe aircraft, on the night of 14th–15th November, 1940, switched to a new system, involving the *X-Gerät*, by which early fire-raising aircraft could release showers of incendiaries accurately over the aiming point, setting the city on fire—in this case Coventry. The main force of bombers would then have little difficulty in identifying the target. The final development by the Germans in the radio-beam war was the introduction in February 1941 of *Y-Gerät*: a radio signal beamed out from a German ground station was picked up by the bomber's equipment and retransmitted back to the ground station; the time-lapse provided an accurate gauge of the aircraft's exact location over England. Two years later, this technique, as *Oboe*, was to provide the most powerful weapon in Bomber Command's arsenal during the Battle of the Ruhr.

The deployment and technical equipment of the German path-finder wing *K.Gr.100* was in every way an object lesson for Bomber Command in girding itself for the first major offensive against German industry in the Battle of the Ruhr. By the light of fires started by the *K.Gr.100* Heinkels navigating by *X-Gerät* beams, the remaining main force squadrons were easily able to find their targets and aiming points: *I./L.G.1* was allotted the Standard Motor Company as its target, together with the Coventry Radiator and Press Company; *II./K.G.27* was to attack the Alvis aero-engine works; *I./K.G.51* the British Piston Ring Company; *II./K.G.55* the Daimler Works; and *K.Gr.606* the gas holders. Out of 550 aircraft despatched, 449 arrived over Coventry, which was only meagrely fore-armed, although reliable British Intelligence sources had provided the Government with two days' fore-warning of the impending attack. The bombers dropped 503 tons of high explosive and 881 incendiary canisters.

The second object lesson which R.A.F. Bomber Command was to learn from Coventry was that the greatest damage to industrial production was occasioned by the destruction of water and gas mains and electric power supplies; thus twenty-one vital factories were severely bomb-damaged, of which no fewer than twelve were connected with the aircraft industry. But the paralysis of public utilities caused the total stoppage of nine other vital factories which would otherwise have been operating very soon after the raid. This damage in Coventry was accomplished at the price of 380 lives among the population and of course the cathedral was burnt down.

This phenomenon was to be the very fundament of R.A.F. Bomber Command's area offensive; the equivalent of thirty-two days' industrial production had been lost in Coventry, not so much by damage to factories as by the incidental gutting of the city centre. Moreover, experts advised the Government that had the Luftwaffe repeated its attacks on two or three consecutive nights, taking into account the ease with which the by then helpless and defenceless city could have been identified and attacked by night, with the fires from previous attacks still showing clearly, the city might have been put out of action permanently. The Germans, however, were still finding their feet in the air war; thus the Coventry attack was deliberately drawn out from 10.15 p.m. until nearly 6.00 a.m. next morning, while the usual length of the most successful R.A.F. raids on German towns was cut down to about ten to twenty minutes by the end of the war, resulting in a saturation of the target areas with fire bombs which the German fire-services were unable to master.

There is, in fact, little doubt that had the 449 German bombers been charged with predominantly incendiary loads, had they been routed over the target area in great concentration in the way that we shall come to see was employed during the great No. 5 Group attacks on Brunswick, Dresden, and other cities, and had the attack been concentrated on the mediaeval centre of Coventry, as was the case at Dresden, then without doubt a fire-storm could have been generated with at least a comparable loss of life in the city, and very probably with complete paralysis of the industrial life of the city for the rest of the war; this was an opportunity which the Germans mercifully missed. Only once, recalls Sir Arthur Harris, did a Luftwaffe raid ever approach fire-storm conditions: during an unusually heavy fire-raid on London, when the Thames was running a neap tide, the hoses of the London fire brigades had been unable to reach down to the river surface. 'So often the factor which converted an otherwise routine attack into a major catastrophe was just a freak of nature,' he observes, alluding perhaps to the heatwave which had sealed the fate of Hamburg in the summer of 1943.

In December 1940, however, a Committee which had been set up under Mr. Geoffrey Lloyd submitted to the War Cabinet a report on the success of the offensive which Bomber Command had waged against synthetic oil plants since the previous May. Though reduction in oil output had only amounted to some 15 per cent this achievement became very notable when compared with the amount of effort that Bomber Command had devoted to it—only 6.7 per cent of their total operations directed against industrial targets, invasion ports and communications. On these findings Sir Charles Portal, Chief of the Air Staff, urged the destruction of the major seventeen oil plants in Germany, in the belief that this could have a decisive effect on the fortunes of the war. The recommendations made in the ensuing Chiefs of Staff report to the War Cabinet formed the basis of a Directive issued on 15th January: oil was to be the primary target and the bombing of industrial cities and communications subsidiary. This emphasis on oil as a target was to be a recurrent factor in the policy for Bomber Command for the rest of the war and was to become at some stages a source of critical dissension.

Chapter II

BOMBER COMMAND GETS ITS TEETH

FOR Bomber Command and the British Prime Minister the truth about the inaccuracy of their offensive hitherto had dawned slowly, and was revealed to them completely and unambiguously on the date that the private secretary to Professor Lindemann, Mr. David Bensusan-Butt, reported back to Bomber Command: 18th August 1941. Mr. Butt had been shown the entire collection of the R.A.F.'s bombing photographs during a private visit to the Photographic Reconnaissance Unit's base at R.A.F. Medmenham, soon after Christmas 1940; the officers who had made the collection fully realised their significance, and saw that while some senior officers had at first refused to believe the evidence of the cameras, there was a possibility of bringing them to the attention of the Government through Professor Lindemann's secretary. As a direct consequence of his private report to his Professor, Mr. Butt was commissioned to analyse the photographs statistically.

The Butt Report, submitted in August 1941 and presented in melancholy detail, finally confirmed what the neutral free Press abroad had been proclaiming for a year about the impotence of the British bomber force. Of all aircraft recorded as having attacked their targets, only one-third had in fact bombed within five miles; on well-defended inland targets like the Ruhr industrial complex, the success rating sagged to below one-tenth within five miles. It was clearly unrealistic to require Bomber Command to continue to attempt precision night attacks until electronic equipment like that of the German groups was available at least to a part of the Command's aircraft.

On 9th July 1941 Air Vice-Marshal N. H. Bottomley, the Deputy Chief of the Air Staff, issued the first of his many Directives to the A.O.C.-in-C. of Bomber Command, at that time still Air Marshal Sir Richard Peirse:

> I am directed to inform you that a comprehensive review of the enemy's present political, economic and military situation discloses that the weakest points in his armour lie in the morale of the civil population and in his inland transportation system.

The main effort of the bomber force, until further instructions, was to be directed towards dislocating the German transportation system and to destroying the morale of the civil population as a whole. Peirse was left in no doubt as to how he was to achieve this. As primary targets for attack he was allocated Cologne, Duisburg, Dusseldorf and Duisburg-Ruhrort, 'all suitable for attack on moonless nights, as they lie in congested industrial towns, where the psychological effect will be the greatest.'

> We must first destroy the foundations upon which the [German] war machine rests—the economy which feeds it, the morale which sustains it, the supplies which nourish it, and the hopes of victory which inspire it.

The above extract from the Chiefs of Staff memo, 31st July 1941, heralded the approach of the area offensive; the January 1943 Casablanca Directive was in fact barely more than an extension in bolder language of this policy.

An attack on enemy morale, however, required new techniques: an Air Staff memo to Bomber Command commented in September 1941 that the conclusion was irresistible 'that the greater damage achieved by the enemy is caused by incendiarism'. While the Luftwaffe in its attacks on British towns was on occasions dropping 60 per cent of its bomb load as incendiaries, Bomber Command never exceeded 30 per cent. German practice in achieving terroristic aims was to lead off attacks with waves of fire-raising aircraft, dropping incendiaries in a greater volume than the fire services could master—then to follow up with waves of bombers cascading high explosive bombs into the target; these clearly were factors which Bomber Command could profitably imitate. The high explosive bombs, in bursting water mains, would aid and amplify the devastation wrought by the incendiaries. But in 1941 Bomber Command still had no bombs more massive than 500-pounders available, and there was little incentive to develop larger weapons.

Experiments conducted in late 1941 by Professor S. Zuckerman as leader of the Oxford Extramural Unit, and which first came to the public notice as the result of a question in the House of Commons, demonstrated that German bombs, weight for weight, were about twice as efficient as British bombs: furthermore, by detonating standard British 500-pound General Purpose bombs among live goats staked out at various angles in a deep pit, he was able to deduce that 'the lethal pressure for man was between 400 and 500 pounds per square inch'; cross-checks with air-raids on British cities showed this estimate to be of the right order. Previously, the lethal pressure had been placed at around 5 pounds per square inch.

Again, the pressure necessary to cause minimal pulmonary damage in man was empirically placed at 70 pounds per square inch; finally, referring to Professor J. D. Bernal's survey of casualties in German air raids, Professor Zuckerman emphasised that only a small percentage were so close to the bombs that they received direct injuries from the blast wave. Professor Zuckerman was thus able to forecast the average number of casualties which would occur if one ton of bombs were dropped on one square mile of territory of given population density; 'the results of these investigations,' a post-war Stationery Office pamphlet on Operational Research relates, 'became a guide to future bombing policy'. Curiously, although Professor Zuckerman and his team investigated both blast and splinter effects—the latter by firing high-velocity steel balls into rabbits' legs—no Government scientist investigated the lethality of bombs from the aspect of smoke and gas-poisoning which, as we shall come to see, resulted in the raids analysed in this book in at least seventy per cent of all fatalities.

At this point these macabre calculations were taken up by an Admiralty expert on Operational Research, Professor P. M. S. Blackett:

> Static detonation trials showed that the British General Purpose bombs then in use were about half as effective as the German light-case [*i.e.* blast] bombs of the same weight. In the ten months from August 1940 to June 1941 the total weight of bombs dropped on the United Kingdom was about 50,000 tons; the number of persons killed was 40,000, giving 0·8 killed per ton of bombs.

Thus, reasoned Blackett, given the proven lower efficiency of the R.A.F. as well as its inferior weapons, we might hope to kill 0·2 Germans per ton of British bombs dropped. As he had already showed that 'the loss of industrial production . . . and civilian casualties . . . were about proportional,' he implied by his calculations that a continuation of the R.A.F.'s area offensive was futile.

But if Professors Blackett and Zuckerman expected the Air Staff to heed their pessimistic calculations, and to divert industrial resources to an attack on the enemy's submarines—both were noted opponents of the area offensive—they were disappointed. Their calculations, and many others by similarly inclined scientists, were used only as an argument for more powerful weapons and better instrumentation of Bomber Command.

•   •   •   •   •

Clearly it was essential that production of light-case blast bombs should begin as soon as possible, in order to approach the efficiency of the German weapons. Towards the end of 1941 the first 500-pound medium capacity bombs, forty per cent explosive content, came into service; the primary weapon of the area offensive was, however, to be the high capacity bomb, eighty per cent explosive content, thin-walled weapons roughly the size of boilers, produced in 4,000-pound, 8,000-pound and finally 12,000-pound 'blockbuster' sizes.

While Professors Blackett and Zuckerman had thus decisively rejected the possibility of inflicting serious damage on the German populace, the British Prime Minister had consulted a different adviser: Professor F. A. Lindemann, who it will be remembered had had the persistent failures of R.A.F. Bomber Command before him since his Secretary's melancholy discovery of Christmas 1940. He was asked to propound a bombing policy by which Britain could effectively assist her ally in the East.

Lindemann's final report, on 30th March 1942, suggested that there was little doubt that an area bombing offensive could break the spirit of the enemy provided that it was aimed at the working-class areas of the fifty-eight German towns with a population of more than 100,000 inhabitants each.

> Each bomber will in its lifetime drop about forty tons of bombs [minuted Lindemann]. If these are dropped on built-up areas, they will make about 4,000 to 8,000 people homeless.

His conclusion was that between March 1942 and the middle of 1943 it should be possible to make about one-third of the whole German population homeless, provided that the resources of the armament industry were concentrated on this campaign.

The Lindemann minute was passed to Professor Blackett and Professor H. Tizard for comment; both were on record as advocating priority in the aircraft industry for the needs of Coastal Command. Later on, of course, Blackett was to perform a signal service for the Command by his development of the Mark XIV bombsight. Both scientists dismissed the minute as being seriously in error and suggested that Lindemann was overestimating the success of the air offensive by six and five times respectively. Both were overruled.

. . . . .

In view of the controversy which developed over the validity of Professor Lindemann's forecast, it is interesting to observe that at least as far as the raids discussed in this work are concerned, Professor Blackett's estimate of the number of deaths—and thus of the commensurate industrial damage—would have been out by a factor of over 51, while Professor Lindemann's estimate of the homeless would have been out by a factor of only 1·4 (Appendix II).

The Lindemann policy did not require many changes in Bomber Command's tactics for its implementation. As early as 14th February 1942, Bomber Command had been directed that its primary task was to attack residential areas in certain industrial towns, and the following day the Chief of the Air Staff clarified the Annexe listing these towns:

> Ref the new bombing directive: I suppose it is clear that the aiming points* are to be the built-up areas [Sir Charles Portal had written to his Deputy, Sir Norman Bottomley], *not*, for instance, the dockyards or aircraft factories where these are mentioned. This must be made quite clear if it is not already understood.

Bottomley replied that he had specifically confirmed this point with Bomber Command by telephone.

This then was the policy of attacking residential areas which awaited Sir Arthur Harris when he arrived at Bomber Command's underground headquarters at High Wycombe to take up his appointment as A.O.C.-in-C., Bomber Command, on 22nd February, 1942. There can be no more eloquent proof of Harris' innocence of having personally initiated the area bombing of civilian residential districts. The general concept of the Casablanca directive of 21st January, 1943 was worded:

> Your primary object will be the progressive destruction and dislocation of the German military, industrial and economic system, and the undermining of the morale of the German people to a point where their capacity for armed resistance is fatally weakened.

Within this concept the following priorities were listed:

(a) German submarine construction yards
(b) The German aircraft industry
(c) Transportation
(d) Oil plants
(e) Other targets in enemy war industry

* Until the summer of 1944, a bomber's aiming point was invariably the target for attack. With the introduction of 'offset bombing' methods the aiming-points did not necessarily coincide with the centre of the target area; this was the case with the first Bomber Command attack on Dresden.

A directive expressed in such broad terms could clearly be interpreted in many ways. The tactical control of operations was, however, the prerogative of the Commander-in-Chief of Bomber Command, and Sir Arthur Harris clearly indicated his interpretation in a letter to the Air Ministry on 6th March 1943, where in place of the phrase 'and the undermining of the morale of the German people', he quoted it as if it read 'aimed at undermining the morale . . .' a change of wording which 'altered the emphasis of the sentence, though it could not be said that his interpretation was not justifiable.

Bomber Command had not yet attained the degree of precision in night bombing that it was to achieve by the closing stages of the war, and, despite some reservation by the Air Staff on the effectiveness of the area offensive, the Battle of the Ruhr and the Battle of Berlin took place under the terms of this directive.

. . . . .

Now, for the first time in the war, Bomber Command had the weapons and instruments with which it could hope to put this directive into effect. The Telecommunications Research Establishment had successfully developed a new radar navigation device, 9.2-cm *H2S*; a cathode-ray tube in the aircraft showed the general topography below in a pattern of dots of light of varying intensity —rivers showed up black, built-up areas brilliantly light; so far, indeed, had the use of *H2S* progressed that by late in June 1943 the Germans were already in possession of their first captured *H2S* set and were learning the wonders of centimetric radar, ably assisted by a co-operative ex-Bomber Command prisoner, dangerously fast—by 19th May, the Berlin firm of Telefunken had made plans for mass-production of a copy of the vital magnetron, *LMS.10*, which would within a month be produced at the rate of ten per week. Trials of a new computer-linked radio-repeater target tracking equipment for Mosquitos, called *Oboe*, based on Germany's 1941 *Y-Gerät* principles but on the shorter wavelengths in which British technology was vastly superior, had come to a successful conclusion, and it would not be until 7th January 1944 that a crashed Mosquito near Cleve would provide the missing links which would enable German Radio Counter-Measures scientists to interfere with the beams. In February 1942 Commandos in a bold raid on a *Würzburg* radar station on the Normandy coast near Bruneval had captured the parts of the radar equipment which enabled electronic experts in England to ascertain the wavelength on which the German early warning system was operating; within a year these scientists had completed their

37

experiments and were able to fashion *Window*—the anti-radar metal foil—to the correct dimensions and stiffness.

More important perhaps than the mechanical innovations was the favourable climate of public opinion towards the bombing offensive which now existed in England. The Secretary of State for Air, Sir Archibald Sinclair, had carefully stressed that Bomber Command was only bombing for military purposes in all his public pronouncements; any suggestions of deliberate attacks on residential or working-class housing areas were decried as absurd, and on occasion even denounced as attacks on the integrity of the brave airmen who were risking their lives for their country. Close on a hundred thousand airmen knew and recognised that their aircraft were being dispatched night after night with the deliberate intention of setting fire to Germany's cities, that the raid on Mannheim of 16th December 1940 had inaugurated the area offensive against civilian centres; but rightly and properly none of them discussed these operational details outside the service.

Early in 1943 a Bombing Restriction Committee had made its appearance in London with an address in Parliament Hill, but attempts by some Labour Members of Parliament to have its leaflets banned and its members interned were unsuccessful. The real attack on the strategic bombing policy, from the highest governmental and religious quarters in the United Kingdom, was to be delayed until the late Autumn of 1943; by that time three of the most devastating and bloody air raids on Germany had already been executed. The first target which was to experience the full force of R.A.F. Bomber Command, its aircrews fresh and the bomb-aimers undeterred by heavy ground defences, was the twin city of Wuppertal, at the eastern end of the Ruhr, when disaster fell on the night of 29th–30th May 1943. Two months later, Bomber Command's most successful and brilliantly staged offensive against the Hanseatic port of Hamburg marked the first climax in the history of the force. The third great attack of 1943, in which, as in Hamburg, a fire-storm was to be generated by the sudden bursting of hundreds of thousands of incendiary bombs, was that on Kassel on the night of 22nd–23rd October 1943. In this last, as in both the Wuppertal and the Hamburg attacks, circumstances—this time in the form of an ingenious new deception worked by Bomber Command on the night fighter and ground defences, under the code-name of *Corona*—were to assist the bomber crews in making accurate bombing runs, undeterred by defences on a heavy scale.

. . . . . .

For the attack on Wuppertal on the night of 29th–30th May 1943, the bomber crews were issued with a 1941-style red and grey target map of Wuppertal Elberfeld, with the usual concentric rings centring on the city's Electricity Power Plant II; the target map itself, *1 (g)(i) 32*, was prepared from another plan dated 1936. The bomb aimers for this attack were, however, to ignore the ring system and the target brightly marked-in in orange; they were instructed instead to pencil in a cross over the grey residential area of Wuppertal-Barmen, at the eastern end of the city, which was the designated aiming point in an emergency, if, for example, *Oboe* Mosquito markers did not arrive. Air Marshal Saundby has explained that it was in fact common for details like military targets, industrial plants, concentric ring systems, etc., to be marked on target maps for the enlightenment of others than bomb-aimers; previously to using these red-and-grey target maps, the crews had been issued with minutely-detailed Ordnance Survey maps of target cities, sprinkled liberally with overprinted red Maltese crosses, and a heading, *Hospitals are marked* ✠ *and must be avoided*. As Sir Robert Saundby now explains, 'this made it possible to get up in Parliament and say that we marked these things on our target maps, and that the crews were specially briefed to avoid hospitals'.

Much that occurred during the Pathfinder-led attack on Wuppertal-Barmen was to reappear, multiplied many times in violence and effect, during the Pathfinder attack on Dresden—the second of the two—in February 1945; there were many comparisons to be drawn between the two attacks: both were hampered by little ground defences, and both were calculated to exploit a known failing of those crews to whom Sir Arthur Harris contemptuously referred as the 'rabbits' of Bomber Command—the crews who dropped their bombs as early as possible and then scuttled away from the target area. It was recognised that if the marker flares were dropped at one end of the target area, and the bomber stream were routed in along the length of the target, then any bombs dropped early by the 'rabbit' crews would still do useful damage somewhere in the target city. Sometimes this creep-back extended for many miles across the countryside from the aiming point; in one Berlin raid of August 1943 the creep-back was thirty miles long. Thus, in both Wuppertal's case and the planning of the second R.A.F. attack on Dresden, it was planned to exploit this creep-back by setting the aiming point at the most distant end of the target, which, for Wuppertal, was in the heart of Wuppertal-Barmen. The force of 719 bombers dispatched was therefore instructed to cross the town on a heading of 68° and, as this route would take the main force of bombers across the length of the twin city, the bombs would devastate the whole area of the city. Such was the plan of attack.

On this occasion, however, the Wuppertal flak remained silent and in the absence of any defences for the first few minutes, a very heavy concentration of bomb-loads was put down round the aiming point in Wuppertal-Barmen; it appears, from examination of German defence controllers' reports, that although the city's flak defences were well prepared for the advancing bomber formations, they did not expect the attack to fall on Wuppertal, and thus ordered the guns not to fire, so as not to betray the city's location. However, as Sir Arthur Harris had taken the precaution with this attack of leading off the blow with a wave of fire-raising aircraft—a strategy rather similar to that employed by the Luftwaffe with the attack on Coventry in November 1940—the result was that all crews, in the absence of heavy flak defences and with the aiming point marked out not only by the red *Oboe* flares but also by a brilliant concentration of incendiary fires, were able to achieve a high degree of concentration; over 475 crews were found to have dropped their bomb load within three miles of the aiming point in the heart of Wuppertal-Barmen—a total of 1,895·3 tons of fire-bombs and high explosive. Thirty-three aircraft were lost and 71 damaged.

Wuppertal-Elberfeld, in the absence of any appreciable creep-back, was completely unscathed, apart from glass damage; Bomber Command had to return a month later to take in the western end of the twin city. In the absence of ground defences, much the same phenomenon was to be observed in Dresden, where—just as in Wuppertal—an enormous area was set on fire by an early fire-raising attack.

Wuppertal's industrial production was set back by fifty-two days, compared with thirty-two in Coventry; the loss of life, which Professor Blackett insisted would be proportional to the loss of industrial capacity, was in fact greater: in the first attack on Wuppertal-Barmen, 2,450 people were killed (in Coventry the death-roll was 380); the second attack, on Elberfeld a month later, raised the total for Wuppertal to 5,200.

This was the first raid to cause civilian casualties on such a scale in the area offensive, however, and as such attracted special attention from the German war-leaders; even in London there were some horrified murmurs when photographs of the damage to Wuppertal were published. The first leader in *The Times* on 31st May 'recognised and regretted that no matter how accurate Allied bombing of military objectives may be—and the degree of accuracy is very high in the R.A.F.—civilian losses are inevitable'; it reminded those who might nevertheless be tempted to question this apparently brutal use of the bomber weapon that 'it was not questioned in either Germany or Italy when the Luftwaffe was turned loose against undefended Rotterdam in 1940 and killed many thousands of civilians—men, women and children'. For Germany the wheel was apparently turning full circle.

This approach did not, as might be expected, pass unrivalled in Germany: as senior Reich Defence Commissioner—an ex officio role of all Gauleiters for their *Gaue* since 16th November 1942— Dr. Goebbels addressed the mourners at the mass funeral arranged in Wuppertal on 18th June 1943:

> This kind of aerial terrorism is the product of the sick minds of the plutocratic world-destroyers.
>
> A long chain of human suffering [he added] in all German cities blitzed by the Allies has borne witness against them and their cruel and cowardly leaders—from the murder of German children in Freiburg on 10th May, 1940, right up to the present day.

Just as the German raid on Rotterdam had begun to figure more frequently in the Allied statements on the history of the air offensive, so the Germans had more and more recourse to the story of the mysterious Freiburg raid; they even stated it in a White Paper published in 1943 as the start of the bombing offensive by the British or French. However, as the German Führer, his Reich Air Minister and Dr. Goebbels himself had known from the very evening of the Freiburg affair, the three twin-engined bombers which had bombed Freiburg during the afternoon of 10th May 1940, killing fifty-seven civilians and children, were German Heinkel 111s dispatched from the bomber station at Lecheld, near Munich, to bomb the fighter airfield at Dijon in France; they had lost their way in the clouds, and 'attacked Dôle' near Dijon, a specified auxiliary target. In fact the bombs had fallen on Freiburg. The Police President had checked the serial numbers on the bomb fragments, had collected the data relating to the unexploded bombs and had proved conclusively that they came from a case of German bombs, which had originally been delivered to Lecheld airfield. It was a mistake that any operational crew could make in the heat and excitement of its first sortie. But, before six years were out, over 635,000 German civilians were to die in an air offensive for which they now had only their own leaders to blame.

Chapter III

FIRE-STORM

THE battle of Hamburg which began on 24th July 1943 was important not only because it produced the first fire-storm in the history of the Second World War—during the night of the R.A.F. attack on 27th–28th July 1943—but also because it clearly emphasised how even a city in which the most stringent A.R.P. measures had been undertaken was not immune to fire-raids on the largest scale, if the ground defences were not in the position to deter the bomb-aimers from releasing their bomb loads accurately around the aiming point. During the Battle of Hamburg, the device which did, of course, secure the temporary immunity for the bomber formations was the simple *Window* technique, the mass release of quantities of metal foil strips, some 27 centimetres in length, which successfully jammed the German *Würzburg* gun-laying radar equipment.

During the first raids on the city during the Battle of Hamburg, therefore, the target was again effectively without ground defences and was doomed to suffer an even worse fate than Wuppertal. In the four main raids of the Battle, 7,931 tons of bombs were released on the city, nearly half of them incendiaries. Magnificently prepared though the city was for air raids on the largest scale, a catastrophe could not be averted.

During the first years of the war, air-raid precautions in Hamburg had been advanced to a degree unknown in other German cities. By the time of the Battle of Hamburg, 61,297 of the 79,907 cellared buildings in Greater Hamburg had been shored up and splinter-proofed; but a further 42,421 buildings, mostly in the more water-logged areas of the city, had no basements—without water-proof tanking, they would have flooded too easily. For these areas a costly shelter-and-bunker-building programme was launched. In accordance with the Führer's shelter-building Programme of August 1940, a honeycomb network of wall-breaches (*Mauerdurchbrüche*) connecting adjacent basements had been constructed; by 1941 this work was virtually completed.

Every method of securing emergency supplies of water in the event of a major conflagration had been exploited: swimming pools, rainwater tanks, wells, industrial cooling-towers and tanks, empty oil-storage tanks, even the cellars of blitzed buildings had been flooded with water and prepared for emergency use. The camouflage of the city's main features had also proceeded apace: the outline of the Alster lakes was changed and a dummy Lombards-brücke railway bridge was built across them several hundred yards away from the real one; the Central Railway Station was completely masked from view and in early 1943 an extensive screen of smoke-generators round the U-boat pens was installed.

During this period, fire-prevention experts had advised on the clearance of attics and roof-spaces, on the construction of incendiary proof ceilings in commercial and industrial premises and, in the closing months of 1942, on thorough chemical fire-proofing of roof timbers and attics.

Astute though these precautions were, and profound though the foresight of the Hamburg City Fathers had been in promoting these projects and A.R.P. schemes, all were doomed to collapse under the weight of the three heaviest raids of the Battle of Hamburg; the fourth, on 2nd–3rd August 1943, fought through under almost impossible weather conditions, failed to achieve any degree of concentration at all. The first raid caused enormous fires which had not been extinguished even after twenty-four hours; the citizens of Hamburg, heeding the advice of the City leaders, had providently accumulated large stocks of fuel for the winter in their cellars, and when the coal and coke caught fire it could not easily be quenched. In addition to this, the Police Praesidium was gutted and the A.R.P. control room was 'engulfed in fire'.

Control on this occasion was unaffected, and a speedy transfer of control to the Security Police control room was effected; although the telephone service broke down, it was swiftly superseded by motor cycle despatch-riders. By the time that the All Clear sounded at the end of the first raid, some 1,500 citizens had been killed; worse was however to follow.

> The continuation of the first raid by daylight and nuisance raids until the morning of the 27th disclosed the enemy's intentions [reported S.S. Major-General Kehrl, who, as Police President, was ex officio Hamburg's A.R.P. director]. When the fifth alert was sounded during the night of 27th–28th July, 1943, we were not surprised, but the weight of the raid exceeded even our expectations.

By the time that the All-Clear was sounded at 2.40 a.m., 2,382 tons of bombs had been dropped; it is interesting to note in this connection that during the two R.A.F. Bomber Command raids on Dresden, 2,978 tons of bombs were dropped, with a further 771 tons from American Flying Fortresses in the third blow, ten hours later. However, in Hamburg a large number of liquid-filled bombs had been dropped, in consequence of which fires broke out not only in the attics and the upper floors, which, as we have seen, had been specially fire-proofed, but right at the foot of the buildings. With 969 tons of incendiaries claimed dropped on Hamburg, the proportion of fire bombs was considerably higher in this second main force raid than previously: forty minutes after zero hour it was recognised that Germany's first fire-storm had begun. Parallel again to the Dresden triple blow, the area on which the bulk of the bombs fell during this fire-storm raid on Hamburg was the most heavily built up and densely populated area of Hamburg, with a resident population of 427,637 inhabitants, and an additional population of thousands of refugees bombed out of the area hit three nights before.

It was during this, the second main force Bomber Command raid on Hamburg during the Battle, that the largest toll in human life was exacted from the populace: in the four Hamburg districts which formed the fire-storm area, Rothenburgsort, Hammerbrook, Borgfelde, and South Hamm, the appalling fatality rates were 36·15 per cent, 20·10 per cent, 16·05 per cent and 37·65 per cent of the resident population. During the whole Battle, as the Police President reported on 1st December 1943, the known dead totalled 31,647, of which 15,802 could be identified immediately (6,072 men, 7,995 women and 1,735 children). That could not be regarded as a final figure for Hamburg's losses, as the centre of the city was still in ruins.

At the end of 1945 the U.S. Strategic Bombing Survey's *A Detailed Study of the effects of Area Bombing on Hamburg* suggested a corrected figure of 42,600 killed and 37,000 seriously injured; the Hamburg *Statistisches Landesamt*, after investigating the final numbers of missing people, arrived at the estimated total of over fifty thousand dead in the Battle of Hamburg. Unfortunately none of these authorities provide an estimate of casualties among military personnel on active service in Hamburg; an educated guess would suggest a figure of the order of one thousand dead.

·   ·   ·   ·   ·

While undoubtedly the Battle of Hamburg had contributed to the Casablanca Directive's target of 'the progressive destruction and dislocation of the German economic and industrial system', by the time that the final All Clear echoed across the now rain-soaked and wrecked city in the early morning hours of 3rd August 1943, the British attacks had between them taken the lives of the greater part of 50,000 civilians, a figure not far short of the 51,509 given as the most authoritative estimate of the total number of people killed by bombing in Britain. When rescue teams finally cleared their way into hermetically sealed bunkers and shelters, after several weeks, the heat generated inside them had been so intense that nothing remained of their occupants: only a soft undulating layer of grey ash was left in one bunker, from which the number of victims could only be estimated as 'between 250 and 300' by the doctors; doctors were frequently employed in these gruesome tasks of enumeration, as the German Reich Statistical Office was up to 31st January 1945 most meticulous about compiling its statistical tables and data. The uncommon temperatures in these bunkers was further testified to by the pools of molten metal which had formerly been pots, pans and cooking utensils taken into the shelters.

The task of recovering the bodies was allocated to the *Sicherheits und Hilfsdienst*, the Rescue and Repair Service, which was organised in five divisions: fire service, comprised of local fire-brigades—as distinct from the para-military national service; *Instandsetzungsdienst*, the repair service for fractured gas mains and severed electricity and water supplies and for dangerous demolition work; the medical service, organised by the German Red Cross; the decontamination service, for counter-measures during Allied gas-attacks; and finally the veterinary service for tending wounded livestock and pets. The S.H.D. cordoned off a 2½-mile-square dead zone, embracing the whole of the fire-storm area's seat; the access streets were sealed off with barbed wire and dry masonry; this measure was necessitated both by the undreamed-of accumulation of corpses inside this area, and by the belief that public recovery operations would injure civilian morale.

One hundred and eighty-three factories were destroyed out of 524 and 4,118 out of 9,068 smaller ones, 580 industrial plants were wrecked, the transport systems of all types were wiped out and 214,350 out of 414,500 homes were destroyed. Approximately 180,000 tons of shipping were sunk in the port, and twelve bridges were wrecked.

The Reich Armaments Minister, Albert Speer, told Hitler shortly after the raid that if another six major German cities were to be similarly devastated, he would not be able to maintain armaments production, but in his May 1945 interrogation he said that he had underestimated the capacity for recovery.

Air Vice-Marshal Bennett in his memoirs wrote:

Unhappily nobody seemed to realise that a great victory had been won, and certainly nobody realised its effect on the German people at that time. It was an opportunity that we missed. Whatever the chances of success might have been, it would certainly have been worth while to have weakened German morale by some appropriate political action.

But chief among retrospective comments, Sir Arthur Harris has said that Bomber Command could not then have repeated the Hamburg catastrophe on six major cities in quick succession.

This first big success of R.A.F. Bomber Command pitted against a single German industrial city had been made possible largely by the paralysis inflicted on the German ground and fighter defence systems by the use of *Window*; the second major success, again occasioning a fire-storm in·a huge industrial city, was on the night of 22nd–23rd October 1943, when the target was Kassel, centre of German tank production and the locomotive industry. The tactic which hindered German efforts at defence on this occasion was not a mechanical device like *Window*, but the combination of the diversionary raid principle—which had been introduced in increasing measure into the air offensive since the Battle of Hamburg—and a completely new deception tactic, code-named *Corona*: well-trained German-speaking personnel, broadcasting from the big monitoring post at Kingsdown in Kent, were to issue false instructions to the growing German night fighter force, which would delay them, or even cause them to accept the diversionary attack as the main force target for the night; a secondary duty for the *Corona* broadcasters was the transmission of false weather reports to the German night fighters, which caused them to land and disperse.

On the night of 22nd October, a main force attack on Kassel was timed to commence at 8.45 p.m. while at 8.40 p.m. a spoof raid was timed to commence on Frankfurt-am-Main. Aided by skilful use of *Corona* for the first time, the bombers were able to deliver a very concentrated attack on the city virtually unhindered by night fighter defences; only after the city had been set well on fire by the first waves did the night fighters arrive back from a fruitless chase to Frankfurt, and by then the attack could not be halted. As late as 8.35 the guns in Kassel were informed that the 'most probable target' was Frankfurt, and when at 8.38 the report came through that Frankfurt had been attacked, the Kassel flak defences dropped their guard.

A total of 1,823·7 tons of bombs was dropped on Kassel that night, and of 444 bombers no fewer than 380 were plotted to have scored hits within three miles of the aiming point. Within thirty minutes of the zero hour, Germany's second fire-storm had emerged. Once again the destruction of the city's telephone system was to herald the disaster which only a fire-storm could entail.

A preliminary report on the damage effected by the raid listed 26,782 homes as totally destroyed, with over 120,000 people homeless; in anticipation of what will be said later in this book, it is of interest to record here that in comparison the fire-storm raid on Dresden totally destroyed 75,358 homes. The Kassel Police President's final report of 7th December 1943 reported that sixty-five per cent of all homes were no longer habitable; damaged and destroyed buildings included 155 commercial and industrial establishments, and 16 military and police barracks. The Kassel raid did however provide a classic example of the theory underlying the area offensive, in the chain reaction dislocation which first paralysed the city's public utilities, then halted even the undamaged factories. The city's electricity was supplied on the one hand by a City power station, and on the other by the Losse power station; the former was destroyed, the latter halted by destruction of the coal-conveyer; the city's low-tension grid was destroyed anyway: thus, although with the loss of only three gas-holders the undamaged gasworks was not in itself unserviceable, and the gas mains were not beyond repair, without electricity to drive the gas-works machinery, the whole Kassel industrial area was deprived of its gas supply. Similarly, although the five water pumping stations had not themselves been damaged, without electricity they were paralysed. Without gas, water or power supplies, Kassel's heavy industry was crippled.

.   .   .   .   .

Although a fire-storm approaching the scale of that in Hamburg had emerged in Kassel, the death-roll of certainly less than 8,000 was remarkably low. Indeed the preliminary report of 30th November cited an interim figure of 5,599 dead; by the time of the Police President's report six days later, the figure had risen to 5,830, of which 4,012 were identifiable. This figure included 150 military personnel (whether they were on leave or on active service was not stated) and nine members of the A.R.P. police. On 30th October 1944 the Director of the Henschel locomotive works wrote in his own report that the total death-roll in Kassel was near 8,000; it is not certain from where he gained his information. The United States Bombing Survey in 1945 cited a figure of 5,248, lower than any of the German estimates. The population was 228,000.

47

In Hamburg the deathroll had approached 43,000 to 50,000; in Dresden it was to be more than twice as big. The question which needs to be studied is how Kassel, with its notoriously inefficient Gauleiter Weinrich, managed to escape the fate of these two other fire-storm cities. The answer most probably lies in the measures of extended A.R.P. precautions taken throughout the city; thus, soon after the National Socialist election victory in 1933, a thorough slum-clearance programme had been exploited to clear giant escape routes through the suburbs which could be used in the event of a city fire; this was, it should be emphasised, even before the war had begun. Again, a positive consequence of the famous raid on the Ruhr Dams on the night of 16th–17th May 1943, as well as later U.S.A.A.F. raids on Kassel, was that the centre of Kassel —which had been partly flooded by the breaching of the Eder Dam—had been evacuated; only 25,000 indispensable residents were left there, and for these large concrete bunkers were erected.

Like Hamburg, Kassel had been provided with an extensive independent fire-hydrant system, and the chemical fire-proofing of roofing timber had functioned so well that even during the fire-storm raid fire bombs had in many cases in the suburbs of Kassel burnt out harmlessly among the roof-timbers so treated without setting fire to them; this was undoubtedly a factor in preventing the spread of the fires. In addition to the chemical fire-proofing, the Kassel house-owners, like all others, had been required by the hastily passed *Luftschutzgesetz* Air Raid Precautions Act—of 31st August 1943—to provide in every house fire-syringes, grappling hooks, ropes, ladders, first-aid chests, beaters, fire-buckets, water-tubs, sand-boxes, shovels, paper sand-bags, spades, and sledge-hammers or axes, which were all to prove their worth on the night of 22nd–23rd October 1943. Again, and with great foresight, sand dumps had been located ready for laying causeways of sand across roads and streets: the asphalt was expected to melt in the heat.

Nevertheless, in spite of all these precautions, in spite of the rigid observance by the population of all the regulations and doctrines laid down by the A.R.P. authorities, well over 5,000 people were to lose their lives that night in the fires. Of the victims a total of seventy per cent had been asphyxiated, the greater part of them by poisonous carbon monoxide fumes. In fact so many people had died of poisoning, and their bodies had turned such brilliant hues of blue, orange and green, that it was at first assumed that the R.A.F. had for the first time been dropping poison gas bombs in this raid; steps for suitable retaliation were taken; post-mortem examinations by German doctors refuted this charge, and the air offensive was spared this hateful new development. (See Appendix 1.)

Fifteen per cent had met more violent deaths. The remainder, being completely carbonised, were not analysed.

On account of the considerable number of unidentifiable victims on the one hand and of missing people on the other, the city authorities organised a Missing Persons Bureau, which employed within a few days a staff of 150 to 200.

The Police President expressed alarm in his Report at the numbers yet again killed by asphyxiation, although for the most part they had suffered a peaceful death, 'slipping into unconsciousness and finally succumbing without a struggle to death'. This was, he suggested, the inevitable consequence of the policy which had been 'hammered-in' during the first three years of the war, that the safest place during air raids was the air-raid shelter. Only since the Battle of Hamburg had attempts been made to counter this fatal advice.

Many of the victims had probably had every intention of escaping from their shelters, but had missed the right moment for this undertaking; the correct moment, during the Kassel raid, would have been some forty minutes after the start of the attack when the Inner City was still just passable and the fire-storm was still only emerging, the Police President explained, adding:

> It is easy to understand how many people, especially the elderly folk and the women and children, could not pluck up enough courage to desert their shelters at the moment when the bombardment was still in progress.
>
> All this testifies [he concluded] to the urgency of instructing people much more convincingly than hitherto in the vital need to evacuate shelters and bunkers even while major conflagrations are still raging, if they are in the danger area. This is not the place for anxiety that a too-clear depiction of the terrors of the fire-storm may demoralise the civilian population . . .

This view differed markedly from the express policy of Reich Propaganda Minister Dr. Goebbels, on whose conscience must lie the responsibility for the greater part of the civilian death-roll in the ensuing fire-storms in Germany. A few days after delivering the funeral oration at Wuppertal-Barmen in June he had privately declared:

> If I could hermetically seal off the Ruhr, if there were no such things as letters or telephones, then I would not have allowed a word to be published about the air offensive. Not a word!

For many Kassel citizens, therefore, as for the citizens of Darmstadt, Brunswick and finally Dresden, the first experience they gained of fire-storms and conflagrations so large that, as in the case of Kassel, 300 fire-brigade units could not contain them, was when the bombs fell and they discovered that they themselves were right at the heart of a fire-storm in their own home city.

.   .   .   .   .

As the winter of 1943 approached, the forces aligned against Bomber Command were not entirely those under the command of the German flak and fighter divisions; a controversy about the ethical issues involved in night area bombing was mounting both within and without the Government. In public, as we have seen, the Government's statements had been designed to assuage the suspicions of uneasy minds. When the B.B.C. news bulletin had reported in May 1942 that numerous workers' dwellings had been successfully destroyed during the 1942 attacks on Rostock, an Independent Labour M.P. had asked the Secretary of State for Air whether the Royal Air Force had been instructed 'to impede and disorganise the German effort by the destruction of workmen's dwellings?' Although this Question had been framed some five weeks after the acceptance of the Lindemann minute discussed above, and although ten weeks had passed since Sir Charles Portal had directed that Bomber Command's aiming-points were to be 'the built-up areas, *not* for instance the dockyards or aircraft factories where these are mentioned', Sir Archibald Sinclair felt justified in replying that 'no instruction has been given to destroy dwelling houses rather than armament factories'.

Similarly, when Mr. R. Stokes, the Labour M.P. for Ipswich, who was a veteran campaigner against the area offensive, asked on 31st March 1943, at the height of the Battle of the Ruhr, whether British airmen had been instructed to 'engage in area bombing rather than limit their attention to purely military targets', Sinclair replied that 'the targets of Bomber Command are always military'. Sinclair must have been as aware by this time as any of the thousands of Bomber Command personnel of the exact siting of the pencilled crosses on the aircrews' target maps, but, as he explained to Sir Charles Portal in a minute sent on 28th October 1943, it was only thus that he could satisfy the inquiries of the Archbishop of Canterbury, the Moderator of the Church of Scotland, and other significant religious leaders who, on learning the truth and condemning the area offensive, could undoubtedly impair the morale of the bomber crews and hence their bombing efficiency. This explanation satisfied the Chief of the Air Staff, but not Sir Arthur Harris, or apparently Sir Robert Saundby, both inveterate opponents of hypocrisy and firm believers in the propriety of the area offensive; Harris was even compelled to point out that the effect on his crews of the continued Ministerial negation of any area offensive could be just as unfortunate: aircrews might form the independent impression that they were being asked to perform deeds which the Air Ministry was ashamed to admit. Whether or not this prolonged air offensive against civilians in Germany was immoral, Sir Arthur Harris never feared to proclaim both his intentions and his methods to the world, frequently to the acute embarrassment of the Air Ministry, as when he declared that his ill-fated Battle of Berlin would continue 'until the heart of Nazi Germany ceases to beat.'

At a later date in the war into this argument stepped the R.A.F. chaplain at Headquarters, Bomber Command in High Wycombe: Canon L. J. Collins, who was a relative by marriage to Sir Arthur Harris and who had been appointed to the Chaplaincy at the Command in September 1944. He had organised an actively attended Christian Fellowship group there.

Late in 1944, when this closed controversy was nearing its climax, he felt called upon to organise under the auspices of this group a series of political lectures, on moral subjects, for the senior Bomber Command officers. One of the first lectures was at Collins' own suggestion delivered by Stafford Cripps, the Minister of Aircraft Production and a Christian moralist. Sir Arthur Harris refused to attend personally and appointed his Deputy C.-in-C., Sir Robert Saundby, to receive the guest and Chair the meeting, to be held in the Command's Air Staff Conference Room.

The Minister of Aircraft Production took as the unfortunate text for his after-dinner lecture, attended by some hundred senior officers and men, the words 'God is my Co-Pilot.' Eloquently he pressed the argument that those responsible, the Government as well as Bomber Command, should always be sure before sending a bombing mission to Germany that it was really essential for military purposes. 'Even when you are engaged in acts of wickedness,' he insisted, 'God is always looking over your shoulder.' For a leading politician in the midst of one of the Command's heaviest air offensives this implicit condemnation of the Command's methods was remarkable; but for the Minister of Aircraft Production to adopt thus openly such a partisan view was more than many of the officers present were prepared to tolerate. A lively discussion ensued. A

Wing Commander on the administrative staff, who innocently asked whether they were to assume from Cripps' lecture that he had little faith in Sir Arthur Harris' bombing policies, was treated by Cripps as a Q.C. would treat a hostile witness, as Saundby recalls—held up to ridicule and contempt. The meeting was already developing into an ugly verbal brawl, when another officer queried whether Cripps' obvious lack of sympathy for the air offensive against Germany was the explanation for his apparent lack of success as Minister of Aircraft Production, and was that why the Command had experienced inordinate delays in dealings with the Ministry.

Before Stafford Cripps could reply, Bomber Command's superior planning once again outmanoeuvred its enemy, even though he had thus seized the initiative. Sir Robert Saundby, who was, in fact, the air officer who had originally formulated the brilliantly successful *Corona* deception strategy, depressed a hidden bell-push under the table and at once a straight-faced meteorological officer appeared, brandishing the latest 'meteorological report', which forecast 'severe fog' in Gloucestershire, to which the Minister had to repair that same night; the report had indeed come at a providential moment, but, suspecting nothing, the Minister of Aircraft Production hastened for home. There must have been many officers in the audience that night who were well aware of the existence and practice of *Corona*; it was to the credit of the Command that none of them betrayed the secret by premature hilarity.

Sir Arthur Harris was naturally upset by the scene which had occurred, even though the opportune fog report had saved further damage to relations with the Ministry of Aircraft Production; later he tried to rectify the harm he considered to have been caused by Cripps, by inviting his Personal Assistant, T. D. Weldon, a tutor in Moral Philosophy at Magdalen College Oxford, to lecture on 'The Ethics of Bombing' to his senior officers; this lecture was, as Saundby recalls, almost as obscure as that of Cripps, lightened only by the innocent inquiry at the end by Canon Collins whether he had mistakenly assumed the title of his lecture to be 'The Bombing of Ethics'.

.   .   .   .   .   .

The exchanges in public were by the end of 1943 hardly less lively, if less enlightening than those behind the barbed wire and concrete of the Bomber Command establishment. On 1st December Mr. Stokes made his last attempt until 1945, after the Dresden tragedy, to elicit an admission by Sinclair that a policy of area bombing had been adopted. He demanded to know whether in fact the objectives of the night bombers had 'been changed to the bombing of towns and wide areas in which military targets are situated?' Sir Archibald Sinclair was forced to sidestep the burden of the question and, referring to his reply of 31st March, assured him that 'there has been no change of policy'. Bomber Command's policy had indeed not changed, but Mr. Stokes, dissatisfied with this obscure reply, persisted with his Question and demanded whether it would not be 'true to say that probably the minimum area of a target is now sixteen square miles?' With more sarcasm than objectivity the Air Minister replied that his honourable Friend could not have listened to his answer: 'I said there had been no change in policy'.

When Mr. Stokes, with remarkable tenacity, demanded to know the area in square miles in which the 350 blockbusters recently dropped on Berlin had landed, he was informed that the question, predictably, could not be answered without giving useful information to the enemy.

Mr. Stokes: Would not the proper answer be that the Government dare not give it?

Sir A. Sinclair: No, sir. Berlin is the centre of twelve strategic railways; it is the second largest port in Europe; it is connected with the whole canal system of Germany; and in that city are the A.E.G., Siemens, Daimler-Benz, Focke-Wulf, Heinkel and Dornier establishments; and if I were allowed to choose only one target in Germany, the target I should choose would be Berlin.

Mr. Stokes: Does not my right honourable Friend admit by his answer that the Government are now resorting to indiscriminate bombing, including residential areas?

Sir A. Sinclair: The honourable gentleman is incorrigible. I have mentioned a series of vitally important military objectives.

Mr. Emanuel Shinwell interjected that he wished to applaud the efforts of H.M. Government to bring the war to a speedy conclusion, and the view that any measures which would hasten the end of the war were morally acceptable appears to have prevailed for the rest of the Debate. And when the Church, in the person of Dr. Bell, Bishop of Chichester, did in early February 1944 protest vigorously about the air offensive—he had learned of the horrors of Hamburg and the other great cities from neutral sources while in Sweden—popular opinion refused to take him seriously.

CHAPTER IV

THE SABRE AND THE BLUDGEON

THE summer of 1944 produced one further illuminating if unintentional exposition of the theory of the area attack, this time by the German Air Force; in June, the V-weapon offensive against London began.

Its effect was almost as immediate as it was unscheduled; *Crossbow* (the code word for attacks on V-weapon launching sites) became an added objective, and at times top priority for the bomber forces, competing with the intensity of the offensive against French railways targets, a vital component of the *Overlord* landings in Normandy. Forty per cent of the 1,000-pound-bomb production was vested in factories in the London area, and the assault of V weapons caused so much damage that output was seriously affected. These bombs were primarily used for the bombing of precision targets, which again adversely affected the railway plan. This plan had for some time been a cause of dispute between the Allies. In April the Prime Minister had become increasingly worried by the number of casualties among the French civilians that the railway plan would involve, and finally protested to Roosevelt. Replying on the 11th May, Roosevelt merely said that the decision should be left to the military commanders, and plans went ahead without further protests, though aircrews were warned by Eisenhower to keep civilian casualties to a minimum.

The supreme control of the Anglo-American strategic bomber forces had been transferred from Sir Charles Portal to the Supreme Commander, General Eisenhower, in April 1944, in view of the approaching need for close co-operation between the forces for *Operation Overlord*. Under the directive issued by Tedder, Eisenhower's Deputy, on 17th April, 1944, the role of Bomber Command was loosely described as to 'disorganise German industry', which could be interpreted as an authority to continue the area offensive in which Sir Arthur Harris so firmly believed. Instead, however, responding to the wishes of Eisenhower and Tedder, Sir Arthur Harris's efforts were devoted firstly to the co-operation with *Overlord* and then to the oil plan. One influencing factor may have been the crippling losses in crews and planes incurred by area bombing at this time, which was mainly directed against Berlin, and which culminated on the night of 30th–31st March when 95 of the force of 795 bombers failed to return from an attack on Nuremberg.

Post-war research has suggested from at least three different sources that this impressive night-fighter success at Nuremberg was the consequence of a security leak at a Bomber Command station; at least one P.o.W. being interrogated at the *Dulag Luft* clearing house for Allied airmen near Frankfurt was informed by the Chief Interrogating officer on the afternoon of the Nuremberg raid that the Germans knew that Nuremberg was the target for the night, and that the bombers were to follow a curiously direct route out.

During these summer months Bomber Command were not therefore able to carry out an area offensive on a scale comparable to that of the great 1943 battles. The oil plan intensified during June and July, becoming top priority, and when in July an attempt was made to saturate a German city with a succession of heavy raids, the reprisal went off at halfcock: by the time of the third, and final raid, in this case on Stuttgart, some No. 3 Group stations were even employing bombs earmarked for scrapping before 1940, charged with World War I explosives or Amatol 65. The bulk of the explosive dropped in these three Pathfinder-led raids on Stuttgart consisted of small General Purpose bombs, already proved to be of little worth by Professor Zuckerman three years previously. The only innovation was the introduction of a large number of J-bombs, thirty-pound petrol-jet bombs, designed to throw a thirty-foot jet of flame.

As an attempt at reproducing the Hamburg catastrophe the Stuttgart series were a total failure; the city presented a notoriously indeterminate *H2S* image, surrounded as it was by a bowl of low-lying hills. The timing was poor, the concentration weak, the marking hazy; the only significant success during the attack on the night of 24th–25th July 1944, the first anniversary of the Battle of Hamburg, was the destruction of the Observations Corps operations room, with the deaths of eight officers and forty Luftwaffe girls. The failure of the attack, delivered by 614 bombers, was reflected in the low death-roll: the Police President reported a provisional figure of 100 dead, 200 missing, and some ten thousand homeless, in an attack lasting 35 minutes. For the complete series, the Stuttgart Statistical Office provided post-war data: in the three raids of 24th, 25th and 28th July 1944, a total of 898 people were killed and 1,916 injured.

But on one night barely six weeks later, a force of only 217 Lancasters was to deliver such a concentrated raid, under much less favourable conditions, that in thirty-one minutes after 10.59 p.m. on the night of 12th September, 971 people were killed and 1,600 injured; the heart of the city was in this raid 'completely wiped out'.

The notable dispersal of effort in the three Pathfinder-marked raids of July, compared with the later single raid of September in which the Pathfinder Group played no direct part, is attributable to two factors: on the one hand, the first three attacks were executed during the embargo on high explosive wastage on German cities; on the other hand, the last attack was delivered by No. 5 Bomber Group, marking by its own distinctive low-level technique, while the first three had relied on the radar-placed marker flares of the No. 8 Group Pathfinders.

The success of this Stuttgart raid as an area attack—No. 5 Group's 230 sorties had achieved rather more than had the 1,662 sorties of the whole Command in July's series—was a grim augury for the remainder of the air offensive against the German cities. No. 5 Group's speciality of conspicuous and accurate low-level visual marking was contrary to all the doctrines in which the Pathfinder Commander believed. He had even protested, earlier in the year, that low-level target marking was impracticable: 'It was virtually impossible to map-read over densely built-up areas at low level', he protested when a plan to dive-mark Berlin in this way was being discussed; for his pains, he had had his crack Pathfinder Lancaster Squadrons 83 and 97 confiscated by Sir Arthur Harris and presented together with 627 (Mosquito) Squadron to Air Vice-Marshal Ralph Cochrane, the A.O.C. No. 5 Group, with effect from 6th April. All three squadrons were to discharge cardinal duties in the execution of the first of the three major raids on Dresden in 1945.

All three again made their debut as a No. 5 Group force in the first low-level visual marking attack on a German city on the night of 24th–25th April 1944. The target was Munich, and while the main force of 260 Lancasters dog-legged its way across France towards South Germany, and a full-scale Bomber Command diversionary attack on Karlsruhe was decoying the bulk of the fighter force, Group Captain G. L. Cheshire, in a courageous low-level dive across the heavily-defended Munich marshalling yard had dropped his red marker bomb in the heart of the station, some four minutes before zero hour. Three other Mosquitoes repeated the marking at the same time on his V.H.F. radio orders. The bombing began one minute early, and ended twenty-nine minutes later, 663 tons of incendiaries and 490 tons of high explosive having been dropped, of which no less than ninety per cent were estimated as having hit the target.

The feint towards Southern France appears to have failed to deceive the defences: the bomber formations were plotted by the Observer Corps entering the Continent over the Somme estuary at 11.55 p.m., the Increased Alert had been signalled at 12.31 a.m., with the Air Danger 28 stage reached four minutes later. In fact the Munich flak batteries had opened fire as early as 1.25, with zero hour still twenty minutes away: presumably they were firing at the eleven 627 Squadron Mosquitoes dropping *Window* in advance of the main marker force. Although the Provisional Police Report on the raid, issued next day at 10.00 p.m., placed the casualties at thirty people dead and six missing—a remarkably low figure which was later corrected, but only to 136—the damage to the city was impressive: the Central Station, the Eastern Station, the Arnulf-strasse marshalling yards, the Central Post Office, and the Laimer Station were reported very badly damaged. Buildings destroyed included three Army buildings, five police barracks and eight A.R.P. barracks. Success on this scale was the consequence of a closely controlled attack by main force bombers with accurately placed target indicators to aim at.

The idea of using a Master Bomber over the target to direct bomber crews and to encourage them had first been mooted by Air Vice-Marshal Bennett on 2nd December 1942, when he sent out Squadron Leader S. P. Daniels, one of his leading officers, to lead an attack on Frankfurt, with, however, only standard radio equipment by which to communicate with the main force. Unluckily, the weather on that occasion was very poor, and the Master Bomber could barely make himself heard above the atmospherics; all crews had been briefed to listen out when over the target area, but many reported in their post-raid interrogations that they had heard only 'muttering' over the target. Nevertheless, it does both the Path-finder Group and Squadron Leader Daniels an injustice to suggest, as do the Official Historians, that the Master Bomber technique was 'first evolved by Wing Commander Gibson in the dams raids', or that the Peenemünde attack was the 'first occasion upon which [it] had been applied to a major attack.' The Frankfurt authorities failed to realise that Bomber Command had even intended to attack the town, and no bombs were recorded within the city boundaries. In Darmstadt, however, seventeen miles to the south, the Police

President recorded the deaths of four citizens in the heaviest raid of the year. This Master Bomber experiment was wholly unauthorised and Sir Arthur Harris ordered Bennett not to repeat it; the dangers were too obvious. When, however, Air Vice-Marshal Cochrane, the A.O.C. of No. 5 Group, had been planning the raid on the Ruhr dams some six months later, Harris had raised no objection to the use of V.H.F. radio equipment for communication.

.   .   .   .   .

On 29th August 1944 an attack delivered by No. 5 Group on Königsberg was to lay the foundations for the fire-storm raids on Darmstadt, Brunswick, Heilbronn, and finally Dresden. The Group was by now operating largely as an independent force, with its own pathfinder squadrons, its own meteorological flights, its own post-raid reconnaissance aircraft, and, perhaps most important of all, an all-Lancaster force of bombers. For the attack on the port of Königsberg a new 'offset' marking and bombing technique was developed. The 189 Lancasters approached the target on three different pre-instructed bearings, while two early pathfinder Lancasters loaded with red target indicators identified and marked the aiming point, a distinctive railway yard in the southern city. Although the main force of bombers was to aim from the same single marking point, the three different approach angles and timed overshoots resulted in effect in three aiming points for the cost of only one successful marking attack; this was no small consideration when the target was as highly defended as Königsberg, and especially advantageous as the marking point lying to the windward of, and outside, the area of attack would not be obscured by smoke or swamped by incendiary fires. Of the 480 tons of bombs dropped, 345 tons were fire-bombs, of the small and potent four-pound thermite type; the bomb load which each Lancaster could carry was small on this occasion in view of the eleven hours and twenty minutes of the flight. During an unsuccessful attack on Königsberg three nights before, the Group had been required to drop clusters of J-bombs and they had turned out to be as ineffective in the Baltic port as they had been in Stuttgart a month before or in Darmstadt on 25th August.

Zero hour was at 1.07 a.m. on 30th August for Königsberg, but it took twenty minutes before the Master Bomber, Wing Commander J. Woodroffe, was satisfied; in spite of unpredicted low cloud over the target area, the markers were both within four hundred yards of the marking point in the railway yards. The Master Bomber's instructions over the V.H.F. were clear and concise, and by 1.52 when the last bombs fell, 435 acres of a total built-up area of 824 acres had been destroyed: 134,000 people were homeless and 21 per cent of the industrial buildings had been seriously damaged.

.   .   .   .   .

When the time came on 11th September for No. 5 Group to mount an attack on Darmstadt, a still further improvement in this technique of 'offset bombing' had been effected. The city was technically a difficult target to attack, as the industrial areas weı ⁚ well scattered around the periphery of an extended residential and commercial zone in the centre; to have attempted to harm the industrial areas by scattering bomb loads round a central aiming-point and hoping—as was standard Pathfinder Group practice—that the overspill would affect the industrial suburbs, would have been a disastrous dissipation of effort, especially with such a small force of bombers.

To many Germans the attack on Darmstadt came as a surprise. They themselves had accorded it a very low A.R.P. rating, and the lack of fire-fighting equipment was a direct cause of the high casualties. It will be illuminating here to describe how it came about that an attack was delivered on this city at all, for it provides a well-authenticated example of the sources of information upon which the Air Ministry target committees relied. At the beginning of June, an elderly widow who before the war had lived in Darmstadt, fleeing in 1938 like so many Germans before the National Socialist anti-semitic measures, found herself living in the same block of flats in Surbiton as an R.A.F. Wing Commander then attached to the Targets Selection Committee of the Air Ministry. She mentioned to him that she had observed a large factory 'making submarine optical components' being constructed near to her home in Darmstadt just before she left Germany, and asked how it was that the town had not been the subject of a major R.A.F. attack. As the Targets Selection Committee expressed a certain degree of interest in this report, the Wing Commander was requested to inquire after more details of military installations or industrial plants in the neighbourhood.

It was as a result of his final report on the town to this Committee that Darmstadt appeared on the weekly target lists compiled by the Combined Strategic Targets Committee, and that Bomber Command was instructed to deliver an attack on that town. Darmstadt was not only a centre of the chemical industry and of optical factories at this time, however: although the Air Ministry was not aware of it, there was in the city an academy for training V-2 technicians.

The line attack developed by Air Vice-Marshal Cochrane was specifically related to the attack on Darmstadt. In the western outskirts of the town was a large and prominent rectangular Cavalry Exercise Ground, built on a chalky subsoil, for it emerged conspicuously white on reconnaissance photographs; it was this parade ground which served as the marking point for the attack. No. 627 Squadron, whose motto was fittingly 'At First Sight', and who had persistently distinguished themselves by their bold low-level visual marking attacks since Munich, had provided 14 pathfinder Mosquitoes both for the visual marking and for dive-bombing attacks on individual outlying factories like the I.G. Farben plant. Wing Commander Woodroffe was again Master Bomber.

At 10.25 the sirens sounded the public air raid warning in Darmstadt. The *Drahtfunk* warning service signalled:

Heavy enemy bomber formations approaching from Oppenheim East and Heidelberg North. Acute danger for Darmstadt.

At 11.25 p.m. the *Fliegeralarm* was sounded. By 11.45 the first bombs were already falling. The fire-watching posts reported that there appeared to be no definite centre of the attack. They were correct: the 240 Lancasters had been briefed to approach the clearly marked Parade Ground on two different bearings; not only was the force thus divided into two sections, but each squadron had been ordered to bomb on a different overshoot over the marking point. The intended result was that two wide lines of attack would extend across the city in a V shape from the western marking point, taking in the whole city area. In this way sticks of bombs were calculated to saturate the whole administrative section of the town and its residential areas. Of the 240 Lancasters dispatched 234 attacked, dropping 872 tons of bombs within forty minutes, including 286,000 thermite fire bombs, and nearly two hundred 4,000-pound blockbusters. Although the left-hand line went partly astray, the operation was a major success and it was clear that Bomber Command would never need to return to Darmstadt.

.   .   .   .   .

Once again the post-raid report drawn up by the town's Police President provides a documentary description of the attack: the raid on the night of 11th–12th September was recorded as having been distinguished from all previous minor raids by the massed and concentrated bombing. The fire-storm which emerged after about one hour embraced the entire Inner City, even igniting buildings damaged only slightly by blast. Immediate rescue operations were out of the question, as the streets and squares were inaccessible. Even the external fire-brigades trying to penetrate to the city centre were forced back by the lack of water and by the unbearably fierce heat radiation, which threatened both the men and their vehicles. The forty-per-cent complete slaked-lime fire-proofing of roof-timbers, which in Kassel had prevented a spread of the fire-storm area, in Darmstadt proved worthless. The doors and windows which had been broken down by blast and decompression waves now gave access to the fires on every floor, and buildings were gutted not only from the roof downwards, but from the ground floor up as well.

By about 2.00 a.m. the fire-typhoon in the streets had exceeded hurricane force ten or twelve, and any kind of movement in the open was out of the question; the typhoon subsided only slowly towards 4.00 a.m. In consequence, the inhabitants of this area were unable to save themselves; an unfortunate circumstance of the Darmstadt fire-storm raid was that successive detonations from a wrecked munitions train on the railway sidings to the south of the town centre discouraged people from deserting their shelters in time, as it was generally believed that the attack was still under way.

The whole Inner City was destroyed by this one small attack—only 240 heavy bomber sorties despatched—and the devastation reached 78 per cent; if the less damaged suburbs of Arheiligen and Eberstadt are included, the destruction totalled 52.4 per cent. The British Bombing Survey, more objectively than their American contemporaries, estimated from photographs that 69 per cent of the total built-up area was destroyed, 516 acres of a total of 745. In a city with 115,200 inhabitants, 21,487 homes had been destroyed, rendering homeless 70,000 of the population. In the Old City, only five buildings had escaped destruction: the prison in Rundeturm-strasse, 'provided with a blue-lamp to spare it from air raids'; the tavern called 'The Crown', a butcher's shop next to it, an architect's house a little further away, and the rear buildings of St. Ludwig's catholic church. As Darmstadt had been only a second-degree A.R.P. zone (*L.S.-Ort 2. Ordnung*) no expenditure was made by the Reich on air-raid bunkers, but only on unimportant measures of construction, including three rescue centres and 54 public air-raid shelters.

The unprotected citizens, accordingly, suffered more severely than their luckier counterparts in Kassel, and later Brunswick, as we shall see. The number of registered dead was recorded as 5,500 with certainty, of which 1,800—a total therefore of 32.7 per cent—were unidentifiable because of total incineration; again no figures for casualties among military personnel on active service were included.

> Considering the scale of this catastrophe the final death roll will be much higher [the Police President emphasised] especially as no fewer than 4,500 people have been reported as missing. In fact the total figure will be even more than that, as events have already shown that whole families with all their members have been killed, whose disappearance will as a result never be reported.

The Statistical Yearbook of German Municipalities states a final figure for the Darmstadt death-roll on this one night as 12,300. The town's Statistical Office places the figure between 12,000 and 15,000. The United States Strategic Bombing Survey gives an estimate of 8,500.

The cause of death was predominantly—in some 90 per cent of the cases—asphyxiation or burning.

For the first four days after the attack the recovery of the victims presented considerable difficulties, as there were no vehicles left within the town for their removal. Only with the arrival of a Transport Unit of the Speer Organisation was the situation alleviated. The same scenes which had greeted the rescue troops penetrating the gutted streets of the fire-storm areas of Hamburg and Kassel now met the eyes of the rescue gangs in Darmstadt: the streets were strewn with naked, brilliantly hued corpses, or charred objects some three feet long, which looked like logs, but which had been human beings.

On 24th September the Roman Catholic Bishop of Mainz celebrated a Requiem Mass for the Darmstadt citizens who had lost their lives in the forty-minute No. 5 Group attack on the town.

.   .   .

With the attack on Bremerhaven on 18th–19th September 1944, the line attack was further adapted to suit the peculiarly elongated port, which extended eight miles along the eastern shores of the Weser estuary; the problem, it will be remembered, was similar to the problem of the attack on the twin city of Wuppertal. The Pathfinder group would probably have relied on some degree of creep-back; the line attack of No. 5 Group however was a more certain method of destroying the whole city; this time one marking point, but with five approach lines, sufficed for the whole attack; the marking force was able to mark the chosen spot in the northern end of the city with great speed: Zero hour was to be 9.00 p.m., but as early as 8.58 p.m. the Master Bomber was able to broadcast the instruction to the main force of Lancasters to 'come in and bomb'. As a result the bombers, which were now *Window*-ing at the rate of five bundles per minute, a much heavier rate than had been thought sufficient at Hamburg thirteen months previously, were not kept unnecessarily orbiting over the heavily defended port area and only two aircraft, one of them a Mosquito, were lost during the whole attack, while the remaining 208 of the 213 despatched were able to drop their 863 tons of bombs—including no fewer than 420,000 thermite bombs—in a very concentrated attack. The British Bombing Survey reported from investigation of reconnaissance photographs that of a total built-up acreage of 375 acres, 297 were totally destroyed: that represented seventy-nine per cent destroyed. This was the first occasion on which Bomber Command had turned its attention to the port; the Command was not troubled to return again. No. 5 Group's tactics were rapidly nearing perfection.

It is surprising that these raids, which were among the most effective executed by the Command, have hardly rated any attention in any of the official accounts published on the course of the air war.

Air Vice-Marshal Bennett in his memoirs dismisses all these raids, as it were, in one breath:

> In the rest of 1944 No. 5 Group sometimes joined in with the rest of the Command on proper P.F.F. marking [*i.e.* No. 8 Group marking] but otherwise attacked on their own a large variety of small targets, most of them comparatively undefended, such as . . . Darmstadt, Königsberg, Heilbronn, etc.

He also records that they 'went to' Brunswick twice. The three first raids, involving the deaths of over 24,000 civilians, had been carried out at the cost of only some 670 sorties by No. 5 Group.

· · · · ·

Although only 561 citizens were in fact killed by the No. 5 Group attack on Brunswick of 14th–15th October 1944, its analysis is important in the context of the later raids on Dresden; Brunswick was the first successful exposition of the Group's sector-attack technique, the technique finally selected for the first raid on Dresden four months later. As Air Vice-Marshal Cochrane explained to his station and flight-commanders prior to the attack, in the usual loudspeaker link-up peculiar to the Group, the intention was to saturate each square yard of the target sector with an equal weight of bombs: the fires would then break out swiftly and would be so widespread that the fire brigades would not be able to master them. Instead of a limited number of aiming lines and timed overshoots, as had been the case at Königsberg, Bremerhaven and Darmstadt, the Brunswick raid would involve each of the 233 Lancasters attacking over the single marking point on a different heading and with a different timed overshoot; in this way a fan-shaped sector could be devastated evenly right across the centre of the city. The marking point was in the south of the city, and the attacking force would fly in a northerly direction across Brunswick.

Zero hour for Brunswick was set at 2.30 a.m. on 15th October. Once again a large part of the force was carrying the petrol-jet J-bombs of which the Command seemed to have an inexhaustible stock. By 3.10 a.m. a medium-strength fire-storm had arisen in the area bounded by the Brunswick Woll-markt, Lange-strasse, Weber-strasse, and light pieces of furniture, tables and chairs were being sucked up by the tornado; violent whirlwinds whipped up the dust and showers of sparks and burning embers were driven before them through the streets. The fire area embraced the whole Inner City, with the exception of small districts round the Central Station, the Town Hall, and the August Gate. It was just in this area however that six giant bunkers and two public air raid shelters, with about 23,000 people now trapped in them, had been built.

Once again the telephone service had been destroyed, and the despatch rider service was unable to operate under these conditions; the city's fire-brigades had already gone into action independently in various parts of the city and as a result it was only towards 5.00 a.m. that sufficiently powerful fire-fighting detachments could be assembled to risk the dangerous and seldom tried 'water-alley' technique, which seemed to be the only hope of reaching and rescuing the 23,000 trapped in the heart of the fire-storm area.

A group of high-pressure fire-hoses was to be fought forwards under a constant screen of water into the heart of the fire area: the front and sides of this 'alley' would be protected from the fierce, radiated heat by veils of water from overlapping jets of water; obtaining water-supplies presented considerable difficulties for this, because although water supplies and hydrants as such were at hand nearby, they were in the fire-area itself. Similarly, the pressure in the hoses had to be reinforced several times by auxiliary pumps in the hose-system; all the time both pumps and hoses were endangered by collapsing buildings and the heat radiation.

Nevertheless, in spite of time wasted in constantly having to shift the pumps to safer locations, by 7.00 a.m., four and a half hours after the raid had begun, the bunkers were reached. As the doors were unbarred and unlocked, the rescuers heard the sound of 'many people talking quietly but nervously under their breath.' All the shelterers were still alive. The evacuation of the 23,000 people was effected, with the people forming an endless human chain along the inside of the water alley to the areas of relative safety outside the fire-storm zone, without any casualties.

The fire-service teams did not always have the same good fortune: in the air raid shelter in Schöppenstedter-strasse 104 people were recovered, of whom only nine could be revived. In this case, although the shelter itself was undamaged, the cause of death was the familiar fire-storm one: asphyxiation. Nevertheless, with its advanced state of A.R.P. measures, and the courage of its fire-fighting teams, the city of Brunswick had been able to avert a major tragedy.

So great was the extent of physical damage, however, that although only the one Bomber Group had taken part, the city authorities recorded that over a thousand aircraft had been responsible. Some 4,500 firemen fought for six days to control the last fires, repeatedly being driven under cover by renewed air-raid warnings; as they sheltered, the fires they had nearly extinguished blazed into flames again as fiercely as before. Only on 20th October were the last fire-services returned to their home towns. During the forty-minute sector-attack No. 5 Group had dropped a total of 847 tons of bombs on the city; the results, expressed in bare statistics, were remarkable: 80,000 people were immediately homeless of a population of 202,000; of a built-up area of 1,400 acres, 655 acres were totally destroyed. The city's gasworks, power station and water-works were wrecked, as were the telephone network, the tramlines and railways. One official account of the raids complains: 'Even those heavy industries in Brunswick which had not been badly hit in the attack of 15th October were more seriously affected than ever before by the loss of personnel, either killed or too pre-occupied with the domestic problems of survival to report for work.' There can be no more convincing support for the theory of the area attack than this; unfortunately not all area attacks were performed with such a low loss of civilian life. Apart from this Brunswick operation,

J-bombs were able to cause a major conflagration only during the 4th December 1944 attack on Heilbronn; the same sector attack technique evolved by Air Vice-Marshal Cochrane and his Base Commander, Air Commodore H. V. Satterley, was used, with a forked marshalling yard as the marking point. Over 7,000 of the town's 77,569 inhabitants were killed in the one attack, with many thousands missing. It was an ominous augury for Dresden that both the Master Bomber and his Deputy, the Marker Leader on this attack, were to perform the same rôles at Dresden.

As a precursor of the Dresden raids, however, the night of 14th–15th October not only brought the devastating sector-attack on Brunswick; that same night, the other major technique which was to signalise the end of Dresden four months later was demonstrated in a 'triple-blow' on Duisburg by a total of 2,068 bomber sorties: the first blow was delivered during the day by more than one thousand bombers; then during the hours after midnight the whole force apart from No. 5 Group returned to the Ruhr port and executed a crushing double blow, the two halves of the attack separated by an interval of just under two hours, so that night fighters would be grounded and exhausted, or refuelling, by the time of the last attack.

As it turned out, on this night not only the German night fighters were exhausted. Such was the pressure under which the R.A.F. ground crews were working in bombing-up aircraft for 2,068 sorties in one day that of the total, 9,708 high-explosive bombs (not including 'cookies') which fell on the Duisburg A.R.P. zone, no fewer than 1,336 failed to explode.

Heavily defended though Duisburg was, and hardened though the population was to Allied air attacks, the casualties were heavy: 1,521 Germans were killed, with a further 746 reported missing; 183 prisoners of war and foreign labourers were also among the dead.

With the successful execution of the Brunswick and Duisburg attacks, the stage was set for the February 1945 area attacks on population centres which were to culminate in the Dresden tragedy: the prevailing winds of public opinion would no longer be offended by Bomber Command attacks on this scale. Bomber Command now disposed over a long-range and independent air weapon capable of striking at distant targets, even as distant as Dresden, with great accuracy and violence; and, while No. 5 Group had perfected the sabre of its sector-attack, Bomber Command had fashioned the bludgeon of the triple blow.

PART TWO

THE HISTORICAL BACKGROUND

CHAPTER I

DRESDEN THE VIRGIN TARGET

LATE in 1944 the possibility of an air attack with the capital of Saxony as its specific target came under the direct cognizance of the Prime Minister for perhaps the first time. In October the Air Staff suggested with his approval that the Soviet Air Force might be requested to attack Dresden, although it is not clear from published references to this request whether the city area itself or the nearby Ruhland synthetic oil plant was meant; current practice was to refer without distinction to Dresden and Ruhland, thereby according to the Saxon capital an industrial significance of which, as we shall see, it was not entirely worthy. In spite of the representations made by the British Military Mission in Moscow, the recommendation was not followed up by the Soviet Air Force—which did indeed dispose a small strategic bombing force, as the Reich capital, Breslau and Königsberg—as well as numerous other Central and East German cities—were later to discover.

In spite of its having appeared on a draft directive discussed with Sir Richard Peirse as early as 1940 the city did not suffer its first air attack, until 12.36 p.m. on 7th October 1944: some thirty bombers of one American Bombardment Group had attacked the Dresden industrial area as a secondary target during an attack on the oil refinery at Ruhland. By the time that the city's sirens had sounded the All Clear at 1.27 p.m. that afternoon, the western suburbs of Dresden-Friedrichstadt and Dresden-Löbtau had been considerably damaged; the air raid was a local sensation and it is recorded that enterprising schoolchildren cornered all stocks of bomb fragments to sell as souvenirs, while coach-owners ran special excursions to the blitzed streets; nothing like this had ever happened in Dresden before. A total of 435 people died, mostly workers in the small factories of Seidel & Naumann and Hartwig & Vogel. Casualties inflicted on French and Belgian labourers in these plants were heavy too. Many *Arbeitskommandos*—working detachments—of Allied prisoners operating in the railway yards suffered severely, a number of Americans in one detachment particularly being killed; other prisoners of war were drafted in to take their places. Several

69

previously idle *Kommandos* of prisoners were put to work on salvage operations in this area. Nevertheless, the local inhabitants unanimously agreed among themselves that the bombing was the result of some unfortunate mistake by an Allied navigator and this early blow did nothing to shatter the enormous confidence of the Dresden people that their city was not going to be attacked.

For the British prisoners of war in the city in these pre-February 1945 weeks life could not easily be bettered. The Dresdeners were familiar with the English from pre-war days, when the city had been a cultural centre, and made many friends among the prisoners— a large section of which were from 1st Airborne Division contingent captured at Arnhem.

> The Germans here are the best I have ever come across [wrote one soldier, captured at Anzio, on Boxing Day, 1944]. The Commandant is a gentleman, and we are allowed an extraordinary amount of liberty in the town. The *Feldwebel* has already taken me to see the centre of the town. Unquestionably it is beautiful—I would like to see more of it.

The war seemed very far away from Dresden.

Not endowed with any one great capital industry like those of Essen or Hamburg, even though Dresden was of a comparable size, the city's economy had been sustained in peacetime by its theatres, museums, cultural institutions and home-industries. Even by the end of 1944 it would have been difficult to have singled out any one plant of the kind of major importance which occasioned air attacks on other less fortunate German towns and cities. In the Dresden-Striesen suburb, about three miles from the city centre, Zeiss-Ikon had an optical factory; elsewhere in the city, in Freiberger-strasse, was a Siemens glass factory; in Dresden-Niedersedlitz, five miles to the south-east of the city centre, and in Radeberg, nine miles to the north-east, were two Sachsenwerk plants; these two plants employed some five thousand workers on the manufacture of radar and other electronic components for sets being manufactured by A.E.G. in Berlin; in Grossenhainer-strasse, a long road leading northwards out of Dresden-Neustadt, was the Zeiss-Ikon Goehlewerk plant— built in 1941 of strong reinforced concrete with blast-proof windows and other astute A.R.P. measures; this factory was, by the time of the raids, employing 1,500 men on the manufacture of anti-aircraft shell-fuses for the German Navy. In Dresden-Friedrichstadt were two big factories supplying Germany with a large proportion of its cigarettes.

The Arsenal five miles to the north of the city centre, on which so much stress was placed in subsequent Air Ministry bulletins—though, to be fair, it was never mentioned by Bomber Command in its Weekly Digest—had, in fact, been an arsenal earlier on, in the First World War, but during a small-scale fire on 27th December 1916 it had been totally destroyed when a munitions train caught fire and exploded. On the site of the former Arsenal in Dresden, there was a new Industrial Estate with firms manufacturing a diversity of products including tin boxes, radio cabinets, soap, baby powder, tooth-paste and, according to local rumour, bombsights and navigation devices for aircraft. The remainder of the city's war industry was equally diverse, including a gas-mask factory producing some 50,000 masks per month, several breweries and two small firms manufacturing components for Junkers aircraft engines and cockpit parts for Messerschmitt's Augsburg plant. Research into V-2 rocket-motor injection nozzles was also carried out in the Dresden Technical University. But none of these factories or plants listed was within the area marked out for R.A.F. Bomber Command's two devastating night attacks.

Dresden was not by any means an open city, and had never been declared as such. An American Air Force historian has established to his own satisfaction, by an exhaustive study of German and Allied papers, that in addition to Dresden's significance as a major transportation centre there was an 'entire series' of other reasons why it was a major and bona fide military target, and was 'so considered by the German military and civilian authorities'.

Dresden had become a key point in the German postal and telegraph system, and there is little doubt that the obliteration of the postal installations in the city would hamper communication between the Eastern Front and the rest of the Reich; the permanent staff at the Central Post and Telegraph offices in the heart of the Inner City had been reinforced by some hundreds of Reich Work Service and War Auxiliary Service personnel to cope with the increased traffic; hundreds of British prisoners had been impressed into the German Postal service as labourers in the Post Office sheds in the Rosen-strasse goods-station, where they were forced to work in shifts round the clock unloading mailbags and sorting packages.

At the time of the attack, however, the city's strategic significance was scarcely marginal, and it is questionable whether at that stage of the war Dresden was likely to become, for example, a second Breslau; it was not until 14th April that the Gauleiter of Saxony,

Reichsstatthalter Martin Mutschmann, officially declared Dresden a fortress.

.   .   .   .   .

Historically, Dresden had been of some importance as a centre for the administration of military and, later, air force operations. In 1935 Dresden became the headquarters city of *Luftkreis III*, Air District III, from which Colonel Bogatsch, the Supreme Commander of the Saxon anti-aircraft artillery batteries, controlled various flak-regiments in Dresden, Gotha, Wurzen and Rudolstadt; a year later his authority was extended to include new flak-regiments formed in Weimar, Merseburg, Breslau and Dessau, and in 1937, as German rearmament progressed apace, the *Luftkreis* was extended to embrace new flak-regiments being organised for the defence of Jena, Leipzig, Chemnitz, Liegnitz, Halle, Wittenberg and Bitterfeld; the Rudolstadt regiment II./23 was dissolved.

On 30th November 1938, the German flak artillery was re-incorporated and extended to place the flak regiments under the control of the newly organised *Luftgaukommandos*—Air Zone Commands.

Colonel Bogatsch was now given the command of *Luftgaukommando IV* in Dresden, with headquarters in Dresden's General-Wever-strasse, not far from the Central Station. A separate Breslau *Luftgaukommando* was organised, No. VIII; already the military importance of Dresden as a control centre was declining. With the outbreak of war in 1939, the duties of the Dresden *Luftgaukommando* were primarily performed by Berlin's *Luftgaukommando III*, with which it was united.

In 1918, Dresden had been the headquarters of *Wehrkreis*—Army District Command—*IV*, and near the defunct Arsenal in the northern outskirts of the town there was an extensive complex of barracks and parade-ground installations. In the hills to the north-east S.S. troops under S.S.-General Alvensleben had blasted an underground command bunker into the Mordgrundbrücke rock face. This too was a target of a clearly military nature, but hardly one for strategic air forces.

In recognition of the city's apparent lack of military significance, the Reich government had turned as early as 1943 to Dresden as a haven for administrative departments and commercial offices, especially as the pressure from air attacks on the Reich capital became more severe; typical of this trend was the decision to move the Berlin Grossbank Head Office to Dresden with its whole administrative staff. But even by February 1945 there were no signs that the Reich government itself would be transferred to the city, although with the fall of Berlin such a move might have been contemplated.

Throughout the middle years of the war, the Dresden *Luftgaukommando* had stationed strong flak defences round the city, but, as we shall see, when the years passed without their springing into action more than twice, the Air Zone Command not unreasonably accepted that the batteries were being wasted in Dresden and had them dispersed both to the Eastern front and to the defence of the Ruhr.

Thus arose the widespread, positive, but fatal legend of Dresden, the city that would never be bombed. On the one hand, the Dresden people were convinced by the authorities' lack of action in A.R.P. programmes and by their disposal of the city's flak defences that there would be no attack, and on the other hand their pathetic confidence in the good intentions of the British and American governments reassured them that a city housing daily increasing numbers of civilian hospitals and military dressing stations would never be the object of an attack. The Allies might attack one or other of the remoter industrial suburbs, it was admitted, but never the city centre.

> The Dresden population [the Head of the Home Office Intelligence Section was to minute in 1947] appears to have believed that an understanding existed between ourselves and the Germans that we would spare Dresden if Oxford was not attacked.

Some people circulated a rumour of leaflets dropped by the Allies in which it was promised that, as Dresden was to be the post-war capital of a new and united Germany, the city would not be attacked; others asserted that the British Prime Minister had relatives living in or near the city. That the city had not even been the subject of the nuisance raids by Light Night Striking Force Mosquito formations appeared to lend even more credence to these rumours; tragic and pathetic though they appear to us now in the knowledge of the fate that was awaiting the city, the rumours were nevertheless believed not only by the 630,000 permanent residents of Dresden, but by the city's own officials, and were impressed in turn upon the hundreds of thousands of evacuees who were to flood into the city when the Russian invasion broke in the East.

. . . . .

The Dresden flak defences had been the responsibility of the city's *Luftgaukommando*—Air Zone Command—*IV*; as it is of some significance to consider whether the city was in February 1945 an undefended city within the meaning of the 1907 Hague Convention, it will be necessary to examine the establishment and subsequent total dispersal of the city's flak batteries, before the date of the triple blow.

German flak was predominantly operated on two scales, the light flak positions and the heavy flak batteries. Light flak was provided primarily by 20-mm. calibre machine guns—although 37-mm. and 40-mm. calibre guns were also classed as 'light flak'—and seldom scored damaging hits above seven thousand feet; with its familiar green and yellow tracer shells it was used primarily as a defence against low-flying intruders which would otherwise be immune from flak defences. The heavy flak batteries provided an often deadly defence against high-altitude bomber formations by using an A.A. version of the 88-mm. guns which were the capital weapon of German artillery planning.

From the summer of 1943 there had been two genres of heavy flak in the city, the 88-mm. guns and the less efficient 85/88-mm. *Flak m 39 (r)* guns. Among the standard 88-mm. heavy flak batteries at that stage of the war in Dresden were the 1/565th stationed in Dresden-Übigau, near to the Autobahn bridge across the River Elbe; the 2/565th on the Heller parade ground near Dresden-Klotzsche airfield; the 3/565th in the hills to the south of the city, stationed to be exact in Kohlenstrasse, Dresden-Räcknitz, and later enlarged—by cannibalising the others—to a *Grossbatterie*; the 4/565th on the high ground between Rochwitz and Gönnsdorf; and finally the 5/565th in Altfranken to the west of the city.

In addition to these standard pieces, achieving muzzle velocities in excess of 4,000 feet per second, the Dresden flak commander disposed over a number of captured Russian 85-mm. guns, rebored to the 88-mm. calibre and put into action as '85/88-mm.' anti-aircraft artillery. The standard German 88-mm. gun, as the British Army was painfully to discover in June 1941 in the Western Desert, was also serviceable as an anti-tank weapon; it was even capable when fired horizontally of piercing 202-mm. armour plating at a range of 1,000 yards and more. For Dresden this dual utility was to prove fatal as the Soviet tank offensive in the East gathered momentum, and first the 88-mm. batteries, then even the inferior 85/88-mm. batteries, too, were dismounted and rushed into action in the East. About this Soviet offensive and its both oblique and direct contribution to the Dresden tragedy more will be said in due course.

During such time as the flak was in Dresden, the Russian pieces were concentrated more towards the city centre than the heavier German guns; the 203/IV 85/88-mm. battery was stationed on the Elbe embankment at Vogelwiese; the 204th was in Wölfnitz; the 217th in Radebeul; the 238th in Seidnitz; the 247th in Rochwitz— all of them captured Russian guns. Of these, Battery 203/IV on the Elbe Embankment was closest to the city centre; the battery was equipped with six of the 85/88-mm. guns with radar predicted fire-control equipment. Four of these guns were manned by day by Hitler Youth schoolboys from the city's famous Kreuzschule, to-gether with a permanent crew of soldiers; by night the other two guns were manned by shifts of workers from the factories.

Not surprisingly, the Dresden flak had little chance in the early years to demonstrate its potency: private records indicate that the 3/565th battery was the first to fire in anger, and then only on 28th May 1944, when the U.S.A.A.F. was attacking nearby oil installations; on 24th August 1944 the flak was able to fire again during an attack on Dresden-Freital, and again on the 11th and 12th September—if only in a mild barrage.

In October 1944, however, the process of disbanding the Dresden flak was commenced: the 203rd battery was dissolved and merged with the 217th to form a single *Grossbatterie* in Radebeul; only once did this *Grossbatterie* open fire, during the American attack on Dresden on 7th October. There is a note of pathos in the recollection of one of the Hitler Youth boys, himself on duty as a radar fire control officer, of the wild attempts of the flak to counter the attack; his own steel helmet was much too large for him, and the throat microphone he wore was much too loose for his neck:

The gun barrels were bristling in all directions when we were told to put up a barrage [he recalled]. The boys in our crew were all so young and weak that Russian prisoners had to be used for loading the guns. All in all the Dresden flak was not the élite of the Reich defence.

Fortunately, he added ironically, there was no flak left in Dresden when the big attacks came; had there been, then he too would have been destroyed with the city.

During the winter of 1944 to 1945, with the renewed Soviet offensive on the Eastern front, and Allied armour now thrusting into Germany all along the western frontiers, the demand for the dispatch of Dresden's flak batteries to bolster these sagging defences became too insistent to ignore; nor was Dresden the only city thus to suffer: the United States Strategic Bombing Survey's summary report points out that in January and February of 1945 alone, some three hundred flak batteries were moved to the Eastern front to be used for anti-tank fire. By the middle of January 1945 only the concrete pads remained to mark where the flak batteries had once been in Dresden; only papier-mâché dummies remained on the hills outside to defend the city.

The batteries which had waited in vain for an onslaught on Dresden were by the start of February dispersed throughout the length and breadth of the Reich. Battery 207/IV was transferred to Halle; others were sent to Leipzig and Berlin. The 88-mm. flak was sent into action on the Eastern front, where it cannot have achieved much. Battery 4/565 was sent off to the Ruhr, where it served as an A.A. battery during the almost continual air attacks up to the end of March 1945; on 1st April it was converted to an anti-tank battery and took part in the defence of Hamm, near where it was finally overrun, ten days later, by the American infantry. Of the crew of Dresden Hitler Youth schoolboys, half were killed in this final gallant stand; the story of the end of the Dresden flak batteries, defending anything but the city from which their youthful crews had been impressed, is one tinged with tragedy, but also with heroism.

.   .   .   .   .

By the beginning of February 1945, the capital of Saxony was therefore virtually an undefended city, although the Allied Bomber Commands might well plead ignorance of this. In addition the city was, as we have seen, devoid of first-order industrial, strategic or military targets-in-being. Sir Arthur Harris and Lieut.-General James H. Doolittle, his American counterpart, were however concerned less with possible interpretations of international law than with winning the war, when they set out to attack Dresden as part of the offensive against Eastern population centres.

Sir Arthur Harris has observed that the only international restriction which he considered to be binding on him and his Command during the war was an agreement dating back to the Franco-Prussian War, which prohibited the release of explosive objects from gas-filled dirigibles; this restriction, as he points out, was rigidly complied with throughout the Second World War by Bomber Command.

All this is, however, trespassing seriously on chronology, and it is necessary first to observe how it came to pass that one of Germany's most treasured and beautiful cities, a city housing by then well over a million civilians and refugees, in addition to the servicemen billeted in the town and its barracks, finally came to be attacked, in the fourteen hours and fifteen minutes that were to commence at 10.15 p.m. on the night of 13th February 1945.

. . . .

During the first weeks of 1945, the German Army Command Headquarters found from intelligence sources that the Russians were apparently preparing for a new major offensive across the River Vistula, a front which had remained quite stable since the conclusion of the Soviet summer offensive of 1944. Massive Soviet forces, estimated to outnumber the German defenders by more than ten to one, were observed in concentration in the areas of Baranov, Pulavy and Magnusev. It was clear that a new, and this time possibly fatal, offensive was about to be launched. Colonel-General Guderian, Chief of the German General Staff, appealed to Hitler for troops to be withdrawn from Kurland and sent into action on the Vistula front; Hitler categorically refused this demand and would not permit the Army Commanders to shorten their fronts either. The situation on the Eastern front was clearly going to prove dangerous, none the less, because several German divisions had been withdrawn from this front and East Prussia already, during the winter of 1944 and 1945, with sections being transferred to Hungary and sections to the Western front in the Rhineland.

The German High Command were soon to learn the lessons that they themselves had taught the luckless French in 1940, when panic-stricken crowds of refugees had jammed the roads behind the battle zones. On 20th January, 1945, the German High Command's secret situation report recorded that 'refugee columns are getting in the way of our own troop movements.'

It was the responsibility of the local Gauleiters to organise mass evacuation of the civilian population from battle areas, and experience had already demonstrated that the prospects of the evacuees of reaching safety depended only on the despatch with which the evacuation operation was implemented; in this respect, the Gauleiters as political leaders were at variance with themselves as Reich Defence Commissioners: the whole German civilian morale was founded on the doctrine of Final Victory, and it was difficult to reconcile final victory with being forced to leave one's home and possessions overnight to the enemy; some Gauleiters, like Erich Koch of East Prussia, had solved this dilemma by refusing any discussion of evacuation measures in the province's capital, Königs-berg; thus when the weight of the two R.A.F. Bomber Command attacks on the city in August 1944 had constrained the city's

Oberpräsidium to appeal to Koch to order the evacuation of all non-combatants from the city, he was empowered to refuse, and did. He did not wish to spread alarm and despondency among the populace. On the other hand, the Gauleiters of Wartheland and Danzig/West Prussia had drawn up secret plans to deal with mass evacuation, which were to stand them in good stead.

The resulting fate of the East Prussian population who did obey the Gauleiter's embargo on evacuation was an object lesson not only to the other Gauleiters but also to the citizens of all other areas likely to be overrun by the Soviet Army. On 16th October 1944 the first mass Soviet offensive along a front of eighty-five miles had threatened the very heart of East Prussia, and the first hordes of refugees and evacuees were sent reeling southwards; many thousands arrived in Dresden, considered to be the Reich's 'safest air-raid shelter'. In spite of the exhortations and threats of Gauleiter Koch, about twenty-five per cent of the population had fled from East Prussia, some 600,000 people; the town dwellers, together with women, children and invalids from rural areas had been evacuated en masse to Dresden and other Saxon cities, as well as to Thuringia and Pomerania.

The Saxon capital, which before the war had a population of 630,000, was soon palpably overcrowded. It was the prologue to the final tragedy of Dresden: there were few Germans who now desired to stay behind in the path of the Russian troops. The October offensive in East Prussia demonstrated to Gauleiters and citizens alike that Germans might expect short shrift from either Soviet troops or armoured division commanders; the streams of evacuees arriving in Saxony and Western Silesia brought with them eye-witness stories of Soviet atrocities committed against German civilians who had not been evacuated in time. On 20th October, for example, Soviet tank commanders had caught up with a column of refugees streaming out of the East Prussian district of Gumbinnen; the whole column had been wiped out when the commander ordered his tanks to proceed straight over the refugees and their vehicles. The Gumbinnen affair came to signalise to the Germans what awaited them if their leaders did not order the evacuation of the battle zones in time.

· · · · ·

The sudden launching of the massive Soviet offensive on Central Germany, on 12th January 1945, was to bring in its wake atrocities more degrading than this first Gumbinnen affair; but it had served to terrify the population and an even wilder reluctance to stay near the battle areas developed.

On 12th January the 1st Ukrainian Front, commanded by the ruthless but brilliant Soviet Marshal I. S. Koniev, broke out of the Baranov bridge-head on the Vistula and started a massive push in the direction of Silesia. On 13th January the 1st White Russian Front, under the command of Soviet Marshal Zhukov, broke out of the bridge-heads at Pulavy and Magnusev; his tank columns were headed for Lodz and Kalisch. A simultaneous attack on East Prussia, where the offensive had stagnated since the October onslaught, was mounted by the 3rd White Russian Front under Soviet Marshal Chernakovsky, with the capture of Königsberg as its aim; on 15th January the plan to detach East Prussia from the rest of the Reich was put into operation, with a 2nd White Russian Front push towards Thorn and Elbing.

Now the westward movement of evacuees, which had hitherto been only a moderate trickle, swelled overnight to a flood-tide which the area Gauleiters could no longer stem. An exodus of five million Germans from Eastern Germany had begun, an exodus voluntary as yet, but destined with the end of the war to yield to the most brutally enforced mass expulsion in the history of Europe, though dwarfed by the Nazis' genocidal treatment of the Jews.

Inevitably the greater part of the responsibility for this sudden westward surge of evacuees through Saxony, both marching columns of Allied and Russian prisoners of war and countless treks of civilian refugees fleeing from the Soviet terror, must lie with the local Gauleiters of the areas upon which the weight of the great Soviet offensive of January 1945 fell. At the beginning of 1945 some 4,700,000 German nationals—ethnically German—had been living in Silesia, the province to the immediate east of Saxony. As the news spread from town to town, the German evacuation of Silesia too began. One section of the population headed south-westwards over the mountains into Bohemia and Moravia; another larger section trekked along the main Autobahn into Saxony; the first major city across the provincial boundary would be Dresden and, whether they had friends there or not, there most of the evacuees intended to stay. During the autumn months of 1944 the fame of the Russian troops' revenge actions on the East Prussian population had spread far: fore-warned was fore-armed and, now that the Soviet invasion of Silesia had begun, the whole Eastern population needed no second encouragement to leave the path of the invaders; Gauleiter Hanke, however, was to make one final attempt to slow the headlong rush of people from his Gau, as we shall see.

· · · · ·

79

On 16th January 1945 the city of Dresden was for a second time the object of an Allied bombing attack, when part of a force of some 400 Liberators of the 2nd Air Division (United States Strategic Air Force) attacked the 'Dresden oil refinery and marshalling yards'. On the previous day a new Directive, No. 3 for the Strategic Air Forces in Europe, had been issued by the two Allied air commanders according first priority to attacks on the enemy petroleum industry, and second priority to the destruction of enemy lines of communication, with 'particular emphasis' on the Ruhr. The Eighth Air Force Target Summary recorded 133 effective sorties against Dresden's marshalling yards, in an attack commencing at noon: bombs fell accurately along the Hamburger-strasse side of the Friedrichstadt marshalling yards, with damage to some railway installations. The bombing of one Group, the 44th (Liberator) Bombardment Group, went rather wide and a target photograph showed its bomb pattern bursting in the grounds of the Freidrichstadt-Krankenhaus and the hospital buildings. Each of the Liberators dropped eight 500-pound R.D.X. high-explosive bombs. The flak had been extremely heavy on the way to the target and although over Ruhland the flak was 'heavy' the crews bombing Dresden from 22,000 feet were moderately surprised to experience no opposition from the city. This attack claimed 376 victims in the city; among the casualties was the first recorded British death: a British private from the second largest working detachment was killed on his way to hospital.

That is the first casualty and—I hope—the last [recorded the *Kommando's* British spokesman in his diary]. But with around 170 men, from this *Kommando* alone, working every day in the town, and with the strong possibility of a blitz, it is by no means impossible that there will be further casualties.

While the German civilians were buried in a mass-funeral in one of the city's cemeteries, the Army District Command in Dresden, in surprisingly strict observance of the Geneva Convention, paraded the city garrison and the unfortunate British soldier was buried 'with full military honours and a British and German guard of honour' at the Military Cemetery in Dresden-Albertstadt, as the Camp Leader informed the bereaved parents. In Dresden the war was still being conducted with an almost old-fashioned chivalry.

．　　　．　　　．　　　．　　　．

On the same day, 16th January, the German Army Group *A* pressed for the immediate evacuation of the Silesian area, and between 19th January and 25th January the first great caravans were assembling in the main towns and cities of Silesia and beginning the long trek west.

Unlike the mass evacuations of Berlin and the Ruhr, under the pressure of R.A.F. Bomber Command's night offensive—1,500,000 had been evacuated from Berlin and about 2,000,000 from the Rhine province by the end of 1944—this was a flood-tide of humanity unleashed on the very largest scale and within a startlingly short space of time: within seven days five million German civilians were to have been uprooted from their ancestral homes, were to be streaming westwards along the roads and highways carrying all their remaining property and chattels in boxes and bags and camping out in the open air night after night in spite of the below-zero temperatures. Just as the mass exodus from Silesia was gathering momentum, Gauleiter Hanke of Silesia intervened. He had observed with dismay the depletion of the labour force for the important Silesian industrial plants; now he ordered that women and children only were to be evacuated; all others, particularly those employed in industry, were to stay at their jobs to the last. This decree inflicted appalling burdens on the remaining columns of evacuees fleeing westwards, who were now deprived of all able-bodied men to assist in the journey; at the same time it accounts for the disproportionately high number of female casualties among the refugees who finally stopped in Dresden.

On 19th January, Hanke ordered the evacuation of Namslau in Lower Silesia and designated Landeshut as a reception area for the townsfolk and the Sudetenland for the rural population. On 20th January the Soviet armour reached Kattowitz, Beuthen, Gleiwitz and Hindeburg, and in defiance of Gauleiter Hanke's decree a small scale evacuation by the nearby German population began. On 22nd January the first Russian units crossed the River Oder between Brieg and Ohlau; all main railway lines westwards out of Breslau, the capital of Silesia, were closed. Now the only escape lay along a southerly route through Ratibor and Neisse, and soon these railways were burdened with thousands of women and children fleeing to Dresden and Saxony. The industrial population, however, had to stay at work to the last moment; cases occurred where even as Soviet troops were fighting for possession of the collieries, German miners were still working the coal face below. Other areas were more fortunate. Of the 700,000 inhabitants of the area between Oppeln and Glogau, a timely evacuation order on 20th January saved 600,000 from the Russians; the remainder, ethnically Polish, considered they had little to fear from the invaders.

On 21st January the Gauleiter ordered the evacuation of Trebnitz; as soon as the evacuation decree was promulgated, the whole German population descended on all available means of transport and flooded westwards; being a largely rural area, farm carts and wagons were available for the families to travel westwards in, despite the bitter cold which was to mark the first two months of 1945. As it was generally believed that the Soviet armour would be halted for some time on the Oder, the reception areas designated for the evacuees were only just to the west of the river, in localities including Liegnitz, Goldberg and Schweidnitz. Providentially, the military commanders insisted however that these areas were much too close to the battle zone and had the civilians displaced a further thirteen miles to the west of the river: soon after, the Russians bridged the Oder, and the flight to Saxony began afresh. It was as though fate were conspiring to ensure that by the time that the middle days of February arrived, the maximum number of refugees would be sheltering in the capital city of Saxony.

. . . .

There was quite a large number of Allied prisoners of war in Dresden at the time of the attacks. R.A.F. Bomber Command was dependent on the International Red Cross for precise information on their location in or near prospective targets; Sir Arthur Harris has stated that in the case of Dresden no such information was contained in Bomber Command's dossier on the city.

The War Office admit that the last report on the British camps in Dresden was received from the Protecting Power in January 1945, when there were sixty-seven working detachments within the immediate Dresden area, forming *Stalag IVa*; added to these were seven American detachments, each considerably larger than the British ones, reported after a visit to Dresden by a representative from the Swiss Legation in Berlin between 15th and 22nd January. The exact statistical position is further complicated by the numbers of Allied and Russian prisoners temporarily in the city while in transit from Eastern territories being overrun by the Soviet armies; the British government published soon after the triple blow on Dresden a list of Allied camps in these territories known to have been overrun; of the nineteen camps listed, several are known to have been passing through the city at the time of the attack; others, like *Stalags VIIIb* and *VIIIc* from Oppeln and Sagan respectively, which were also evacuated through Dresden, are known to have reached the city only after the attack; *Stalag VIIIb* was evacuated from Oppeln on the Oder on 26th January but did not arrive until 20th February, after three weeks on the march. *Stalag VIIIc*, with 15,000 prisoners, was also routed through Spremberg to Dresden. The measure in which the city's population of Allied prisoners grew during February is shown by a report by the International Red Cross on a visit to Dresden's *Stalag IVa* on 22nd February, which showed that there was by then a total of no less than 26,620 prisoners of war interned there, including 2,207 Americans.

.   .   .   .   .

On 26th January the first officially organised refugee trains from the East began to arrive in Dresden. Over a thousand Reich Labour Service girls (R.A.D.w.J.) were waiting at Central Station to help unload the elderly and invalid refugees and their baggage from the passenger and open goods trains, and to assist them in finding food and temporary lodgings; then the emptied trains were hauled back to the East to pick up more refugees. Day and night the unloading, victualling and re-directing of refugees continued in Dresden, the tempo increasing until finally R.A.D.w.J. girls, Hitler Youth units, League of German Girls units, National Socialist Welfare Service (*N.S.V.*) and *Frauenschaften* women's associations were all engaged in refugee welfare work. Many of the city's biggest secondary and grammar schools were shut down for conversion into military and Luftwaffe hospitals; within a few days of the Soviet invasion the Dreikönigs, Vitzthum and State Grammar Schools had been thus converted, as well as the boys' secondary schools in Dresden New Town, Dresden-Johannstadt, Dresden-Plauen, Dresden-Blasewitz and the girls' secondary schools in Dresden New Town and Dresden-Marschnerstrasse; the schoolchildren thus released had to work on refugee duty in the stations too. On 1st February large-scale employment of school units at Dresden New Town station began, the senior schoolboys being required to work all night from 7.55 p.m. until 8.00 a.m. the following morning tending the ailing refugees arriving on every train from the East.

In the course of the mass evacuation of the East, the regions of Glogau province, Fraustadt, Guhrau, Militsch, Trebnitz, Gross-Wartenberg, Oels, Namslau, Kreuzberg, Rosenberg and the eastern areas of Oppeln and Brieg had been virtually completely cleared of German civilians. The existing transport system westwards was hopelessly over-burdened, but the Party's Welfare organisation was able to establish moderately efficient food stations at intervals along the route to Dresden to alleviate the distress caused by hunger and the bitter cold.

Now the first great fears were awakened among the German citizens of Breslau, the metropolitan capital of Silesia. Fortunately, the city of Breslau was in January 1945 already underpopulated, with only 527,000 inhabitants; the evacuation of over 60,000 non-essential civilians had already been carried through since the autumn of 1944 when the city had been declared a Fortress. On 21st January the distant thunder of the artillery bombardment of Trebnitz had been heard in Breslau, and the city's remaining women, children, elderly folk and invalids had been enjoined to leave for the west. As the existing train service was hopelessly inadequate, over 100,000 people had to set out literally on foot for the west; in the absence of farm carts and wagons which had evacuated the predominantly rural populations, the industrial populace had no alternative but to walk. It would take some weeks for them to reach Saxony, where the larger part of them was heading.

Nor were German civilians alone in being evacuated from Breslau, which was destined to become the scene of bitter fighting until the besieged city surrendered on 6th May; the Government, in preparing for the siege, ordered the evacuation of many administrative and military installations to Dresden from Breslau. Thus, the complete Radio Breslau transmitting station was dismantled and transported to Dresden, with orders to reinforce the low-powered Dresden city radio station and at the same time to convert it to the former Breslau wavelength, so as to camouflage its location; in the event the lorries carrying the transmitter equipment arrived in Dresden only on the afternoon before R.A.F. Bomber Command's first attack, and suffered the fate of the rest of the city. The competent *Luftgaukommando* for Breslau had also been transferred to new quarters in Dresden.

The untimely end of the Radio Breslau transmitters was paralleled by the more regrettable fate of 158 valuable oil paintings; the Dresden art galleries had long been emptied of the treasures which had made the city famous in peace-time, but during the evacuation of the territories east of the Elbe, it was decided that the castles and châteaux in which the majority of Germany's art treasures had been stored for the duration of the war should be accorded first priority. Thus it came about that on the late afternoon of 13th February an elderly art restorer, in charge of two furniture vans loaded with 197 oil paintings, including works by Courbet, Böcklin and Rayski,

84

drove into Dresden after a day-long journey from Schloss Milkel and Kamenz; the drivers refused to continue that night to Schieritz, the district west of the Elbe where the paintings were to be stored again, and the lorries were parked on the Elbe Embankment near the Brühl'sche Terrasse, which within a few hours was to become the heart of the fire-storm area.

.   .   .   .   .

By the time that the encirclement action began at Breslau during the night preceding the Dresden raids, however, only 200,000 civilians remained in the city; the bulk of the population had escaped to Dresden and to other towns and cities in the Reich. Of those Breslauers who remained, some 40,000 were to be killed during the bitter street fighting and in Soviet air raids. The events in the East augured ill for the future of Dresden, and only the prisoners of war, cut off from the general mood of confidence in the city, appear to have realised the vulnerability of Dresden as a refugee traffic centre:

> Although Breslau is directly to the east of us [recorded a Dresden prisoner on 28th January], there has been no railway bombing, and German traffic has been flowing quite freely. Marvellous organisation on our part or the Russians. I don't know which!

CHAPTER II

THUNDERCLAP

THE impressive speed of the Soviet advance in the East, and
the accompanying Soviet Orders of the Day heralding the
fall of one Eastern town after another, could not for the
Western Allies have been more embarrassing: the long-awaited
Crimea conference, on which so much for the future of post-war
Europe was to depend, was thus to open apparently with a display
of Soviet might on the grandest scale and, compared with the
advances of Soviet Marshals Koniev and Zhukov in East Prussia
and Silesia, the Western Allies' achievements in Italy and recent
struggle in the Ardennes must have seemed paltry indeed.

Clearly the political leaders of the West would be hard pressed
to bargain from a position of strength when the Yalta Conference
opened. In these circumstances it was natural that the Allied
Governments should have turned in the final synthesis to their by
now massive bomber weapon as a means for impressing upon the
Soviet Union that although sections of the Western front were
wavering, on the German 'home front' the Allied offensive was as
crushing as any mounted by Soviet armour in the East. The British
government was especially in a parlous position when it came to
negotiating with the Soviet Premier: President Roosevelt, already an
ailing man, showed little positive concern for the future boundaries
of Eastern Europe.

The winter weather in Europe was, however, as unfavourable for
bombing operations as it was for the comfort of the columns of
refugees reeling westwards; it remained to the Joint Intelligence
Committee to make a positive suggestion for the most effective
employment of the Allied bomber forces. This was a modification of
a plan previously projected under the code-name *Thunderclap*.

In July 1944 the Chiefs of Staff had discussed the possibility of
making Berlin the target for a blow of 'catastrophic force' on morale,
military, political—and civilian. The suggestion had been put to
the Prime Minister and then embodied in a detailed memo submitted by Sir Charles Portal to the Chiefs of Staff on 1st August,

the memo which the Official Historians have justly termed the 'title-deed' of the Dresden operation. As an alternative to Berlin,

> immense devastation could be produced if the entire attack was concentrated on a single big town other than Berlin and the effect would be especially great if the town was one hitherto relatively undamaged.

In the opinion of the Foreign Office, the Political Warfare Executive and the Ministry of Economic Warfare with whom *Thunderclap* had been discussed and agreed in principle, such an attack might hasten an imminent victory or determine one which seemed in the balance.

But on the advice of the Joint Planners' Committee the plan was shelved until such time as the Joint Intelligence Committee might consider the circumstances favourable for a reappraisal of its possibilities. In reports on 25th January, 1945, the J.I.C. presented in detail an appreciation of the new Soviet offensive on the Eastern front in the light of which *Thunderclap* was re-examined. It was the view of the Committee that the assistance which the Allied strategic bomber forces might be able to afford the Russians during the next few weeks justified an urgent examination of the possibilities of using them in this way. This report of 25th January emphasised especially the need for concentration on oil targets. The bombing of tank factories—which were understood to be supplying the armoured divisions on the front direct—should, moreover, take precedence second only to this top-priority oil offensive. The Committee reported finally on the possibility of interfering with German attempts to rush reinforcements to the Eastern front (although this was in fact hardly a serious threat at this stage of the war, as we have seen above by Hitler's response to Colonel-General Guderian's appeal); the committee suggested a bombardment of communications targets, and in particular a 'heavy and sustained' bombardment of Berlin. This was, however, the first report to draw express attention to the possibility of assisting the Russians on the Eastern front, and if only accorded the least priority rating, the attack of communications had been mooted in this context.

In a second report the Joint Intelligence Committee examined *Thunderclap* in more detail as a means of assisting the Russians, since the original plan of a shattering blow to undermine morale, they averred, would not be decisive even if timed to coincide exactly with a favourable stage of the Russian advance. One of the drawbacks to a report of this nature, for which the Committee cannot be blamed, is that the Soviet General Staff did not keep the Western Allies informed in advance of their forthcoming military operations: the great Soviet invasion had started, it will be recalled, on 12th January; yet it was not until 25th January that the J.I.C. issued these detailed reports on it. It might be observed that a minimum delay of at least thirteen days between the launching of a new Russian offensive and the earliest delivery of a 'simultaneous' *Thunderclap* blow on a German city would serve not to underline the close mutual co-operation between East and West, but rather the opposite.

The J.I.C. believed that if such an attack were to be planned in relation to circumstances already prevailing on the Eastern front, the strategic bomber forces might yet be able to assist the Soviet offensive in a way that would make it at least appear to the Germans that mutual co-operation between East and West was a reality (the Germans would have exploited any obvious rift between the Allies). Great confusion could be caused behind the German lines by an attack on a refugee-crowded Berlin; a heavy flow of refugees fleeing from a blitzed Berlin, added to the treks already surging westwards from the Soviet invasion territories, would surely 'interfere with the orderly movement of troops to the (Eastern) front, and hamper the German military and administrative machine'. In addition to these tactical considerations, this second J.I.C. report was of the opinion —significantly in view of the forthcoming Yalta conference—that there might be a 'political value' in demonstrating to the Russians 'in the best way open to us', a desire to assist them in their current offensive.

.   .   .   .   .

With what appeared to be a positive policy thus clearly mapped out for the Allied Strategic Air Forces, the British Air Ministry was not slow to act on this report; the Deputy Chief of Air Staff at once telephoned Sir Arthur Harris to acquaint him with the report's recommendations and to discuss its implications. Though Harris affirmed that he regarded Berlin as already being 'on his plate', Sir Norman Bottomley pointed out that as the full *Thunderclap* plan for a shattering blow on Berlin was now projected, Harris would have to co-ordinate his operations with the United States Strategic Air Forces, and in all probability consult with the Chiefs of Staff as well. In this conversation, according to the minute sent by Bottomley to the Chief of Air Staff, Sir Charles Portal, on the following day, Sir Arthur Harris suggested supplementary attacks on Chemnitz, Leipzig and Dresden which, equally with Berlin, would share the task of housing evacuees from the East, and which again were focal points in the communications systems serving the Eastern front.

It was peculiarly ironic that Sir Arthur Harris should now be consulted on a plan to put the full strength of Bomber Command behind an area offensive, since he had long advocated in vain to the Air Staff the policy of continuing the general area bombing as the key to the collapse of Germany, in preference to the bombing of precision targets. The Government and Air Staff from the early days of the war had been aware of the possibilities of area bombing as a means of striking at the heart of the German war economy, as well as of its attendant psychological effects, and indeed, the efforts of Bomber Command during the years 1943–4 had been largely directed towards the bombing of cities; at this stage of the war, however, the success of the air offensive against oil plants waged by Sir Arthur Harris and the Americans, under the direction of S.H.A.E.F., in the summer of 1944 convinced the Air Staff that the continued top priority of this oil offensive could have a decisive effect on the war before the end of the year. Harris, however, maintained the importance of continuing the area offensive as the means of undermining and dividing Germany both materially and morally, as opposed to the impossibility of operating on a set schedule needed for precision target bombing in the uncertain weather conditions.

Despite the listing of oil as top priority throughout the autumn of 1944, during the months October to December fifty-eight per cent of Bomber Command's operations was directed against cities. (The proportion of fourteen per cent against oil plants represents a larger effort than the figure suggests because of the precise nature of the targets.) In a letter to Sir Charles Portal on 1st November, Harris pointed out that within eighteen months Bomber Command had virtually destroyed forty-five out of the leading sixty German cities, and suggested the destruction of the remaining untouched targets: 'Magdeburg, Halle, Leipzig, Dresden, Chemnitz, Breslau, Nuremberg, Munich, Coblenz and Karlsruhe, and the further destruction of Berlin and Hanover.' This proposed change of priorities was not, however, ceded to Harris by the Air Staff and the deadlock over strategic policy continued.

In the middle of January, with the unleashing of the new Russian offensive, Harris in a letter to Portal of 18th January, brought matters to a head, again expressing his dissatisfaction with the policy of selective targets required by the oil plan and advocating the destruction of 'Magdeburg, Leipzig, Chemnitz, Dresden, Breslau, Posen, Halle, Erfurt, Gotha, Weimar, Eisenach and the rest of Berlin'—a shifting of emphasis from industrial to Eastern cities. The letter concluded that Portal should 'consider whether it is best for the prosecution of the war and the success of our arms, which alone matters' that Harris should remain in his Command. Faced with this ultimatum Sir Charles Portal had to make the unpleasant choice of losing a Commander-in-Chief at a critical stage in the war, whose standing with his Command was extremely high, or virtually unresolving the current deadlock over priorities. He chose the latter, and, in a letter of 20th January, asked Harris to remain but to observe the existing priorities despite his lack of faith in them.

It was in these circumstances that less than a week later the revival of *Thunderclap*—a highlight in the concept of area bombing—was to receive the highest possible stimulation. For quite independently of Bottomley's conversation with Harris, within a few hours the Prime Minister was forcibly expressing his personal concern about the bombing of East German population centres.

It is to be presumed that by the time of his intervention on the evening of the 25th, the Prime Minister had read through the J.I.C. reports on the new Soviet offensive and the possible application of the *Thunderclap* plan. That day, moreover, other facts had become relevant to his consideration of the reports. The London newspapers were recounting the harrowing scenes in East German cities as refugees flooded in from Breslau and Silesia as well as from East Prussia before the onslaught of the Russian army; nevertheless, as *The Times* reported on the morning of the 25th, German radio commentators were claiming that despite all the refugees streaming through Berlin the Reich capital had not been dislocated. Above all, the Russians had that day crossed the Oder near Breslau and no doubt news of this had quickly reached Whitehall. The military situation on the Eastern front seemed conducive to the urgent consideration of the J.I.C. reports.

That evening the Prime Minister telephoned the Secretary of State for Air, Sir Archibald Sinclair, for information on projected plans for dealing with the situation in East Germany. Of this conversation Sinclair's assistant private secretary recorded that the Prime Minister demanded to know what plans R.A.F. Bomber Command had laid for 'basting the Germans in their retreat from Breslau'.

In the light of Mr. Churchill's insistence on the urgency of the

East German situation, rapid consultations at the Air Ministry were necessary. On the following morning the Chief of Air Staff, who had now received Bottomley's report on his conversation with Harris the evening before, minuted his Deputy that subject to the oil priority and the need for attacks on jet factories and submarine yards they should use

> available effort in one big attack on Berlin and attacks on Dresden, Leipzig, Chemnitz, or other cities where a severe blitz will not only cause confusion in the evacuation from the East but will also hamper the movement of troops from the West.

The plan would, of course, have to be agreed between the Anglo-American Combined Chiefs of Staff, and with Sir Arthur Tedder, the Deputy Supreme Commander. Even though almost complete control of the strategic bomber forces had been transferred from S.H.A.E.F. to the Combined Chiefs of Staff in the previous autumn, the Air Staff were by the beginning of 1945 anxious about the amount of direct army support being demanded of the bomber forces. At the Quebec Conference in September 1944, on Sir Charles Portal's recommendation, the control of strategic bombing operations was given to the Combined Chiefs of Staff subject only to General Eisenhower's powers of command over emergency requirements for the land battle. In view of the rapid developments taking place in the strategic situation at that time, Sir Charles Portal had said:

> It may become desirable in the immediate future to apply the whole of the strategic bomber effort to the direct attack on German morale.

The psychological moment for this blow could be considered best by the Combined Chiefs of Staff and best taken advantage of if they directly controlled the bomber forces.

However, despite the J.I.C. reports and the obvious success of the Russian invasion, Portal doubted in his minute of 26th January whether the time for *Thunderclap* on a full scale had yet come, or if it would be decisive. He also doubted the worth of large-scale bombing of communications in the hope of delaying German reinforcements to the East.

Sir Archibald Sinclair, having consulted the Air Staff, replied in a minute of 26th January to the Prime Minister's telephoned demand—as he understood, for plans to disorganize the enemy military retreat before the Russian offensive. Sinclair advised against this on the grounds that such troop movements 'in a large scale retreat westwards to Dresden and Berlin' were more suited to attacks by the Tactical Air Forces, particularly in view of the fact that precise intelligence on troop movements was not available, and that such attacks should be co-ordinated with the Russians as the targets were within their tactical area.

In view of Sir Charles Portal's recommendations, therefore, he was advocating the continuance of the oil plant attacks whenever the winter weather permitted such precision target bombing, and when the weather was unsuited—area bombing.

> These opportunities might be used to exploit the present situation by the bombing of Berlin and other large cities in Eastern Germany such as Leipzig, Dresden and Chemnitz, which are not only the administrative centres controlling the military and civilian movements, but are also the main communications centres through which the bulk of the traffic moves.

He concluded by saying—in view of Portal's comments on the need for prior consultations—that the

> possibility of these attacks being delivered on the scale necessary to have a critical effect on the situation in Eastern Germany is now under examination.

In spite of the detailed and convincing arguments marshalled by Sinclair for a continuation of the oil offensive, the Prime Minister at once replied:

> I did not ask you last night about plans for harrying the German retreat from Breslau. On the contrary, I asked whether Berlin, and no doubt other large cities in East Germany should not now be considered especially attractive targets. I am glad that this is 'under examination'. Pray report to me tomorrow what is going to be done.

The immediate result of this hard reply was to stampede the Air Staff—whose Deputy Chief, Sir Norman Bottomley, was acting for Sir Charles Portal prior to the latter's departure for Yalta—into issuing an instruction in a letter to Sir Arthur Harris which would make it inevitable that the Eastern population centres, including Dresden, would soon be the object of a modification of *Thunderclap*. Bottomley recalled his telephone conversation two days before with Sir Arthur Harris, in which an attack on Berlin, and other attacks on Dresden, Chemnitz and Leipzig had been touched upon. He enclosed with his letter to Harris a copy of the J.I.C.

reports of 25th January in which the plan for delivery of a *Thunderclap* attack on Berlin had been examined, but added that Sir Charles Portal did not think it would be right to attempt attacks on Berlin on the *Thunderclap* scale in the immediate future, as it was doubtful whether such an attack, even if done on the heaviest scale, with consequent heavy losses, would be decisive. Portal had, however, agreed that, subject to oil, Bomber Command should use all available effort in one big attack on Berlin and related attacks on Dresden, Leipzig, Chemnitz or any other cities where a severe blitz would not only cause confusion in the evacuation from the East, but would also hamper the movement of troops from the West.

Sir Norman Bottomley concluded his letter to Harris with the formal request that—subject to the qualifications still imposed on the execution of this attack on the Eastern population centres by the 'overriding claims of oil and the other approved target systems within the current [i.e. No. 3] directive', and as soon as moon and weather conditions permitted—Bomber Command was to undertake such attacks, 'with the particular object of exploiting the confused conditions which are likely to exist in the above mentioned cities during the successful Russian advance'.

The moon conditions were unlikely to be favourable much before 4th February, and the Prime Minister was informed of this immediately after Bottomley's letter had been transmitted to Sir Arthur Harris; on the following day, 28th January, the Prime Minister formally acknowledged the message. Clearly he had secured his immediate aim: soon after 4th February, at the climax of the Crimea conference, he would be able to produce a dramatic strike on an Eastern city which could hardly fail to impress the Soviet delegation. He could not foresee that even with the arrival of favourable moon conditions, nine days—and the end of the Yalta conference—would pass before the weather too was favourable for such a long-range operation.

By 31st January the plan for a joint Allied attack on these Eastern cities had been taken a stage further when as a result of meetings between the Chief and Deputy of Air Staff, Sir Arthur Tedder and General Carl Spaatz, the Commanding General of the U.S. Strategic Air Forces, a new order of priorities was agreed. Directive No. 3 to the Strategic Air Forces, in operation since 15th January, seemed to discourage the possibility of attacks on Eastern targets, stipulating as it did that 'the Strategic Air Forces based in the United Kingdom will place particular emphasis upon the Ruhr' lines of communication. The principal German synthetic oil plants were still top priority for the Allied bomber forces, but as far as the strategic bombers operating from Britain were concerned, the second priority was now switched from the Ruhr communications to attacks on Berlin, Leipzig, Dresden and the other Eastern population centres, designed to dislocate the refugee evacuation from the East and to hamper troop movements. General Spaatz accordingly instructed Major-General J. H. Doolittle's Eighth Air Force which, like Bomber Command, had its headquarters at High Wycombe, to attack Berlin, apparently within this plan.

In reporting on this agreement to Sir Charles Portal on 31st January, who was now in Malta with the Combined Chiefs of Staff prior to the full tripartite conference at Yalta, Sir Norman Bottomley added that the Russians in view of the speed of their advance, particularly towards Berlin, 'might wish to know of our intentions and plans for attack of targets in Eastern Germany'. There is, however, no evidence that the raid on Dresden was ever specifically discussed with the Russians at Yalta, and the Russians have denied that any information about Bomber Command's area attack reached them through the usual channels of communication, the British Military Mission in Moscow. One reason for this may have been the complication that since Lt.-Gen. M. B. Burrows had left Moscow in November 1944 as Head of the Mission, the British Government, as a reaction from the coolness with which the Mission was being treated in Moscow, had not replaced him.

General Spaatz specifically requested that the minute, from Bottomley to Portal, in which something close on the American bombardment of area targets was clearly broached, should also be shown to General Laurence Kuter, who was deputising at Yalta for the convalescing General H. H. Arnold, Chief of the American Army Air Forces. It is probable that Spaatz was seeking some endorsement of this new policy from a higher authority. Not until 13th February, however, was the message seen by General Kuter, by which time the American Eighth Air Force heavy attack on Berlin had already taken place. Sir Norman Bottomley's letter of 27th January clearly called for major raids, and it was thought that the best results were achieved by co-ordinated attacks instead of a single blow, using Eighth Air Force daylight methods in conjunction with Bomber Command's night bombing force. The idea behind this was that if the American day-raid started fires it would assist Bomber Command to successfully follow up the attack by night. In practice this was rarely possible because weather conditions by day tended to differ from those by night. The Eighth Air Force attack on Berlin of February 3rd had originally been planned as part of such a combined operation, and the arrangements for it would be provisionally agreed by Sir Norman Bottomley and General Spaatz.

In retrospect it is not difficult to surmise the nature of the joint approach to this programme of attacks made by the British and American bomber forces. The Americans would not permit their bombers to be sent for any purely terror-raids directed solely against the German populace; they could hardly refuse a reasonable request to direct their bombers to attack military targets in the heart of residential areas, although they were aware of the imprecise nature of these attacks when delivered blind, as during these early winter months they invariably were. Blind American attacks upon aiming points in residential areas would be just as widespread as blind night attacks delivered by British bombers on the residential areas themselves; senior Bomber Command officers have in fact insisted that as radar marking methods were far more precise by night, blind daylight attacks were even more widespread than radar-marked night ones.

At this time, the idea that Dresden was an important industrial city appears to have been only superficially accepted. The War Office department responsible for briefing the Chief of the Imperial General Staff on all air matters fully endorsed the attack on the German synthetic oilplants, but viewed with the gravest suspicion the strategic air offensive on German cities; when the Russians had appealed in general for an Allied air attack on communication centres, a map was produced indicating some of the communications centres which might be included in this request. One of the towns listed on this communications map was Dresden, as it was just possible to put it in this category. However, it was certainly not an important industrial centre; indeed, the information which the department had to supply to the C.I.G.S. about Dresden was that it was not being used so much as a transport centre by the German Army as by vast numbers of refugees from the Soviet front.

.   .   .   .   .

On 2nd February, the Vice Chiefs of Staff in London informed the British Chiefs of Staff, who were still engaged in the Combined Chiefs of Staffs' Conference in Malta that they approved the new priorities. They had amended them slightly to include tank factories, but still as second priority after the synthetic oil plants came Berlin, Leipzig, Dresden and allied cities 'where heavy attack will cause great confusion in civilian evacuation from the East and hamper

95

reinforcements'. Air raids on the Ruhr-Cologne-Kassel traffic complex were relegated to third priority rating. When the dust and debris of the triple blow on Dresden which was to follow had settled and the outside world had learned of the extent of the tragedy, we shall see how there was some dispute as to whether the American Eighth Air Force had been following the original Directive No. 3 or the above-described proposed directive. General Spaatz avers that at no stage was the U.S. directive for attack on 'military objectives' departed from; in the case of Dresden this was to be the marshalling yards.

The new priorities were in one respect apparently observed by the U.S.St.A.F. on the afternoon of 3rd February, when a crushing blow was delivered on Berlin by nearly 1,000 'Forts'. As had already been planned, the Fortresses attacking Berlin were allocated military objectives to aim at, but in the heart of the residential and business areas; German reports quoted in Sweden claimed that over 25,000 people had lost their lives, including heavy casualties among the refugees.* On 8th February at his Allied air commanders' conference, General Spaatz was able to draw attention to the spectacular results his bombers had achieved in this Berlin attack, while he added that it was suspected that the '6th Panzer Army' was on its way through the capital to reinforce the Eastern front. It is not known whether at this stage of the war General Spaatz was aware of the proven inaccuracy of Eighth Air Force air raids delivered on instruments alone as a result of bad weather; his subordinate officer commanding the Eighth Air Force, Major-General J. H. Doolittle, should certainly have been aware of this; he had been informed in a minute of 26th January that the Force had an average circular probable aiming error during the blind air attacks of about two miles, which 'necessitated drenching an area with bombs to achieve any results'.

On 4th and 5th February the weather prevented further long-range operations, and on the 6th compelled a diversion from an attempted precision attack on oil targets to the associated secondary targets in the marshalling yards at Chemnitz, thirty miles south-west of Dresden, and Magdeburg. Some 800 tons of bombs were dropped on each city, in compliance with the general spirit of assisting the Russians. Clearly the time when bombs would be falling on Dresden from either British or American bombers was not far off.

*Although the U.S. Official History refers to this Swedish claim, the actual casualties may have been lower; the German High Command War Diary records that less than a thousand died.

On 7th and 8th February heavy bomber forces were detailed for daylight operations over Germany, but on both occasions the missions were scrubbed because of deteriorating weather conditions. On 7th February, too, a Labour M.P., Edmund Purbrick, demanded to know when Chemnitz, Dresden, Dessau, Freiburg and Würzburg 'which have had little or no experience so far in this connection' would be bombed. Mr. Attlee replied that no statement could be made on future operations; he could hardly have revealed, even if he had known, that plans for the bombing of two of these cities were already in hand with Bomber Command (and probably with the Eighth Air Force also) in accordance with Bottomley's letter of 27th January. The area bombing offensive against German cities was on the threshold of its climax.

With the Soviet armour halted temporarily at the Oder, the refugee tide descending on Dresden had ebbed to a trickle. Then, on 8th February, Soviet armies crossed the Oder in strength, and the regions immediately west of the Oder became bloody battle-fields; the refugees who had only days before thought themselves safe in these regions, now joined a headlong rush for the West again; at the same time a pincer movement to seal off Breslau was launched by the Soviet troops.

The panic-stricken evacuation of Western Silesia too now began. Of 35,000 inhabitants of the town of Grünberg, thanks to swift Party evacuation orders, all but 4,000 escaped in time. Other towns were less fortunate: Liegnitz had already been declared a reception area for refugees from towns east of the Oder; its normal population of 76,000 was multiplied many times by these refugees; 20,000 German civilians were forced to stay behind when Soviet troops occupied the town, which was the second largest in Western Silesia. That such a large proportion of the inhabitants were trapped was the result of the lack, in lower Silesia, of the agricultural transport which had enabled residents of other provinces to escape more readily. The civilians who were left behind in these towns were to suffer fearful atrocities at the hands both of the Soviet troops and of the Polish minority.

The scale of this mass refugee migration, which was both to cause and to characterise the Dresden tragedy, can be only approximately indicated. At the beginning of 1945, the Silesian population had numbered some 4,718,000 people, of which about 1,500,000 either could not escape in time, or being of Polish origin stayed behind. Of the 3,200,000 who took to flight, half sought refuge in the Czecho-slovakian Protectorate, not even suspecting the racialist atrocities which were in store for them after the uprising of the Czechs; the remainder fled further into the German Reich, numbering some 1,600,000. Silesians represented probably eighty per cent of the displaced people crowding into Dresden on the night of the triple blow; the city which in peacetime had a population of 630,000 citizens was by the eve of the air attack so crowded with Silesians, East Prussians and Pomeranians from the Eastern front, with Berliners and Rhinelanders from the West, with Allied and Russian prisoners of war, with evacuated children's settlements, with forced labourers of many nationalities, that the increased population was now between 1,200,000 and 1,400,000 citizens, of whom, not surprisingly, several hundred thousand had no proper home and of whom none could seek the protection of an air-raid shelter.

On the afternoon of 12th February, with the arrival of the last official refugee trains from the East in Dresden, the city was nearing its maximum population. The first official refugee trains westwards would run some days later. Still the refugee columns were pouring into Dresden on foot and packed into horse-drawn carts, a continuous stream of humanity trudging along the *Autobahn* from the East. Not all the people in this endless column of refugees were civilians—some were soldiers who had lost their units on the front. Military police patrols were stationed at the outskirts of the city both to control this *Rückstau Ost*—Flood-tide East—of refugees, and to redirect the soldiers to assembly areas. Significantly, the Soviet belief that Dresden itself was being used as an assembly centre for these troops is not supported by the evidence. The military police directed the troops to assembly areas *outside* the city for re-grouping. The refugees too were being diverted round the city, as the approach roads were by now blocked with long convoys of horses and carts; refugees on foot were permitted to enter the town, but warned to move on again within three days.

Very few of these Eastern peasant refugees had ever heard an air-raid siren before; for six days before the triple blow, the air-raid warnings did not sound in Dresden; most of the refugees were simple agricultural people, who had lived remote from the ugly manifestations of modern warfare, in their farming communities in the Eastern marchlands. These were the peasants who would unwillingly have benefitted from the *Lebensraum* policies which their Führer had mapped out for them in the East; now they were to become the victims of the horrors of the war which Nazi aggression had unleashed in Europe.

The appearance of the name of Dresden as a specific target for attack came as a surprise to the Command's Intelligence Staff. Since 1944, in addition to the Directives issued from time to time to the two Allied bomber commanders, Bomber Command had received a weekly target-priority list from the Combined Strategic Targets Committee, a joint committee including representatives from British and American air force authorities, and the S.H.A.E.F. Intelligence sections; Bomber Command normally selected its targets from these weekly lists, according to the weather conditions and similar tactical considerations; sometimes to be sure, attacks were specifically asked for on particular targets not listed by the C.S.T.C., but in these cases Bomber Command was invariably given the reason for the emergency. Dresden, however, had not yet appeared in these weekly target lists.

Bottomley's instructions were passed as a matter of routine to Bomber Command Intelligence Section to prepare provisional plans for attacks. Within a few days, however, the inclusion of Dresden had been queried. They had, of course, a dossier on Dresden. While this showed, for example, that there were a large number of prisoners of war in the area, there was no detail of their exact whereabouts. There was, moreover, very little to show that Dresden was a city of much industrial importance, or that it was being used on a large scale for troop movements. The usual precise information on flak defences was missing. In particular the Intelligence Section asked for guidance on what targets were to be selected as aiming points.

In view of this, Sir Robert Saundby thought that perhaps the importance of Dresden in the present programme had been over-rated. On the authority of Sir Arthur Harris he therefore queried the order with the Air Ministry. In the light of their information, he suggested, its inclusion ought to be double-checked before they went ahead. The chiefs of Bomber Command did not query orders lightly, and when such occasions arose they would speak to Sir Norman Bottomley or his representative on the scrambler telephone. Formerly Bottomley had dealt with the query and telephoned Saundby back in a matter of hours. In this case, however, he was told that the matter would have to be referred to a higher authority.

It was not for several days that the answer came through. Sir Robert Saundby was informed by scrambler telephone that Dresden was to be included in the order, and that the attack was to take place at the first suitable opportunity. He understood that the attack was part of a programme in which the Prime Minister was personally interested and that the delay in answering the query was because it had been referred to Churchill in Yalta. It should, perhaps, be noted, however, that Sir Charles Portal was also at Yalta, and that the query may well have been dealt with by him alone, especially in view of the fact that the new priorities were under discussion at the time. Sir Robert Saundby understood that the Russians had specifically asked for an attack on Dresden and assumed that this request had been made at Yalta.

The Official Historians found no evidence of this request. On the other hand, the B.B.C.'s news bulletin of 14th February which described the raid as 'one of the more powerful blows at the heart of Germany which the Allied leaders promised at Yalta' could have given support to a belief in its existence.

The Russians deny it, and it would seem more probable that the confirmation of the order to attack Dresden was given in a general spirit of compliance with the memorandum tabled at Yalta by the Soviet Deputy Chief of Staff, General Antonov, on 4th February, in which he suggested that the Western strategic bomber forces might deliver air attacks on communications near the Eastern front; mentioned in particular were attacks designed to paralyse the centres of Berlin and Leipzig. There is no evidence either that a request came through the usual liaison channel, the Military Missions in Moscow. General Deane, the Head of the American Military Mission, who at that time was also at Yalta, has no recollection of any such Russian request, but points out that this does not exclude the possibility of a request having been made through another channel. In another context, however, Dresden was specifically mentioned at Yalta. The question of a boundary line for operations of the Soviet and Allied Air Forces had been in dispute for some time, and at Yalta on 5th February General Antonov proposed a bombline running through Berlin, Dresden, Vienna and Zagreb. The towns through which it ran were to be allotted to the West for air operations, though General Kuter observed that this would prohibit operations on industrial and communications targets in the neighbourhood of Berlin and Dresden. No agreement was, however, reached.

.   .   .   .   .

Once the order to bomb Dresden was confirmed Sir Arthur Harris raised no further objection to carrying it out. As he comments in his memoirs *Bomber Offensive*:

The attack on Dresden was at the time considered a military necessity by much more important people than myself.

Not for about a further week, however, was the Meteorological Section at Bomber Command able to forecast weather favourable for a long-range thrust into Central Germany; thereby, it might be argued, the whole political advantage of a raid on Dresden was lost. Without doubt the Prime Minister was as pre-occupied at the end of the Crimea conference, on 11th February, as he was at its commencement, and there was no reason why once he had pressed for such raids he should now call them off.

Out of the three towns specified in Bottomley's order, apart from Berlin, Dresden became a primary consideration, not only on account of the emphasis which had been given it when the original order was confirmed, but also because the chances of the weather being favourable for such a long-range attack at this time of the year were in fact extremely slim, and if conditions proved at all suitable the opportunity would have to be seized immediately.

On the 12th February the Eighth Air Force considered the weather would allow them to attack Dresden on the following morning. A signal was dispatched to Major-General Edmund W. Hill in Moscow, head of the aviation section of the American Military Mission, asking him to inform the Soviet Army General Staff that the Eighth Air Force would attack marshalling yards in Dresden on the next day, 13th February. By the afternoon of the 12th, R.A.F. Bomber Command had been informed by their American liaison officer that, subject to the weather, the Americans would attack Dresden on the morning of the 13th. In order that this combined operation might achieve its maximum effect Bomber Command would therefore have to attack on the night of the 13th.

The American airmen had already been briefed for their attack on Dresden, when the whole mission was cancelled—as General Spaatz recalls, on account of the bad weather. At any rate, Major-General Hill in Moscow was again cabled to inform the Soviet Army General Staff that on the following day (i.e. 14th February), if weather permitted, the Eighth Air Force would attack the marshalling yards in Dresden and Chemnitz; this was what in fact did come to pass. But in the meantime, the U.S.St.A.F. had been spared the necessity of making the first-ever massive attack on Dresden; this fate would now most probably fall to R.A.F. Bomber Command.

On the morning of the 13th, however, a cable from General Kuter in Yalta arrived at General Spaatz's headquarters. The question of the new priorities had now come to his attention and the burden of this cable was to enquire whether this proposed new Directive authorised 'indiscriminate attacks on cities'.

This may account for the fact that the new Directive was in fact never issued, although the new priorities it embodied had been agreed by Spaatz and Bottomley, approved with a slight amendment by the Vice Chiefs of Staff, and confirmed by the British Chiefs of Staff on 6th February. Bottomley in accordance with Portal's recommendation, suggested to Spaatz that the new Directive should be issued. There is no doubt that the priorities it would have embodied had been verbally agreed between Spaatz and Bottomley at the end of January; in fact, this Directive was never formally issued by the Combined Chiefs of Staff, and General Spaatz has said that the Berlin and Dresden attacks were carried out within the terms of Directive No. 3.

On the 13th, at the daily early morning conference, presided over by Sir Arthur Harris, it was reported that the weather conditions would be favourable for an attack on Dresden. The Air Ministry's meteorological section predicted that although the sky would be overcast along most of the route to Dresden, the cloud tops were expected to lower to 6,000 feet beyond five to seven degrees east. In the Dresden and Leipzig areas there was a chance of breaks to half cover, and there was a 'risk of thin cloud layers spreading over between 15,000 feet and 20,000 feet'. The meteorological report added that Bomber Command's airfields would be 'generally fit' for landing by the time the bombers returned from the nine-hour flight to Dresden.

The decision to adopt Dresden as a target for that night was therefore taken and the programme passed over to S.H.A.E.F. for clearance chiefly in connection with the general military situation. This clearance had become routine since *Operation Overlord* with the need for close co-operation between land and air forces, and was an important formality—in the case of Dresden because of the speed of the Russians' advance. Shortly before 9 a.m. Air Marshal R. D. Oxland, Bomber Command's Liaison Officer at Supreme H.Q. confirmed the clearance and the executive order for the attack on Dresden was issued. The 'severe blitz' in Bottomley's order of the 27th January, and re-affirmed in Saundby's telephone conversation with the Air Ministry, was now translated into practical effect in the planning of the attack.

The raid on Dresden had ceased to be the object of messages and minutes between politicians and committees; now it was an affair of machines and men, of bombs and flares, of briefing officers, pilots and bomb-aimers. 'With considerable misgivings,' relates Sir Robert Saundby, 'I had no alternative but to lay on this massive air attack.'

PART THREE

THE EXECUTION OF THE ATTACK

CHAPTER I

THE PLAN OF ATTACK

THE technical and strategic problems that faced Bomber Command in carrying out the 'massive air attack' on Dresden, a city in the heart of Central Germany, could not have been easily resolved at any earlier stage of the war.

The Command had been ordered to deliver a massive blow on the city. But the weather conditions of February 1945 were poor, and for an attack which would involve a nine- to ten-hour flight by the Lancaster force, and which would require standards of timing and concentration on the target rivalling the best that Harris had ever achieved before, the meteorological prospects were of considerable importance.

In the early weeks of 1945 the German night-fighter defence had been of an indeterminate strength. The fighter force was indeed numerically diminishing, and the fighter crews were tired and reaching breaking point. But the area that they were required to defend was also rapidly shrinking, as the invading armies rolled the Reich frontiers further and further into Germany.

For this reason Air Chief Marshal Harris planned the execution of the R.A.F. Dresden attack as a double blow, the value of which he had tested as early as October 1944: the virtue of the double-attack strategy was that fighter squadrons, deceived into believing that the first attack was the main thrust, would be grounded and refuelling by the time that the second bomber stream crossed the Reich frontiers some three hours later. Again, there was the more practical hope that the fire services and other passive defences would be preoccupied by conflagrations caused in the first attack; they would then be swamped and overcome by the second blow.

The third profit from the double-blow is made apparent by the results of the attack on Dresden: any telephonic or telegraphic communications passing through the damaged city to fighter and flak defence networks would be cut off; the defences, both active and passive, would be both paralysed and taken unawares by the second attack. Air Chief Marshal Harris and his tacticians had calculated the optimum gap between the attacks of such a double-blow to be about three hours. If the gap were any shorter, the fighter squadrons might not be properly dispersed; the fires would not have time to take hold in the streets, and the fire-fighting defences would not be overwhelmed in the second attack. If the delay were any longer, the active defences would be refreshed and ready for battle anew, and, knowing the probable identity of the target for the second attack, would be able to inflict more severe losses on the bomber stream.

For some days after Harris had received confirmation of the order to bomb Dresden, a belt of cloud and unpredictable weather covered most of Central Europe. Apart from No. 3 Bomber Group, a force specially trained and equipped for blind daylight bombing on instrument through cloud layers, the whole of Bomber Command was effectively grounded. The end of the Yalta Conference came and went. Sir Arthur Harris's Staff Officers used the remaining days to assemble what material they could in readiness for the attack, but they were still not able to produce the standard H2S comparison photographs, which were not included in the original Dresden file.

Then, on 12th February 1945, the Meteorological Section at High Wycombe were able to promise the two Allied Bomber Commanders reasonable weather conditions over the Continent during the following day, Tuesday 13th.

In the early hours of Tuesday 13th the American crews were briefed for an attack on two alternative targets. If the weather was satisfactory the Flying Fortress crews were to attempt Plan B, the long flight to Dresden, and attack the railway yards and stations there in either a precision visual attack or a blind attack on instruments, as a preliminary to a heavy R.A.F. blow. If the weather closed down Central German operations then the alternative target to be attacked was Plan A, Kassel. But the weather prospects, which had looked favourable the night before, deteriorated suddenly on the early morning of the fated day, and both American missions were cancelled, apparently on that count; ice clouds were blanketing Europe and in Dresden itself a thin frosty snow was drifting down out of the sky. Thus the honour—as it was described to the Master Bomber—of striking the first blow at Dresden, the virgin target, fell to R.A.F. Bomber Command.

Soon after nine o'clock on Tuesday morning, 13th February, having studied the weather reports and synoptic charts, the Commander-in-Chief ordered his Deputy, Air Marshal Sir Robert

Saundby, to lay on the attack on Dresden. The plan of attack had already been decided; it remained only for Saundby to pass the appropriate coded signal to the five Bomber Group Headquarters directly concerned.

The Russian front lay less than eighty miles to the east of Dresden. There must be no chance of any of the Lancasters going astray and dropping their bombload behind the Red Army lines; even less must the target-marking force be permitted any latitude of error. The Royal Air Force's most up-to-date piece of electronic navigation equipment, installed in certain aircraft under the code-name *Loran*, was to be used to make the initial fix on the target area, and low-level visual marking was to be relied on for selecting the correct city for attack.

In the light of what was to happen to a luckless American Bombardment Group during the Flying Fortress attack on the following day, this was a wise precaution.

Loran, a bulky set of American-built equipment in several metal containers strapped into the already cramped cockpit of nine Mosquito high-speed bombers, was originally designed to be installed in Lancasters and used in long-range attacks in the Pacific theatre of war.

Basically a natural extension of the *Gee* radio-beam navigation device, which spun an invisible web of beams across the Western European ether, *Loran* had been designed to work at very long ranges, because *Gee* was only completely efficient if it was used within relatively short distances of the transmitter chains.

Loran, using reflected radio waves from the 'E'-layer, had a range of some 1,500 miles, but the use of 'E'-layers effectively limited its applicability to night flying only. Up to February 1945 it had never been relied on for an R.A.F. operation. Now with the issue of the executive order to bomb a city at a great range and almost within sight of the Russian lines, the highest confidence in the navigation of the target-finding aircraft was required; only *Loran* could provide this. The crews of the Lancaster and Mosquito aircraft fitted with *Loran* were well trained in the operation of their equipment; Bomber Command's navigation chiefs crossed their fingers and hoped that on the night the gear would work perfectly: the English *Gee*-chain radio beams even when unjammed petered out some 150 miles west of Dresden; the signals picked up from the mobile *Gee* transmitters moving up behind the Allied lines were unreliable and weak; even they did not cover Dresden, the target city. The complication involved in navigating successfully to Dresden was that the *Loran* beams would apparently not be picked up lower than 19,000 feet. The Master Bomber and his eight Marker Mosquitos would have to endure a probably very painful switchback dive from 19,000 feet to their normal marking altitude of one thousand feet and less within four or five minutes, if they were to arrive at the target area on time.

The political embarrassment that any mistaken target marking would occasion was clear: the Allied leaders had decided to support the Red Army's advance by attacking population centres; the plan was intended not only as a demonstration of solidarity with the Russians, but also as a timely expression of the terrible striking power possessed by the Western Allies. If when the ashes settled and the smoke pall lifted it was found that the Lancasters of Bomber Command had failed in their mission and hit the wrong target, the embarrassment would be bitter; if the bombers were to strike a city behind the Russian lines the consequences might be more severe.

Harris insisted that *Loran* must be available to the crews responsible for initially finding the city and marking the target area with coloured target indicators. This was the reason why he decided that the initial blow should be struck by the then famous low-level visual technique of Air Vice-Marshal the Hon. Ralph Cochrane's No. 5 Bomber Group. (In fact, command of the Group had one month before passed to Air Vice-Marshal H. A. Constantine, but to all intents and purposes the technique evolved for the Dresden attack was elaborated and developed during the period that Cochrane was at No. 5 Group Headquarters.)

No. 5 Group's own private pathfinders had a good record of reliability in marking; the No. 8 Group Pathfinders had made a poor start in 1942 when a number of wrong towns had been attacked; this was not a reflection on the ability or determination of the crews in Air Vice-Marshal Bennett's Group so much as on the serious shortage in those early days of reliable radar aids to night navigation and blind bombing.

In the first months of the Pathfinder Force's existence they had marked Harburg instead of Hamburg; they had missed Flensburg completely and also Saarbrucken; research into many raids on cities like Frankfurt, which have gone down in an official account as successfully marked by No. 8 Group Pathfinder crews, has found in the city archives and Police President Reports that 'although the sirens sounded that night, not a single bomb fell within the city boundaries'. Until the introduction of *Oboe*, the precision blind target marking equipment, remotely controlled by computers back in England, which could track the position of the marking Mosquitos accurately to within a few hundred feet and order the release of the target-indicator bomb with the same degree of accuracy, the Pathfinder Force was looked at askance by many of the senior officers at Bomber Command Headquarters. *Oboe* reached with difficulty only as far as the Ruhr; even the trailer-mounted *Oboe* stations behind the Allied lines in France and Germany did not reach halfway to Dresden in strength. Moreover, the Pathfinders were completely untrained in visual identification of targets from low levels. Thus Air Chief Marshal Harris selected No. 5 Group's independent pathfinder force to lead the attack on Dresden on the night of 13th February 1945. It was for the eight Mosquito markers from 627 Squadron to use their *Loran* sets to reach the proximity of the city, flying independently of the main force of marker and bomber aircraft; the Mosquitos would be hard pressed to reach Dresden with a target indicator load, and could only adopt an almost direct route, while the Lancasters of the marker and bombing force would be routed out to Dresden by a course taking them to a rendezvous over Reading, then out over the Channel to a point on the French coast by the Somme estuary, from which they would fly due east for some 130 miles; on reaching the 5 degree line of longitude they would then head directly for the Ruhr, setting the sirens wailing throughout Germany's industrial cities. Ten miles north of Aachen, the bombers would head across the Rhine between Düsseldorf and Cologne; at 9.00 p.m., with the bomber formations still surging across the Rhineland, swift Mosquito formations from No. 8 Group's Light Night Striking Force would attack Dortmund and Bonn, to divert the attention of the night-fighter controllers. The Lancasters would meanwhile be skirting by a northerly route round Kassel and Leipzig; fifteen minutes before the attack on Dresden was due to commence, a force of Halifaxes from No. 4 and No. 6 Groups would attack an oil refinery at Böhlen, just south of Leipzig, in a large-scale diversionary move. The Lancasters, however, would be heading south-east, almost following the course of the River Elbe, bearing at high speed downwind towards the target city, Dresden. The whole force would be withdrawn from the attack by a totally different southerly route, passing south of Nuremberg, Stuttgart and Strasbourg.

The illuminating and primary marker Lancasters for the attack on Dresden, supplied by Squadrons 83 and 97, and also equipped with *Loran*, would approach along the same route. These Lancasters were crewed with specially trained radar operators, highly skilled in interpreting the data provided by the *H2S* radar equipment. On the small cathode-ray tubes of this equipment, a rotating time-base provided as a crude shadow-pattern picture of the landscape underneath the aircraft, showing up rivers and large expanses of water as dark patches amidst the green of the land itself and the brilliantly glowing towns. At best *H2S* was only a confirmation of the existence of some city ahead of the bomber; unless, as in the case of Hamburg or Königsberg, there was a sharply defined water-front or system of docks, the town itself would not be readily identifiable from the tube. Dresden on the radar screen was one of the nondescript towns-on-a-river with which Central Germany, both sides of the Red Army front, abounded. Only the characteristic S-bend in the River Elbe made a feature for the radar operators to watch out for. They had no comparison radar photographs to guide them: attacks on other cities had yielded Leica-photographs of the *H2S* screen over the target; the operators could then compare the photographs of the target-image with the image on their screens for certainty. But Dresden had not been attacked by R.A.F. Bomber Command since the introduction of *H2S*. The lack of preparation which characterised this attack on Dresden showed itself none the less in this absence of *H2S*-image photographs.

It was the duty of these 83 and 97 Squadron Lancasters to arrive at Dresden some eleven minutes before zero: while some dropped strings of 3-minute parachute flares across the city, together with make-weights of long-delay high explosive time-bombs, the others would attempt to lob green target indicator bombs, set barometrically to burst at two to three thousand feet above the approximate position of the aiming point, as it appeared on the radar screen. At no time was any attempt at a visual identification to be made by these first waves of bombers over the target. Their task was only to point out the approximate position of the city and the rough location, within a mile or two, of the allocated aiming point. These flares were to guide the eight Mosquito crews, whose task was to search the landscape from only three thousand feet up for the marking point itself, and to mark it with salvoes of red marker bombs.

If the first attack on Dresden was to provide the unmistakable beacon that Harris required for the second blow, the city must be set well on fire. The German engineer directing Civil Defence measures in Dresden at the time afterwards characterised the firestorm phenomena as:

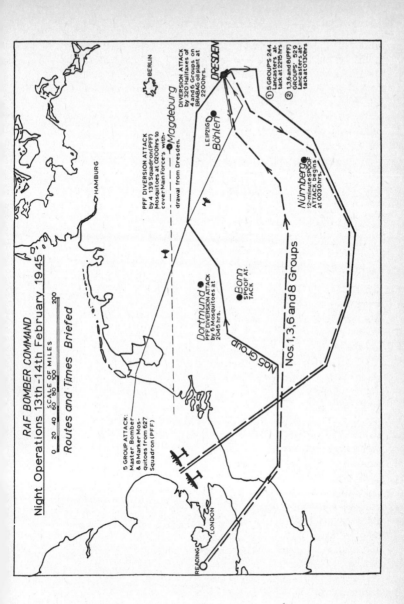

RAF BOMBER COMMAND
Night Operations 13th–14th February, 1945

Routes and Times Briefed

SCALE OF MILES
0 20 40 60 80 100   200

HAMBURG

BERLIN

Magdeburg

PFF DIVERSION ATTACK by 4 139 Squadron (PFF) Mosquitoes at 0200hrs to cover Main Force's withdrawal from Dresden.

DRESDEN

DIVERSION ATTACK by 320 Halifaxes of 4 and 6 Groups on BRABAG oil plant at 2200hrs.

① 5 GROUPS 244 Lancasters attack at 2215 hrs
② 1,3,6 and 8(PFF) GROUPS 529 Lancasters attack at 0130 hrs.

LEIPZIG
Böhlen

Nürnberg
12-minute SPOOF ATTACK by 910s at 0030hrs.

Dortmund
PFF DIVERSION ATTACK by 6 Mosquitoes at 2045 hrs.

Bonn
SPOOF ATTACK

No5 Group

Nos.1,3,6 and 8 Groups

5 GROUP ATTACK: Master Bomber & 8 Marker Mosquitoes from 627 Squadron (PFF)

LONDON

READING

III

a slowly developing series of fires scattered evenly across a large area, fires which were not extinguished by the inhabitants (who preferred to remain in their basements, cowed by the explosions of time-bombs) and which suddenly multiplied and spread as thousands of individual conflagrations united.

This period would take about half an hour or more; Air Chief Marshal Harris calculated that within three hours the fires should have gained a good grip on the centre of the city, provided that there was a strong ground wind and that the incendiary loads were well concentrated within the boundaries of the target sector; three hours would give sufficient time for fire brigades from most of the big cities of Central Germany to come to the assistance of the burning Dresden and to penetrate to the heart of the Old City. In fact this happened, exactly as he planned.

Only the No. 5 Group sector-attack provided the degree of saturation required to start a fire-storm. Every time it had been employed before it had caused a fire-storm of some degree. Previously the fire-storm had been merely an unforeseen result of the attack; in the double-blow on Dresden the fire-storm was to be an integral part of the strategy.

. . . . .

As in all the other more recent major attacks carried out by No. 5 Group, a Master Bomber was required to control the development of the attack.

For the attack on Dresden, the choice naturally fell on No. 5 Group's most experienced Controller, as the Group's Master Bombers were referred to; indeed the Wing Commander selected had himself controlled raids on several larger German cities, including Karlsruhe and Heilbronn, and was an expert in directing the marking and development of sector-attacks. The Marker Leader was also a veteran of the Heilbronn and other sector-attacks. The Master Bomber at Dresden has written since the war in a specialised publication that the Master Bomber was 'in effect the personal representative of the Air Officer Commanding in the target area'. Of Squadron Commander status, he would be given complete control of the attack after most careful briefing. The Master Bomber had a responsible and often hazardous job; he had to remain in the target area for the duration of the attack, often at very low altitude, regardless of the dangers and distractions of the enemy defences. Providing all went well with the attack, the duty of the Master Bomber was to a great extent a psychological one. 'It's not always the instructions you notice so much as the relief at hearing a good English voice getting things organised ahead of you after that long slog through flak and dirty weather', a pilot once remarked after a raid on another city in the Leipzig area. The English elocution of the 'voice' was usually not only good but excellent: Master Bombers and Marker Leaders were sent on short speech-training courses at Stanmore. The Master Bombers of No. 5 Group were all provided by 54 Base at Coningsby, the controlling headquarters for the Group's independent pathfinder force.

At the Headquarters of No. 5 Group, the morning of 13th February was taken up with the final details and the plan for the execution of the double blow on Dresden, so many times prepared, and so many times scrubbed. The Wing Commander in charge of Group Intelligence was forced once again to bemoan the almost total lack of knowledge about the city and its defences: it was suspected, however, that if Dresden was indeed being used for the passage of troops and munitions to the Eastern front then the flak defences might have been reinforced since the last small attack made on Dresden by American bombers on the morning of 16th January 1945.

The presence of convoys of army vehicles passing through the city also prompted the intelligence staff to suspect that the convoys and trains would mount mobile light anti-aircraft guns; these guns, ineffective above 8,000 feet and well below the altitude of the Lancaster forces which were to deliver the first and second attacks on Dresden, nevertheless could be very dangerous for the Mosquito crews, diving across the city at altitudes of less than a thousand feet. At the station briefings a few hours later the airmen would be told that the defences at Dresden were 'unknown'. This was not the only curious feature of the briefing that was awaiting the 6,000 airmen detailed for operations to Dresden on the night of 13th February 1945.

Towards noon the word came through from High Wycombe that meteorologists had predicted a stiff breeze blowing across the city from the south-west. But the teleprinter message added the warning that weather conditions were very unfavourable and only if the timing was kept strictly to the minute could the attack succeed: if the No. 5 Group attack for any reason had to be delayed more than half an hour, the double attack would fail, because the second mission would be scrubbed.

A belt of strato-cumulus cloud was drifting across the whole of Central Europe; the gap in the cloud layer was likely to last for only four or five hours as it passed over Dresden. The skies over Dresden would begin to clear soon before ten o'clock in the evening. Within five hours, the cloud would return. The double attack had to be fitted into that time. In spite of these contrary factors operating against the ultimate total success of the raids, the executive order to bomb Dresden was issued from Bomber Command's underground planning room; it was not the first time that Air Chief Marshal Harris had risked a fiasco, and it was typical of his bold and courageous attitude to decisions like this that he decided to press on then, in spite of his earlier reservation about the instruction to bomb Dresden.

By noon the executive order had been passed to every Group Headquarters. Two hundred and forty-five Lancasters from No. 5 Group were detailed to take part in the first attack, although one fell out later. The biggest contingent of aircraft delivering the second blow was detailed from No. 1 Group, with Headquarters at Bawtry: over two hundred of the Group's Lancasters were asked for; 150 Lancasters from the No. 3 Group Squadrons were despatched to Dresden, and 67 from the Canadian Bomber Group, No. 6; the remainder of the second attacking force was provided from the No. 8 Group Pathfinders: since Dresden was beyond the range of the Group's Pathfinder-Mosquito operations, sixty-one Pathfinder Lancasters, many of them equipped with the latest version of the *H2S*-radar equipment, were detailed to undertake the marking of the aiming points for the second attack. It was expected that this new equipment, the *H2S* Mark IIIF with the six-foot scanner, would provide sufficient ground detail on the radar screen to enable the crews to pick out identifying topographical details more clearly. Ten of these Pathfinder Lancasters were to be provided by 405 Squadron, the Vancouver Squadron of the R.C.A.F.; one of this Squadron's most experienced crews was the only Pathfinder Lancaster crew not to return from the Dresden operation. The largest contingent was to be supplied by the veteran 7 Squadron, with twelve Lancasters in the Pathfinder Force; 635 Squadron provided both Master Bomber and Deputy Master Bomber for the operation, as well as nine other Lancasters; the primary visual marker was supplied by 405 Squadron; 35 Squadron dispatched ten crews, and 156 and 582 Squadrons nine crews each. As 582 Squadron's records are incomplete, no reference can be made to the composition of its Pathfinder crews in the final battle order for the attack on Dresden.

In addition to the attacks on Bonn and Dortmund, Air Vice-Marshal Bennett had also planned for his force to deal with six other targets, including Dresden and Böhlen. Two targets were spoofs only, with crews dropping flares but no bombs on them; at thirty minutes past midnight, however, just as the two formations of bombers, one attacking, one withdrawing, were passing by to north and south of Nuremberg, a force of Mosquitos would deliver a twelve-minute attack on that city; again, at 2.00 a.m., after the last Dresden attack had finished, four very-high-flying Mosquitos —including one of the new Mark XVI pressurised-cabin Mosquitos —of 139 Squadron would each drop four 500-pound bombs on Magdeburg; as the German defence planners were well aware that Bomber Command had been ordered to concentrate to an increasing extènt on Germany's frailest link, her oil production and reserves, it was planned to lead off the night's attack with a small, but positive attack on the synthetic oil plant at Böhlen, ten miles south of Leipzig and not far from Dresden.

The zero hour for Böhlen was set for 10.00 p.m., fifteen minutes before the first blow fell on Dresden. This attack would be carried out by the Halifax squadrons of No. 4 and No. 6 Groups; 320 aircraft were detailed to attack Böhlen, rather over a third being from the Canadian No. 6 Group. The Halifax bomber, four-engined like the Lancaster and having a similar range, had, however, a considerably smaller bomb-load and was being gradually eliminated from the Command: as the attack on Dresden had been ordered as 'a severe blitz' it was appropriate that the maximum force of Lancasters only should be despatched, in order to deliver the maximum load of incendiaries and high explosive. The raid on Böhlen can hardly have been intended as anything much more than an elaborate spoof, in view of the prevailingly unfavourable forecast for raids on small targets like synthetic oil plants.

It was intended that the first attack on Dresden should serve to light it up as a beacon for the crews of the second attack three and a quarter hours later; the second attack, marked by the Pathfinder Group's Lancasters, would follow standard *H2S-Newhaven* technique. With zero hour at 1.30 a.m. on 14th February for the second blow, the Blind Illuminator Lancasters—twelve in number, not counting the 582 Squadron contribution—would make blind runs on their *H2S* radar indications alone across the city at 1.23 a.m., zero minus seven, and drop sticks of flares across the approximate position of the aiming point. At 1.24 a.m., one minute later, the Lancaster of the Deputy Master Bomber would make a bombing run across the city, and attempt, having identified unambiguously the aiming point for this attack, to mark it with his six red target-indicator bombs; the

Master Bomber, orbiting the city to the north-east, would assess the distance between these red flares and the true aiming point, and if they went wide attempt to drop his own red target indicators more accurately, using the first red flares as datum lines. If the Deputy Master Bomber's flares were accurate, then the Primary Visual Marker would put down a load of red and green flares around them to reinforce the marking of the aiming point. The rank and file of Visual Centerer Lancasters, of which there were some twenty in the Dresden operation, would then attack in waves of three at a time, at three- or four-minute intervals throughout the raid, replacing the dying target-marker flares of the preceding marker waves, and at the same time visually centering any wide marking shots.

Provision was also made for the eventuality that cloud obscured the target; if the cloud was moderate, then thirteen Blind Markers (not including 582 Squadron's) would be used to drop green ground marking flares early on; the Master Bomber would check whether the glow was visible through the cloud; if not, then as a last resort eight (not including 582 Squadron's) Blind Sky Markers were laid on, carrying loads of *Wanganui* sky-marker flares of a kind that would emit a red light with green stars; these would have to be released blind on radar data alone to float above the cloud layers on parachutes. Had the cloud been so dense during the second attack on Dresden that sky marking was necessitated, then without doubt the tragedy of Dresden would not have occurred; the weather over Dresden was, however, fine, and neither the Blind Markers nor the Blind Sky Marker bombers were called upon to release their flare loads by the Master Bomber.

The Master Bomber for the second Dresden attack was a very experienced pilot, with more than three tours of operations behind him; once, in November 1944, he had been asked to act as Master Bomber during the disastrous attack on Freiburg im Breisgau, but he had declined, as he had studied at the University there and had many friends in the area around the Freiburg Cathedral which was to be the aiming point for the attack; he had, however, never been to Dresden, and although he deeply regretted the necessity for the destruction of such a fine and beautiful city, he could find no personal reason for objecting.

The executive order to bomb Dresden did not pass unquestioned: soon after receiving it, the Pathfinder Group Commander felt bound to telephone back to High Wycombe to check that his staff had not misunderstood the order; when the order to bomb Dresden was confirmed, Air Vice-Marshal Bennett was able to overcome his doubts about the real nature of the attack and satisfied himself with a discussion of the aiming point allocated to his Group's marker force. Similarly, the Commander of No. 1 Group recalls that he and his senior staff were 'a little surprised' when they read the teleprinter message from Bomber Command Headquarters. Other Group Commanders remember the distinctly reserved note in their Commander-in-Chief's voice when he confirmed the order and gained the impression that he was to a large extent dissatisfied with the whole affair. By evening, when the 6,000 airmen had been briefed, the dissatisfaction had to some extent permeated as far as the lowest levels in the Command.

．　　　．　　　．　　　．　　　．

In the afternoon the Master Bomber for the first attack was called to the Intelligence building of 54 Base for final briefing on the plan of attack. The Base officers had searched in vain for one of the usual target maps prepared for attacks on German cities: target maps at this stage of the war were specially printed plans 24 inches by 18 inches, on which the countryside and city were lithographed in grey, purple and white as an artist's impression of how they looked by night, with the stretches of water and rivers showing up a brilliant white amidst the black and grey masses of the cities and the purple shading and cross-hatching representing variously fields, woods and open countryside; marked on these target maps were the main gun defence positions, the local airfields, and positions of German decoys. The particular target appeared in the middle of the target map, at the centre of a system of black concentric one-mile rings. The target itself would be printed on these target maps in a distinctive orange colour, whether it was the Krupps factory site at Essen, the Focke-Wulf works at Bremen, or the oil refinery at Gelsenkirchen.

For Dresden there was no such target map. Perhaps, as Sir Robert Saundby and Air Commodore H. V. Satterley suggest, this is the conclusive evidence of the absence of any fundamental desire on Air Chief Marshal Harris' part to destroy this city. Had it been otherwise, then, with his usual thoroughness, he would have instructed Bomber Command Intelligence to ensure that adequate photographic cover had been made of the city, with sufficient frequency to ascertain the nature of the target, its defences, and any decoy sites in the immediate neighbourhood. He would have plotted and fixed the position of the Dresden fighter squadrons on the air station at Dresden-Klotzsche.

He would have observed the scale of the military barracks complex to the north of the city and the neighbouring, but now defunct, Arsenal. As it was, all that the Master Bomber and his deputy could be provided with to operate from was a *District target map: Dresden (Germany), D.T.M. No. G.82 1*; this rather outdated target map with which the Master Bomber and his marker force were to identify and mark the marking point for what was to be the climax of the strategic air offensive against Germany was nothing more than a black and white glossy letterpress-printed aerial photograph of Dresden, made up from a mosaic of not very high quality aerial-reconnaissance photographs, dating back to November 1943. Pitiful though this target map was in comparison with the highly superior target maps issued normally to bomber crews for operations in Germany, France and Italy, it did at least show clearly the points from which an attempt at marking Dresden might be made. Curiously, a single black cross was printed on the target map on a large building in the centre of the sector; this building was in fact the Police Headquarters in Dresden, containing in deep concrete bunkers the underground command centre of the A.R.P. staff, headed by Saxon Gauleiter Martin Mutschmann.

The forecast wind was going to blow steadily from the southwest, according to the Meteorological Section at High Wycombe. If the smoke from the burning city was not to obscure the glare of the target indicator candles burning on the ground, they must be to windward of the target area; the bombers would have to release their bombs to the east of the target markers.

The most prominent feature of the city's topography which could be identified on this aerial photograph mosaic was the large sports stadium to the west of the Old City, the central stadium of three, built roughly in a line across Dresden.

The sports stadium selected, the Dresden-Friedrichstadt Sportsplatz, was about 500 feet long and well situated near the lines of both the river and the railway; these might serve the Marker force well as datum lines when searching for the stadium in what promised to be minimal conditions of visibility at Dresden.

The Marker Leader would have to mark this stadium clearly with his single red marker; when the Master Bomber had checked its position, he would order the remaining Marker Mosquitos to back up on it with more red indicators until the whole sports stadium was well marked out with red flares. Then the main force of Lancasters, thundering across the countryside a few miles to the northwest, would be called into the attack. They would almost cross the city

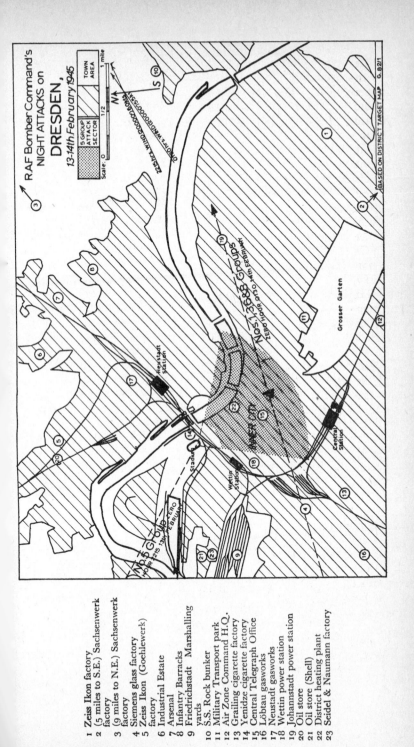

RAF Bomber Command's
NIGHT ATTACKS on
DRESDEN,
13-14th February 1945

5 GROUP ATTACK SECTOR
TOWN AREA
Scale: 0   ½   1 mile

BASED ON DISTRICT TARGET MAP G. 82/1

Nos.1,3&8 Groups
ZERO HOUR on 13-14th FEBRUARY

No.5 Group
HOUR 2215 13th FEBRUARY ZERO

INNER CITY
Grosser Garten

Neustadt Station
Central Station
Wettin Station

 1 **Zeiss Ikon** factory
 2 (5 miles to S.E.) Sachsenwerk factory
 3 (9 miles to N.E.) Sachsenwerk factory
 4 Siemens glass factory
 5 Zeiss Ikon (Goehlewerk) factory
 6 Industrial Estate
 7 Arsenal
 8 Infantry Barracks
 9 Friedrichstadt Marshalling yards
10 S.S. Rock bunker
11 Military Transport park
12 Air Zone Command H.Q.
13 Grailing cigarette factory
14 Yenidze cigarette factory
15 Central Telegraph Office
16 Löbtau gasworks
17 Neustadt gasworks
18 Wettin power station
19 Johannstadt power station
20 Oil store (Shell)
21 Oil store (Shell)
22 District heating plant
23 Seidel & Naumann factory

downwind, training their bombsights on the red glow of the marker indicators on the sports stadium, and after a timed overshoot, varied squadron by squadron and aircraft by aircraft, would release their bombs on the city itself. As the Lancasters each had a different heading briefed on which to fly over Dresden, the result would be that each of the bombers would fan out over the city from the stadium, and drop their bombs in a cheese-shaped sector, stretching eventually from close to the stadium to a maximum radius of 2,400 yards from the marking point. This sector included the whole of Dresden's Old City, and was marked out as the fire-storm area which would serve as the beacon for the Lancasters of the second attack. In fact, as we now know from the local German Director of the Dresden 'Central Bureau of Missing Persons (Dead Persons Department)', it was just this area that became 'the main area of the inferno'. Those who immediately after the end of the first raid made for the open air and the suburbs would have saved their lives. 'Those, however, who waited for the second attack did not come out of this central part of the town alive . . . There were also areas in (Dresden-) Striesen and particularly round Seidnitzer-platz where hardly any-one—if he waited for the second attack—escaped with his life.'

The Master Bomber and his navigator had been instructed that the purpose of the attack was to hinder the railway and other communications passing through Dresden. Even as they studied this 1·28 square mile sector allocated to No. 5 Bomber Group for a precision saturation attack like those for which the group had become famous, it probably did not occur to any of the officers present that in fact there was not one railway line crossing the sector marked out for carpet-bombing: there was not one of Dresden's eighteen passenger and goods railway stations in the sector; nor did the sector include the Marienbrücke railway bridge across the Elbe, the most important one for a long way in either direction.

If this point did occur to the Master Bomber, he did not remark on it during his special briefing. The only detail which stands out clearly in his mind now, eighteen years after the attack, was that at the end of the briefing the Base Commander recalled that before the war he had been to Dresden once and had stayed at a famous hotel on the Dresden Altmarkt, the large square in the centre of the Old City. This square was in the very heart of the sector marked out for saturation in some eight hours' time; it appeared that the Base Commander had been rooked by the hotel staff on his depar-ture. He said he hoped it would be attended to—this light-hearted remark cleared the air. The call sign for the main force of bombers was also imparted: *Plate-rack*. This was not yet another reference to the legendary, but false association of the target city with porcelain: *Plate-rack* was a phrase clear to broadcast and easily identified by main force crews; it was often used. The zero-hour on which all timing would be based was set for 10.15 p.m.

At 10.15 p.m. the first high-explosive bombs should be falling on the Dresden Old City. But before that, the marker force would have to spend ten minutes at least in marking the sports stadium in the western city with their marker flares.

. . . . .

By 5.30 p.m. the eight marker crews had been briefed and each had been issued with one indicator bomb from the bomb dump. Their aircraft had been checked and extra fuel tanks had been strapped into position. A run out to Dresden for the Mosquitos was going to stretch their operational range to the limit of their capacity and extra fuel was being carried only at the expense of fewer target indicators; there was no latitude for error in the marking technique.

As it was, if the Mosquito crews were to reach as far as Dresden, they would have no opportunity for making a wide detour to throw the enemy fighter controllers off the scent: at best they could head for Chemnitz, a few miles to the south west of the target city, and then at the last moment alter course for Dresden. But even so, the direct route in a straight line across Germany was going to take the marker force across several areas well defended with flak.

By 5.30, too, the first squadrons of Lancasters from the No. 5 Group airfields in the Midlands had taken to the air. By 6.00 the whole force of 244 bombers of the first wave was airborne, circling their airfields and setting course for the first route marker, and Germany.

CHAPTER II

THE PLATE-RACK FORCE ARRIVES

Dusk was already falling across England, and many crews must have looked at each other with uneasy anticipation of what lay ahead as they eyed the cloud-heavy skies and read their weather forecast notes. Icing was expected at very low altitudes, electrical storms were forecast, and ten-tenths cloud was covering most of Western Europe. Few of the airmen were relishing the prospect of a nine- or ten-hour flight across enemy-occupied territory in weather conditions like those: the only comfort was that the poor visibility and cloud cover over Germany would keep the night-fighters grounded; only fighters based on airfields where the cloud was not so thick presented a danger to the force.

The nine Mosquitos of the Marker Force contained in their equipment racks some of the most advanced electronic apparatus developed by Western scientists. The apprehension which they felt on viewing the deteriorating weather conditions must have been increased when they recollected their briefing instructions that if they 'got into trouble, they were to head back west, and try if possible to avoid being forced down, or landing, to the east of Dresden; and that they must most certainly destroy the aircraft and everything else. The crews were to land in German-occupied territory in preference to that overrun by the Soviet army.'

At the same time as the marker force aircraft were being loaded with equipment and pyrotechnics for the attack on Dresden, Farnborough scientists were checking over for one last time a special camera fitted on 26th January into the bomb bay of the Mosquito of the Marker Leader, who was also *ex officio* deputy Master Bomber. The camera had been equipped with a high-speed cartridge flash system, designed to take photographs of the target from very low level at one-second intervals, during the actual process of the marking. In this way it was expected that precise photographic confirmation of where the target-indicator bombs had landed would be obtained. The camera was designed to commence operating as the Marker Leader pressed his bomb release, and to continue flashing and taking photographs in a pattern across the target until the film was finished. For the first time the apparatus was to be used on Dresden.

At three minutes to eight on the evening of 13th February, Mosquito KB.401, piloted by the Master Bomber, lifted into the air from the base at Coningsby. At 9.28 p.m. they passed out of range of the *Gee* navigation chains both in England and in France. The west wind was blowing strongly now. Between 15,000 and 20,000 feet over North-west Germany a steady 85-knot gale was hastening the Mosquitos towards their target. Now the navigators had to rely on their own navigation and the correctness of the forecast winds to keep them on track and prevent them wandering across any heavily defended areas until they could pick up the faint signals from *Loran*, the long-range navigation equipment. At 10.00 p.m. the spoof attack on Böhlen was due to start, and a few minutes afterwards the blind radar markers would be dropping their parachute flares and green primary markers over the approximate position of Dresden.

Only at 9.49 p.m. did the navigators finally pick up the *Loran* navigation system's transmission. The navigators required to pick up two of the beams for a positional fix and, while the Master Bomber looked anxiously at his watch, his navigator checked patiently on the *Loran* screen trying to pick up the second beam; higher and higher the Mosquitos were forced to climb, groping in the ether for the elusive radio beam. It was 9.56 p.m. In five minutes or so the flare force would be over Dresden. The Master Bomber's Mosquito was over 20,000 feet up. Then the navigator found the beam he was searching for, and at once obtained the fix he needed. They were fifteen miles due south of Chemnitz. Turning onto a homing course, the pilots of all nine Mosquitos scanned the horizon for the tell-tale flares which would tell them that their calculations had been correct.

The whole of the countryside below them seemed to be swathed in banks of ten-tenths cloud. Above them the cold February sky was clear and starry. But, even as the Mosquitos covered the last thirty miles towards Dresden, losing seventeen and eighteen thousand feet in a matter of four or five minutes, they could see the cloud clearing away exactly as had been forecast by the meteorologists at Bomber Command. At Dresden itself they would find only three layers of cloud over the target: a thin layer of strato-cumulus from 15,000 to 16,000 feet, another layer of cloud from 6,000 to 8,000 feet, and wisps of cloud at 3,000 and 5,000 feet.

At the same time, the edge of the horizon over Dresden was broken by a string of vivid white lights, and a single ball of green fire hanging in the sky. The primary flare force of 83 Squadron Lancasters had arrived. The Primary Green, aimed and dropped by radar over the S-bend in the river Elbe, together with the attendant showers of magnesium parachute flares, was falling exactly over Dresden. From now on the whole attack would develop with terrifying military precision. After the first wave of blind illuminator Lancasters, a second wave marched over the target area, dropping sticks of white flares; this time the bomb-aimers relied on visual methods as well as the data on the radar screens.

Finally it was the turn of the Mosquito marker force, the brilliant red marker bombs as yet still clutched in the bomb bays, to swoop down on Dresden and mark out the sports stadium on which the whole attack depended.

.   .   .   .   .

Dresden lay within the aegis of the German 1st Fighter Division. Divisional Headquarters were at Döberitz near Berlin. Other fighter command divisional headquarters in giant bunkers had been built at Arnhem, Stade, Metz, and Schleissheim. These fighter command centres were referred to by the airmen as 'battle opera houses'.

On entering [wrote a Luftwaffe night-fighter general] one was immediately infected by the nervous atmosphere reigning there. The artificial light made faces appear even more haggard than they really were. Bad air, cigarette smoke, the hum of ventilators, the ticking of the teleprinters and the subdued murmur of countless telephone operators gave one a headache. The centre of attraction in this hall was the huge frosted-glass panel on which were projected by light spots and illuminated writing, the position, altitude, strength and course of the enemy as well as of our own formations. Each single dot and each change to be seen here was the result of reports and observations from radar sets, aircraft spotters, listening posts, reconnaissance planes, and from units in action.

In front of the map, on rising steps like an ampitheatre, were seated, several rows deep, the fighter controllers, who issued the orders to their night fighters, as the battle progressed.

Now Fate stepped in to seal Dresden's destiny. That very morning, 13th February, 1945, the German High Command had issued a new directive to the Luftwaffe, clarifying priorities in the use of aviation spirit: 'Top priority is the operation of fast bomber formations in the front line area by day, and the operation of strafer-aircraft against the same targets by night. On account of the loss of the production of the synthetic oil refineries, the operation of fighter defences is forbidden'. There was no fuel for the fighter squadrons.

On the night of 13th February 1945 the dilemma which faced the fighter controllers in the 'battle opera house' at Döberitz can clearly be seen. Firstly, their information was only very scanty; even their usual enemy radar-transmission monitoring posts, which had picked up the tuning-in and testing of the radar and radio sets during the mornings prior to full-scale attacks, were now blinded by 'curtains' thrown round the eastern coast of the British Isles, and along the Western Front. The German early warning chain along the Channel coast had long fallen into Allied hands; the news of the enemy bombers approaching low across the Allied lines would reach them only as they came within range of radar chains inside the Reich; and then when the threat did materialise on this bleak evening of 13th February 1945, only 244 bombers finally emerged from behind the radar 'curtain'. The problem which faced the controllers was not only: Where are these bombers heading for? but also: What is Air Chief Marshal Harris going to do with his 750 other serviceable bombers tonight? As the Lancaster bomber formation headed deeper and deeper into Southern and Central Germany, joined shortly by another three hundred Halifaxes despatched to Böhlen, the threat became clearer to the controllers; but the order for the airworthy squadrons in Central Germany to take off was given only when it was realised that the third, smaller formation of red arrows on the frosted glass screen in front of them was not the usual nuisance raid on Berlin under way, but was in fact going to pass over either Leipzig, Chemnitz, or Dresden at the same time as the big bomber stream. At this point the controllers ceased waiting for the third major threat, and possibly the real one, to materialise, and decided that the immediate threat was to one of the Saxon cities. Even so, more than one controller must have had serious doubts when he considered the possibility of an attack on Dresden. A first alarmed report from Dresden indicated that one thousand paratroops had landed to the west of the city.

Nevertheless, at about 9.55 p.m. the order reached Dresden-Klotzsche to scramble V/NJG.5, the night-fighter squadron based there. But by then it was too late and the target-marking was already beginning. One of the Me.110 night-fighter pilots based at Klotzsche, a 25-year-old Sergeant who had volunteered for duty in the Reich Defence, described 13th February in his diary as his 'saddest day as a night-fighter pilot'. At midday he had checked and tested his aircraft. The *SN-2* night interception radar device was in perfect order.

> In the evening we received an alarm, the first of the day. Naturally it concerned only the A-crews. The take-off order came much too late. . . .

The A-crews were the eight or ten most successful crews of the squadron. The pilots of the A-crews were finally scrambled at five minutes to ten, at the same time as the Mosquito markers were at 20,000 feet struggling to find the *Loran* beams. It took the Messerschmitt twin-engined night fighters over half an hour to gain attacking altitude, circling over their own airfield five miles from Dresden. The light anti-aircraft gunners at the airfield became increasingly nervous as the sounds of the approaching armada of bombers echoed from beyond the horizon; when the airfield's one searchlight trapped a circling aircraft, at quite a low altitude, all the light guns opened up on it. The plane crashed in flames. It was the anti-aircraft gunners' only success during the night: one of the five A-crew Me.110's piloted by a young Sergeant pilot. Thus ill-prepared the Saxon capital girded itself against the attack. In the whole of Germany, only twenty-seven night fighters had taken off to ward off the mightiest air raid in history.

Three of the Lancasters of the two pathfinder squadrons had been equipped as special Link aircraft; their task was to communicate the instructions of the Master Bomber in Morse to the bomber force if the speech transmitter equipment installed in the bombers should fail or be jammed. Sometimes one of the bomber wireless operators would switch on his *VHF* set by accident, jamming communication between the bombers and the Master Bomber; at other times the Germans themselves were responsible. The Links also acted as means of communication between the Master Bomber and the Group's base in England. Corrected weather forecasts and wind estimations were exchanged between the Master Bomber and the base; on such operations the Master Bomber was required to make a snap judgment of the success of the raid and pass it back to England even as he was still over the target.

On the Dresden raid, the three Link Lancasters were all provided by 97 Squadron. In Link 1, piloted by a Flight Lieutenant, a special wire-recorder had been installed to make a permanent record of the progress of the attack; the record would be produced at the raid assessment inquiry into the execution of the raids on Dresden during the following days: R.A.F. Bomber Command was still eager to learn from its mistakes, and to develop and extend its procedure and techniques.

As the Master Bomber's Mosquito was still approaching the target area, he switched on one of his two *VHF* speech transmitters; now for the first time radio silence was broken over Germany: 'Controller to Marker Leader: How do you hear me? Over.' The Marker Leader replied that he could hear the Master Bomber clearly 'at strength five'. A similar inquiry of the first Link aircraft recorded that communications between Link 1 and Master Bomber were 'loud and clear'. The whole operation would be directed in plain speech; code-words were used only for prime orders like 'Recall', or 'Mission Cancelled'. No acknowledgment was required by the Master Bomber except for the order 'Go home'. The cloud was still quite apparent over the target area; the Master Bomber called up the Marker Leader once more: 'Are you below cloud yet?' 'Not yet,' replied the Marker Leader. He too had just lost nineteen thousand feet in less than five minutes; the navigator in the Master Bomber's aircraft had in fact suffered agonies from ear trouble during the descent. The Master Bomber waited, then asked the Marker Leader whether he could see the Primary Green dropped by 83 Squadron. 'Okay, I can see it. The cloud is not very thick.' 'No,' confirmed the Master Bomber. 'What do you make the base of it?' After a moment the Marker Leader replied, 'The base is about 2,500 feet.' It was time for the marking to begin. The flares were burning very brilliantly over the city now; the whole town looked serene and peaceful. The Marker Leader in his Mosquito inspected the target carefully: to his surprise he could see not one searchlight, not one light flak piece firing. Cautiously he circled the town, picking up his bearings.

As I flew across the city it was very obvious to me that there was a large number of black-and-white half-timbered buildings; it reminded me of Shropshire and Hereford and Ludlow. They seemed to be lining the river which had a number of rather gracefully-spanned bridges over it; the buildings were a very striking feature of the city's architecture.

In the marshalling yards of Dresden-Friedrichstadt he could see a single locomotive puffing industriously away with a short length of goods wagons. Outside a large building which he identified as the Central Station—he had spent the afternoon at Woodhall Spa studying a mosaic aerial picture of Dresden—there was another plume of smoke where a locomotive was struggling to pull a passenger train with some white coaches out into the open air.

Then it was time to begin his first run up on the marking point. Over the Central Station he was two thousand feet up. Now he began to dive sharply; he kept a wary eye on the altimeter: the target indicator bombs were set to burst barometrically at seven hundred feet. If released below that altitude, they would either set the little wooden plane on fire, or not cascade properly.

His eyes tracked the railway lines out of the Central Station, round in a right-hand curve to the river. Just to the left of the railway bridges lay his marking point; now that he was in the position to commence his run, he called out, 'Marker Leader: Tally-ho!' to warn off other markers who might otherwise be commencing marking runs; from two thousand feet the Mosquito dived to less than eight hundred feet, opening its bomb-doors as it entered upon the straight run-in to the aiming point. The first flash cartridge fired as the camera was pointing at the Dresden-Friedrichstadt *Krankenhaus*, the biggest hospital-complex in Central Germany. In its lens the camera trapped the picture of the 1,000-pound target indicator bomb slipping out of the bomb bay, the finned canister silhouetted menacingly on top of a small oblong building in the hospital's grounds.

The Marker Leader levelled out briskly, maintaining a high speed, as he still did not know whether there was any flak to come up, and as the flare illumination of both Dresden and his aircraft was particularly good. The camera flashed a second time: the bomb was a dark fleck above the brightly lit stadium. One of the Mosquito pilots who had not been warned of the new camera technique shouted an involuntary, 'My God, the Marker Leader's been hit,' to his navigator. But at the same moment the first red marker bomb cascaded perfectly into a blaze of light.

The Mosquito swooped across the stadium towards the river at 300 miles per hour. Its camera was still flashing regularly once per second. The third flash was over the hospital's railway siding; a hospital train from the Eastern front was unloading there: now it was recorded for all time on a strip of film before the bombers arrived to blast the sidings from the map. The fourth flash showed the Marker Leader that he was across the River Elbe; a cotton-wool plume of steam coiled up from a single saddle-tank locomotive puffing along the railway running beside the Japanese Palace Gardens. 'Marker Two: Tally-ho!' The second Marker Mosquito was already following the railway lines round, ready to estimate the overshoot of the Marker Leader's red indicator bomb.

At the same time, the Master Bomber checked the three Dresden stadiums on his District Target Map, checked the stadium that had been marked, and announced grimly: 'You've marked the wrong one.' For a moment the *VHF* radio recorded only uncomfortable breathing. Then there was a relieved: 'Oh no, that's all right, carry on.' The Master Bomber could clearly see the red marker flare burning in a brilliant crimson pool not far from the stadium. 'Hello, Marker Leader,' he called, 'that target indicator is about 100 yards east of the marking point.' This initial marking shot was extraordinarily accurate. When one remembers that during the first night of the Battle of Hamburg in 1943, the markers of the official Pathfinder Group were anything from half a mile to seven miles wide of the aiming point, also using a visual technique, the fundamental difference between the standards achieved by the two Bomber Groups can be judged. 'Controller to Marker Leader: Good shot! Back up, then; back up.' 'Marker Leader to all Markers: Back up, back up.' 'Marker Five to Marker Leader: Clear?' 'Marker Two to Marker Leader: Tally-ho!'

The time was six and a half minutes past ten. Zero hour was still nearly nine minutes away, but the target marking point was clearly and unambiguously marked. There remained only for the other Mosquitos to unload their red marker bombs onto the one already burning, to reinforce the glow. The only thing which was concerning the Master Bomber was the visibility of the marker bombs through the thin layers of cloud, especially for the Lancaster bombers who had been stacked in the top height band at some eighteen thousand feet; the Lancaster squadrons had been briefed to approach the marking point at different altitudes to avoid collisions as they fanned out over the city. A specially equipped Lancaster of 97 Squadron had been positioned at eighteen thousand feet over Dresden. This was Lancaster Check 3. 'Controller to Check 3: Tell me if you can see the glow.' 'I can see three T.I.s through cloud,' replied the Check Lancaster. The Master Bomber, thinking that the Check had reported seeing only 'green T.I.s', queried this. 'Good work. Can you see the reds yet?' 'Check 3 to Controller: I can just see reds.'

One after another two more Marker Mosquitos tally-ho'd and dropped their reds on the stadium. The Master Bomber remembered that the Mosquitos only carried one marker each, and warned them to 'take it easy'; they might be needed later on. The time was seven minutes past ten, zero minus eight. The marking had proceeded much better than expected. 'Controller to Flare Force: No more flares, *no more flares.*' One more Mosquito called out its intention of marking the stadium. A trifle impatiently the Master Bomber called out to all the markers: 'Hurry up and complete your marking and then clear the area.' A brilliant concentration of red markers was now burning around the stadium, each marker a pool of burning candles, scattered over a radius of several hundred square feet, too numerous to be extinguished even if there were any Germans brave enough to venture into what must seem to them the very heart of the target area.

In Dresden the *Horizont* flak-transmitter was warning: 'The formation of nuisance raiders is orbiting from Martha-Heinrich 1 to Martha-Heinrich 8; the first waves of the heavy bomber formations are at Nordpol-Friedrich, now Otto-Friedrich 3; their heading is East-North-East.' *MH1, MH8, OF3*—these were all the appropriate squares of the grid overprinted on the flak commanders' plotting charts; in their excitement, however, the speaker had confused the nuisance raiders—in fact the nine Mosquitos of the marker force —with the heavy bombers, and vice versa. Moments later, it dawned on the flak commander of the area that these were in fact the pathfinder Mosquitos arriving from the Chemnitz area, and the heavy bomber formations were approaching over Riesa from the north-west; at once a signal was passed to the local A.R.P. Control Room in the basement of the Albertinum building. The last broadcast report from this Control was a shrill: 'Bombs falling on the City area! Comrades, keep sand and water handy!' But still the citizens had not been warned to take cover.

The Master Bomber made one final check with the Lancaster in the top height band: 'Can you see the red target indicators?' The reply was satisfactory. 'I can see the green and the red T.I.s.' It was nine minutes past ten, zero minus six. The marking was complete, and the Master Bomber wanted the attack to begin at the earliest possible moment; his tanks would only allow him to stay over the target for another twelve minutes. He wanted to witness the commencement of the attack and ensure that all went well.

It was at this moment that the Dresden people, by now cleared from the open spaces and listening apprehensively in their basements and cellars to the sound of the light Mosquitos racing backwards and forwards across the rooftops of the Saxon capital, were informed for the first time of the nature of the real threat to their city. At 10.09 the ticking clock which replaced wireless broadcasts during alerts in Germany was sharply interrupted. The unmistakably Saxon voice of a very agitated announcer broke out of the loudspeakers: '*Achtung, Achtung, Achtung!* The first waves of the large enemy bomber formation have changed course, and are now approaching the city boundaries. There is going to be an attack. The population is instructed to proceed at once to the basements and cellars. The police have instructions to arrest all those who remain in the open. . . .'

In his Mosquito three thousand feet above the silent city, the Master Bomber was repeating over and over into his *VHF* transmitter: 'Controller to *Plate-rack* Force: Come in and bomb glow of red T.I.s as planned. Bomb glow of red T.I.s as planned.'

It was exactly 10.10½ p.m.

The Marker Leader called up the Master Bomber, asking: 'Can I send the Marker Force home now?'

It occurred to the Master Bomber that the Germans might well have a decoy site in the neighbourhood; without a target-map in his possession showing such sites it would not be wise to discount the possibility. 'Controller to Marker Leader: If you stick around for a moment, and keep one lad with yellow, the rest can go home.' 'Okay, Controller. Marker Leader to all markers: Go home, go home. Acknowledge.' One after another Markers Three, Four, Five, Six, Seven and Eight acknowledged: 'Going home.'

The Marker Leader spotted a circling aircraft with its green and red navigation lights on. This was asking for trouble over enemy territory. 'You have your navigation lights on,' he warned the aircraft. The lights did not go out. It must, in fact, have been one of the German Me.110's still circling to gain height; but the Mosquitos were completely unarmed, and short of ramming the fighter, there was nothing that anybody could do about it.

The Master Bomber was still broadcasting to the main force bombers: 'Controller to *Plate-rack* Force: bomb concentration of red T.I.s as planned as soon as you like.'

The guns defending Dresden were still silent. Not even a muzzle flash was to be seen. It began to dawn on the Master Bomber that in fact Dresden was undefended. He could safely order the heavy four-engined Lancasters down to bomb from lower altitudes, thereby ensuring a more even distribution of bombs over the sector marked

131

for attack. He called up the Link 1 Lancaster which was in constant Morse contact with the bombers: 'Tell the aircraft in top height band to come down below the medium cloud.' 'Roger.' By 10.13 the bombs had started falling on Dresden. The Marker Leader called the Master Bomber's attention to the characteristic heaving explosions of the huge 4,000 pound and 8,000 pound high-explosive bombs, designed to smash the windows and rip off the roofs of the highly combustible Dresden Old City buildings, some of them dating back over a thousand years. A vivid blue flash split the darkness as a stick of bombs, falling wide of the target sector, detonated; the crews decided later that an electricity installation must have been hit.

'Marker Leader to Controller: The bombs seem to be falling okay now. Over.' 'Yes, Marker Leader. They look pretty good.' 'Hello, *Plate-rack* Force. That's good bombing. Come in and aim for the red T.I.s as planned. Careful overshoot, somebody! Somebody has dropped very wide.' 'Controller to Marker Leader: Go home now, if you like. Thank you.' 'Hello, Controller: Thank you, going home.' 'Good work, *Plate-rack* Force. That's nice bombing,' commented the Master Bomber.

The Lancasters ran up to the marking point on the stadium squadron by squadron, each aircraft approaching the stadium and the brilliant glow of red marker bombs on a different heading, some heading due south, others almost due east, fanning out across the blazing Old City. The whole of the cheese-shaped sector was a mass of twinkling fires and, here and there, the brilliant flash of the big explosive bombs, churning up the debris and splintering the buildings, lit up the city's rooftops.

By eighteen minutes past ten the patterns of bombs were covering the whole sector, and one or two tell-tale splashes of lights were visible in the dark areas outside. The Master Bomber had seen these bomb loads go down wide too, and now he warned the rest of the force of Lancasters: 'Hello, *Plate-rack* Force: Try to pick out the red glow. The bombing is getting wild now. Pick out the red glow if you can, then bomb as planned.'

He had another three minutes in which he could stay over the city. In the near distance he spotted something else beginning to glow. The red and yellow glow of a German decoy site being vainly ignited. The thing the Germans never realised when they designed decoy sites was that a burning city from the air was an untidy, turbulent mass of billowing smoke, bursting high explosive charges, and irregular patches of myriads of incendiaries; the German decoy sites were built in neat rectangles, the burning 'incendiaries' tidily scattered at regular intervals across the ground. Nevertheless, it was the Master Bomber's duty to ensure that no bomb loads were needlessly drawn astray by decoys. On this occasion he did not consider that the decoy was worth wasting a yellow cancellation-marker bomb on; he merely broadcast to all crews of the remaining *Plate-rack* Force bombers: 'Decoys at twelve to fifteen miles on a bearing 300 degrees true from town centre.' A minute later he repeated the warning: 'Complete bombing quickly and go home. Ignore the decoy fires.'

At twenty-one minutes past ten on the night of 13th February 1945, the Master Bomber called up the Link 1 Lancaster aircraft for the last time, as he turned his Mosquito on to the new bearing which would take him home. 'Controller to Link 1: Send home: "TARGET ATTACKED SUCCESSFULLY STOP PRIMARY PLAN STOP THROUGH CLOUD STOP."'

Chapter III

A CITY ON FIRE

THE measure in which the success of this first attack on Dresden by No. 5 Group, in the late evening of 13th February 1945, was aided by the accuracy of the weather predictions over the target area can be judged by a comparison with the numerically larger attack—320 Halifaxes—on the synthetic oil plant at Böhlen, just 100 miles west of Dresden.

The weather section at Bomber Command Headquarters had predicted that the rift in the cloud layers over Western and Central Europe would be clear over Dresden only for four or five hours. But even as the early marker force had swept into Dresden from almost due west, they were climbing down over the edge of a precipice of cloud for the last 35 miles. Over Böhlen itself, crews reported layers of strato-cumulus cloud. Only the faintest glow of the Pathfinder markers could be seen, and they were widely scattered. In addition to this lack of marking concentration the Germans ignited a series of dummy target indicators some miles away, and the Halifax crews, not being able to distinguish ground detail, were to a large extent misled, in spite of their Master Bomber's warnings. The bombing was dispersed.

Had the same cloud layers been over Dresden just fifteen minutes later when the No. 5 Group bombers arrived at that luckless city, the first attack would almost certainly have failed to achieve the degree of concentration in space required to start the fire-storm.

The records kept by the meteorological post at the local fighter airfield at Dresden-Klotzsche confirm that not only was the initiation of the attack nearly impossible, but that the cloud banks were equally close on the heels of the attacking force at the end of the second blow: thus although at 7.00 p.m. there had been only one-tenth cloud below 10,000 feet, within ten minutes of the end of the second blow on Dresden, at 2.00 a.m. on 14th February, the overcast was obscuring ten-tenths of the sky both above and below 10,000 feet. Into this accurately forecast break in the cloud cover of Dresden, Bomber Command had had to fit two heavy air raids, with an interval of some three hours between them. As Wing Commander M. A. Smith—the Master Bomber of the first attack —confirms: if the first raid on Dresden had been timed ten or fifteen minutes earlier, the whole double-blow undoubtedly would have failed; the Lancasters could not have been kept orbiting for fifteen minutes waiting for clouds to clear.

Thus close was Bomber Command to being cheated of its greatest, climactic success in its area offensive against Germany; and, equally, thus close were Britain's post-war enemies to being robbed of one of their greatest propaganda indictments against her.

.   .   .   .   .

By 10.30 p.m. on 13th February the whole of the first Dresden force was making its way back to England. Ten minutes after the first attack had ended, the bombers ceased *Windowing* abruptly and by losing height rapidly until they were flying at a mere 6,000 feet effectively slid under the horizon of the German panorama radar chains. Only as the No. 5 Group force approached the Allied lines at a point a few miles south of Strasbourg did a slow climb to 15,000 feet commence, the bombers' withdrawal now covered by the new bomber stream coming in over France and Southern Germany— the force of 529 Lancasters due to open the attack on Dresden at 1.30 a.m. Since midnight the crews of these new bomber formations had been cascading *Window* into the air in copious amounts, while the aircraft steadily climbed over the Allied-held territory, finally crossing the front lines at a point some twenty miles north of Luxembourg.

This was a veritable bomber Armada, carrying an even heavier bomb load than had been dropped during the Thousand Bomber Raid on Cologne thirty-three months before. At the head of the bomber stream flew the Blind Illuminator Lancasters, their bomb racks loaded with time bombs and parachute flares, hooded magnesium lanterns set to ignite at 20,000 feet, to light up the countryside for the Deputy Master Bomber to identify the target and mark the aiming point. There were the Blind Marker Lancasters, and the Blind Sky Marker Lancasters; there were the Visual Centerers, spaced regularly throughout the bomber stream. In the van of the attacking force flew squadrons of fighter aircraft equipped for night fighting, and for strafing German airfields; infiltrated in the bomber stream were the Liberators and Flying Fortresses of No. 100 (Radio Counter Measures) Group, each carrying two trained signals experts for duties of a nature which even the other members of the aircrew were not permitted to ascertain, and each loaded with tons of metal-foil *Window* strips.

But if the force despatched to deliver the second blow to Dresden that night was impressive, the mood of the crews was not jubilant. At their briefing they had learned little of the nature of the target they were to attack. On most air stations the briefing had passed without comment and the young bomber crews accepted what their briefing officers told them. After the briefing was over, some of the aircrew who had been to Dresden before the war felt a little unhappy that such a raid was necessary. The trouble had started for most crews when they entered their briefing huts and the station commander had peeled away the brown paper covering the target maps and routing plans on the wall facing them at the end of the huts. The first reaction of most of the crews was awe at the depth of penetration into Germany. The captains and navigators exchanged glances and calculated roughly the duration of flight to Dresden: it would be about ten hours. This would be stretching the limits of the Lancaster aircraft; there seemed to be little point in going such a long way into enemy territory to attack what seemed to be such an unimportant target. Many of the aircrew voiced wonder and surprise that the Russians were not being asked to attack the city themselves, if it was so 'vital' to their front.

The minds of many of the aircrew were put at rest by the varied and imaginative assurances of the intelligence officers. It must be remembered in this context that Air Marshal Sir Robert Saundby, at Bomber Command Headquarters, 'could see no reason for bombing Dresden' as the city 'was not on our Target List.'

Remembered, too, must be the post-war statements of those close to the inner circles of the target planning committees, for example those in the War Office Department responsible for briefing the Chief of the Imperial General Staff on all air matters: Dresden was certainly not an important industrial centre and their information at that time was that it was *not* being used so much as a transport centre by the German Army, as by vast numbers of refugees from the Soviet front. While there is no doubt that this negative intelligence on Dresden as a target for the Allied strategic bombers was common to both War Office and Air Ministry circles and has been supported ever since by the senior officers at Bomber Command Headquarters, somehow the information became distorted by the time it was passed on to the aircrews themselves. The aircrews of No. 3 Bomber Group were informed: 'Your Group is attacking the

German Army Headquarters at Dresden.' Some crews of 75
Squadron even remember Dresden's being described as a fortress
city. Crews were briefed to attack Dresden to 'destroy the German
arms and supply dumps'. They were given to understand that it
was one of the main supply centres for the Eastern front. In No. 1
Group the emphasis appears to have been laid on Dresden's importance as a railway centre. The crews were told that their
designated aiming point was the railway station. The intelligence
prepared by the Headquarters of No. 6 Group, the Canadian
Group, described how 'Dresden was an important industrial area,
producing electric motors, precision instruments, chemicals, and
munitions'. In few of the squadrons were the airmen originally
warned of the presence of several hundred thousand refugees in the
city, or the prisoner-of-war camps containing 26,620 prisoners of
war in the suburbs. The local briefing officers at the stations seem
to have drawn heavily on their imagination; at one air station the
crews were told that they were attacking a Gestapo Headquarters
in the centre of the city; in another, a vital ammunition works;
in yet a third, a large poison gas plant.

For the first time all crews were issued with Perspex envelopes
containing large Union flags, embroidered in Russian with the
words *I am an Englishman*. While this was not, in a number of cases,
absolutely accurate—every Australian squadron in the force was
taking part in the night's operation—it was the best that Bomber
Command could offer the airmen for their personal security in the
event of being forced down behind Russian lines: they were not
offered much other comfort, but warned that the simple Russian
soldiery had the habit of shooting strange militia-men on sight,
whether decorated with the English Union flag or not.

The briefing ended with full instructions on the Pathfinder
marking techniques being used, the call-signs for the Main Force
and Master Bomber, and general warnings. The crews were advised
by bombing leaders to identify the target-indicator flares with care,
not only because of German decoy markers, but also because
Dresden would 'probably burn' and the markers might be swamped
by the other fires. The call-sign for the Master Bomber was given
as *Cheesecake*, for the Main Force of Lancasters as *Press-on*; when the
Main Force call-sign was announced, the usual ripple of laughter
went up—it was an R.A.F. expression which neatly summed-up
the current attitude. The attitude was indeed current among
Bomber Command crews for many weeks: for several of the major
operations into Germany the bombers' call-sign was given as *Press-*

on. It was only with the Dresden raid that some standard details of the briefing were missing. Normally, when a squadron was briefed for what they regarded as a worthwhile target, they raised a cheer when the station commander came to the rostrum to speak, even when the target was tough like Hamburg or Berlin. With Dresden the cheers were absent. With Dresden there seemed to be a definite, perhaps a studied, lack of information on the city and the nature of the defences. Encouraged though they were by talk of Gestapo Headquarters and poison gas plants, many of the crews were distinctly unhappy when they heard about the refugees. One of the squadrons of No. 100 (Radio Counter Measures) Group was briefed in full about the nature of the target; the intelligence officer even suggested, probably not seriously, that the very object of the raid was to kill as many as possible of the refugees known to be sheltering in the city, and to spread panic and chaos behind the Eastern front. This remark, however, did not meet with a jocular reception and to the last man the whole squadron decided to co-operate, but only to the letter of their orders: it was still the practice of a few bomber crews to take along bits of concrete, steel and old bottles to drop on enemy villages and towns as they passed over. Unanimously they voted to show their disapproval for this mission by omitting this practice for the night. This kind of reception was, however, by no means general in Bomber Command for the night's operation; especially in stations where the real nature of the city had been obscured, the reaction 'was the usual light-hearted chaff, probably covering their concern at the distance of the target,' as a bomb-aimer described it.

Unlike most of the air raids on German targets at this stage of the war, the force was carrying about seventy-five per cent incendiaries. While it had been found profitable earlier on in the war to employ a large proportion of incendiaries in attacks, exploiting the latent combustibility of the target, one by one the German cities had been attacked, bombed and destroyed, and in the Ruhr there was hardly a city where hundreds of acres had not been turned into an incombustible heap of rubble. For this reason the bomb loads had included ever larger proportions of high explosives, as the economic value of incendiaries dropped.

With Dresden the opposite was the case: the target was virtually a virgin city and the full 'Hamburg' treatment could be employed against it: first the windows and roofs would be broken by high-explosive bombs; then incendiaries would rain down, setting fire to the houses they struck, and whipping up storms of sparks; these sparks in turn would beat through the wrecked smashed roofs and broken windows, setting fire to curtains, carpets, furniture and roof timbers.

The waves of bombers in the second attack needed only to carry sufficient high-explosive bombs to spread the fires and to keep the heads of the fire-fighters down. Thus the bomb loads of No. 3 Bomber Group were divided into two types: one wave included a 4,000-pound high-explosive blockbuster in each load, and five 750-pound clusters of incendiaries; the second wave included one 500-pound general purpose high-explosive bomb and the 750-pound clusters; in No. 1 Group the bomb loads were slightly different, the incendiary bombs being more usually dropped from small bomb containers—metal trunks in the bomb bays, in which the 21-inch long hexagonal 4-pound thermite incendiaries were stowed—and from which they were released into the wind over the target; these showers of small bombs presented a danger to other aircraft over the target area and possessed no ballistic properties which enabled them to be accurately aimed.

Nevertheless, for targets like Dresden, where the purpose was to set as much of the city on fire as possible, these incendiaries, scattered broadcast across the target, achieved a useful random effect. The No. 1 Group aircraft were carrying seventeen of these trunks and one 2,000-pounder each; another variation was one 4,000-pounder with twelve trunks of incendiaries. Altogether, 650,000 incendiary bombs were in the bomb racks and S.B.-containers of the Lancasters attacking Dresden. None of them was carrying 'phosphorus bombs'; this allegation has been a feature of East German communist propaganda since the war. The whole force had been tanked up with maximum fuel loads, 2,154 gallons of petrol each. After the engines had been tested and run up, and the bombers had taxied from their dispersal areas to the end of the runways, the bowsers were waiting to top up the tanks once again. For two hours after taking-off there would be the sickly smell of petrol inside the aircraft.

The temperature had dropped considerably over the Continent, and many aircraft were troubled by icing. The blue flames of St. Elmo's fire, the static electricity phenomenon, played along the leading edges of the wings and around the spinning airscrews. In many aircraft the cold was so intense that the automatic pilots ceased to function, and faced the pilots with over nine hours' flying on manual control. Mercifully, between the German frontier and the target there was a thick bank of cloud which grounded many of the enemy's night fighters. Soon after passing to the south of the Ruhr the defences there opened up; many crews saw the flak barrage thrown up over the Ruhr cities. The first of the feints laid on by the Pathfinder Commander, Air Vice-Marshal Bennett, was under way: a small attack on Dortmund by Mosquitos of his Light Night Striking Force. Six high-explosive bombs were dropped, of which two failed to explode. In addition, the Liberators of 100 Group, their crews cascading *Window* into the air, patrolled the 8½-degree-east parallel of longitude, generating a screen which the German radar system could not penetrate. At Chemnitz the banks of cloud rolled apart. Chemnitz—now Karl-Marx-Stadt—was not marked at all on the Captains-of-Aircraft maps used by the pilots; perhaps for this reason some were careless about skirting the flak areas there. As the bomber stream, by now partially scattered and far beyond the range of *Gee*, emerged from the cloud formations and passed by the heavily defended city with its huge Siegmar tank engine works, the flak batteries along its whole length began to fire. One after another three Lancasters were hit and began to glide in flames to earth. Others were hit by flak but managed to complete the flight to Dresden.

In the distance the airmen could now clearly see the fires started by the No. 5 Group attack. Indeed, the fires had been visible from over fifty miles away. Some of the Pathfinder crews now admit to having been deeply mortified on seeing the city ablaze; this feeling is explained by the spirited rivalry then existing between No. 8 Group, the official Pathfinders, who were leading the second attack, and No. 5 Group, who had so successfully initiated this double-blow. 'No. 5 Group were known to us as the "Lincolnshire Poachers", or as the "Independent Air Force". We were irritated to see how successful they had been.' Although this sounds callous, in view of the horrors below, it typifies the honest approach of the bomber crews who made the statements, without which this section of the book would not have been possible.

Unlike the Mosquitos and Flare Force of No. 5 Group, the second attack's Pathfinders had no *Loran* equipment and, if the first blow had not been successful, it is unlikely that they would have achieved the necessary concentration on the target; as it was, the attack began only a few seconds late.

Zero hour for the second attack on Dresden was 1.30 a.m. At 1.23 a.m. the Blind Illuminator Lancasters released their sticks of flares across the aiming point, and at 1.28 the Master Bomber arrived; to his horror, he found that the whole of the centre of the city was being swept by a violent fire-storm, making it impossible for him to identify the aiming point clearly; a strong south-westerly

[*Air Ministry Official Photograph*

An R.A.F. reconnaissance photograph of Dresden taken after the attacks. *Lower left:* the Central Station. *At the top of the picture:* the River Elbe with Augustus Bridge; to the left of it the baroque Zwinger Palace; and, immediately below, the dark honey-combed streets of mediaeval Dresden with the rectangular Altmarkt Square in its heart.

During the second attack Lancasters from the R.A.F. Film Unit circled the blazing city; their cameras brought back film evidence of a pall of smoke three and a half miles high.

A reconnaissance photograph of Dresden-Friedrichstadt marshalling yards after the triple blow showing the lines of trains and vast areas of flame in the nearby streets.

[*Walter Hahn, D*

Dresden, 25th February 1945: soldiers driving commandeered farm carts have brought the victims to the cordoned-off Altmarkt Square. After last identification attempts the bodies are stacked on makeshift pyres.

[*Walter Hahn, D*

[Walter Hahn, Dresden

Five pyres were burning simultaneously as these photographs were taken. Scattered across the square can be seen the heaps of ashes waiting to be transported to mass graves.

[Walter Hahn, Dresden

Dresden's fashionable shopping centre—the junction of Prager-strasse and Ring-strasse. In the background looms the Central Station.

Even by the end of 1945 little had been done to clear the ruins: the view of Dresden's Inner
City with the Castle and Hofkirche.

A burnt out tramcar in Dresden at the junction of Moritz-strasse and König-Johann-strasse.

Dresden—the fringe of the fire-storm area: Pirnaischer-platz at the intersection with Ring-strasse.

wind was blowing down there and the pall of smoke from the burning city was obscuring the whole eastern section of the city.

At 1.30 a.m. the Deputy Master Bomber arrived and he too found that the aiming point was obscured by the fires and smoke; as the two Master Bombers had agreed between them prior to taking off that the Deputy should make the first marking run, the Deputy, Wing Commander H. J. F. Le Good, called up the Master Bomber, Squadron Leader C. P. C. de Wesselow, to confer with him on an alternative marking tactic; the question was whether the crews should be advised to concentrate their bombs on the area already burning, or whether the attack should be spread.

As it was out of the question, even with the powerful Illuminator flares, to identify the aiming point through the smoke-clouds and fires, the Master Bomber finally decided on the second course, by which the main force bombing would be concentrated on those areas not affected by the first attack; the Deputy Master Bomber's flares were not used for marking the aiming point, therefore; he (and the Visual Centerers backing up on him) marked first to one side and then to the other of the fire-storm area with the clusters of red and green target indicators, their only concern being to ensure that the bombing did not become too widespread. The bomb-aimer in Wing Commander Le Good's aircraft noted in his log-book afterwards:

> 13/14th February, 1945, Dresden. Nil defences, six red target indicators and four 500-pound H.E. bombs carried; smoke from the first attack prevented marking aiming point.

Wing Commander Le Good himself, an Australian, noted:

> 13/14th February, 1945, Dresden. Clear over target, practically the whole town in flames. No flak.

The Master Bomber and his Deputy did have some talk while they were over the target concerning the railway yards, but the Deputy was unable to see them clearly, in spite of their being to the windward of the burning area. The Master Bomber, therefore, in broadcasting over the standard R/T to the main force *Press-on* crews directed them to bomb first left then right, then over the existing fire and flare areas. Both Master Bombers stayed over the target area throughout the twenty-minute duration of the attack; as the Master Bomber was leaving, he checked again for the railway yards and this time was able to observe in detail the effect of the raid on them; the Squadron Record Book reports that in his post-raid interrogation he stated that the 'marshalling yards to the south-west had escaped major damage'.

· · · · ·

In some areas of Dresden the sirens did sound, but in most districts the power supplies had failed in the first attack, and this second raid took the people totally by surprise. As the Illuminator Lancasters crossed the burning Dresden, some minutes before zero hour, the bomb-aimers could see the roads and *Autobahnen* leading into Dresden alive with activity. Long columns of lorries, their headlights full on, were crawling towards the city. These must have been the convoys of lorries with relief supplies, and the fire-brigades arriving from the other cities of Central Germany; clearly the second component of Harris's double-blow strategy was being substantiated: the annihilation not only of the passive defences of Dresden, but also of a large number of forces summoned from surrounding cities.

> It was the only time I ever felt sorry for the Germans [relates the bomb-aimer of a Lancaster supplied by 635 Squadron]. But my sorrow lasted only for a few seconds; the job was to hit the enemy and to hit him very hard.

Lancasters of the Blind Illuminator force were by then lighting up the whole area with their sticks of parachute flares.

From the German point of view the opening of a mass attack on a city, prefaced by the waves of Pathfinders, must have been an ominous spectacle: the target indicators descending in shimmering cascades glittered hazily over the doomed city with a dread measure of finality. The bomber crews had been briefed to watch out early on for these sky flares going down over the target city; but the flares were scarcely needed. On 14th February 1945 at 1.24 a.m. there was no doubt at all to the crews that they had indeed arrived over Dresden. From one end to the other, Dresden had become a sea of fire. No. 5 Group had been using a high proportion of incendiaries and, in addition, there was a strong wind blowing down there. 'The area was so bright,' an airman wrote in his diary afterwards, 'that we saw our own aircraft all around us, and our own vapour trails as well.'

> The fantastic glow from two hundred miles away grew ever brighter as we moved into the target [wrote another, Jewish pilot of No. 3

Group]. At 20,000 feet we could see details in the unearthly blaze that had never been visible before; for the first time in many operations I felt sorry for the population below.

The navigator of another aircraft from the same Group writes:

It was my practice never to leave my seat, but my skipper called me on this particular occasion to come and have a look. The sight was indeed fantastic. From some 20,000 feet, Dresden was a city with every street etched in fire.

One flight engineer of No. 1 Group describes the brightness by recalling that he was able to fill in his log-sheet, by the light striking down the length of the fuselage.

I confess to taking a glance downward as the bombs fell [recalls a bomb-aimer of another No. 1 Group bomber] and I witnessed the shocking sight of a city on fire from end to end. Dense smoke could be seen drifting away from Dresden, leaving a brilliantly illuminated plan view of the town. My immediate reaction was a stunned reflection on the comparison between the holocaust below and the warnings of the evangelists in Gospel meetings before the war.

The target-indicator flares could be relied on to burn for some four minutes each. For this reason visual centering bombers were programmed to arrive at three or four minute intervals throughout the attack on Dresden. Few of the main force crews were aware of the nature of the aiming point they were attacking; unless they had taken pains to study the intelligence charts and plans in the briefing huts on the previous afternoon—and few aircrew were as keen as that—they were content to aim at the patterns of flares dropped by the Pathfinders, and to follow the instructions broadcast by the Master Bomber:

The Master Bomber was flying much lower than we were [records a No. 3 Group pilot]. He was directing each wave of the attack separately, and was most anxious that we should not waste our bombs on districts which were already well ablaze.

The bomb-aimers were too busy to wonder how they could be destroying a railway station, or a German Army Headquarters, or even the Gestapo building or poison-gas factory which had been received with such popular enthusiasm, if the Master Bomber was constantly directing the main force to release their bombs on different sections of the town. One area that stubbornly refused to catch fire was the Grosser Garten, the large rectangular park in Dresden, comparable in size with London's Hyde Park. Many tons of bombs were wasted in futile attempts to set the park on fire along with the rest of the city; the smoke layers blowing eastwards across the city obscured this part of the target area.

.   .   .   .   .

Once again the German night-fighter force was paralysed. This time the difficulty was not one of lack of fuel, or of lack of preparation at the airfields concerned. The night-fighter pilots at the Klotzsche airfield could clearly see the large fires burning in Dresden, less than five miles to the south. When news reached them through the normal piped *Drahtfunk* channel of another force approaching Central Germany from the south, there was not one of the airmen who doubted that the second attack was heading for Dresden too, thus clearly marked out as a beacon. The Station Commander at once ordered all the night fighter crews into their Me. 110s at 'cockpit-readiness'. The ground crews stood by, and tended the starting equipment.

At 12.30 a.m. the perimeter lighting and flarepaths flicked on, brilliantly silhouetting the hundreds of aircraft parked all round the perimeter track; whole squadrons of fighter and transport planes had been withdrawn to Klotzsche for safety from the eastern front, to prevent their being overrun. But the flarepaths were not for the night-fighters. The Station Commander explained that a flight of transport planes was expected from Breslau, then invested by Marshal Koniev's armies. The flarepaths could be turned off only from time to time. The fighter crews protested that the whole airfield would be destroyed if the bomber crews saw it. The Station Commander was adamant. The flarepaths winked on and off, as though beckoning the British aircraft to attack.

Nevertheless the eighteen Messerschmitt fighters, their tanks fuelled and their guns armed, were ready this time, and warned in advance. This time it was clear that they would have more than enough time to reach the attacking altitude. But first ten, then twenty, thirty minutes passed from the first alarm's being given by *Drahtfunk* and still the green cartridge was not fired.

Thus we waited for our fate, sitting in our cockpits [recalls one of the night-fighter pilots bitterly]. Impotently we watched the whole of the second raid on Dresden. The enemy Pathfinder aircraft dropped their 'Christmas-trees' right overhead, brilliantly illuminating the airfield, overflowing with aircraft transferred from the eastern front.

Wave after wave of the heavy bombers passed overhead, the bombs whistling down into the city. Still the flarepath lights were switched on and off, on and off, waiting for the transport planes from Breslau.

At any moment we expected the airfield to be wiped out. The strained nerves of some of the technicians and ground-crews could not take it: they abandoned their starting gear, and bolted for shelter. We could not think that the airfield would not be obliterated; but apparently the bomber crews had their orders and had to adhere to them; the airfield cannot have been included in their target plans. In the opposite situation, a German formation would scarcely have possessed the discipline not to attack an objective exposing itself in such a manner right by the target area, even when the objective had not been mentioned in the original orders.

Still the green cartridge was not fired. The pilots of the Me. 110s whose ground crews had deserted them climbed stiffly out of their cockpits; then at last the other crews followed. The raid on Dresden was over. They had watched the whole spectacle from an airfield five miles away, and had not been able to take the least defensive action. The Station Commander who, on his own initiative, had ordered the crews to their cockpits, now wearily admitted that he had not been able to contact Berlin-Döberitz to obtain permission to scramble his squadron. The telephone lines through Dresden, he explained, were dead; and for some reason the shortwave radio channel between Döberitz, the Headquarters of the 1st Fighter Division, and the airfield was unusable. The telephone lines, of course, passed through Dresden Old City; the enemy radio communications had been jammed during every major night attack since the introduction of No. 100 (Radio Counter Measures) Group in November 1943. In his diary the German pilot recorded:

> Result: a major attack on Dresden; the city was smashed to pieces. *We* had to stand by and look on. How could such a thing have been possible? People are hinting more and more at sabotage, or at least an irresponsible defeatism among the 'gentlemen' in the Command Staff. Have a feeling that things are marching to their end with giant strides. What then? Wretched *Vaterland*!

.   .   .   .   .

The ground defences were completely silent; many of the Lancaster crews felt almost ashamed at the lack of opposition. Many crews opted to orbit the burning city several times, unworried by any kind of defences. For ten minutes a Lancaster equipped with ciné-cameras circled the target filming the whole scene below for the R.A.F. Film Unit. The 400-foot film, now stored in the film archives of the Imperial War Museum, is one of the most grimly magnificent records to come out of the Second World War. But this film provides the final conclusive evidence that Dresden was undefended: no searchlight, no flak appears on the film throughout its length. 'When we came to the target area at the end of the attack it was obvious that the city was doomed', remembers the pilot of a No. 3 Group Lancaster which had been hit and delayed by flak over Chemnitz. Originally briefed to arrive at Dresden five minutes before the end of the attack, their Lancaster was now over ten minutes late. Clearly theirs was the last aircraft over the target.

> There was a sea of fire covering in my estimation some 40 square miles. The heat striking up from the furnace below could be felt in my cockpit. The sky was vivid in hues of scarlet and white, and the light inside the aircraft was that of an eerie autumn sunset. We were so aghast at the awesome blaze that although alone over the city we flew around in a stand-off position for many minutes before turning for home, quite subdued by our imagination of the horror that must be below. We could still see the glare of the holocaust thirty minutes after leaving.

Another No. 3 Group pilot on the way home was so impressed by the persistent red glow in the sky behind that he verified the aircraft's position with the navigator: they were over 150 miles from Dresden. Instead of growing dimmer, the fires beyond the horizon seemed to be getting brighter. In his diary afterwards, the pilot noted:

> It was the first time the R.A.F. bombed the city—I don't think it will have to be done again.

Even the Air Ministry was impressed by the scale of the fires they had started in Dresden. An Air Ministry Communiqué announced that the fires were visible 'nearly 200 miles from the target'. Nearly 650,000 incendiaries had been dropped on the city, both loose, from canisters, and in clusters. Hundreds of 4,000-pounders and 8,000-pounders had been in the bomb loads. At first it was announced that the night's operations, in which 1,400

Bomber Command aircraft had been involved, had cost only sixteen aircraft, a loss of rather more than one per cent.

But by 8.20 p.m. next day the casualties had fallen to six Lancasters; ten had landed, short of fuel, on the Continent. The most successful night raid in the history of Bomber Command, involving the deepest penetration into Germany, had been made at a casualty rate of less than half of one per cent. At 6.49 a.m. on the morning of Wednesday, 14th February 1945 the Air Ministry Communiqué began to rattle out of teleprinters throughout the English-speaking world:

FLASH: LAST NIGHT BOMBER COMMAND DISPATCHED 1400 AIR-CRAFT STOP THE MAIN OBJECTIVE WAS DRESDEN STOP MESSAGE ENDS 06.50 HRS., 14.2.1945.

For Dresden however, it was not the end. For Dresden, the onslaught was just beginning anew. A new force of American bombers was already lifting into the air. The principal target for the 1,350 Flying Fortresses and Liberators was to be Dresden once again. The third heavy attack within fourteen hours was under way.

CHAPTER IV

THE TRIPLE BLOW COMPLETE

I N Moscow, the news that Dresden was to be attacked by the
British and American Air Forces was received without comment
by the Soviet Army General Staff. On 12th February 1945, the
chief of the aviation section of the American military mission in
Moscow, Major-General Edmund W. Hill, had announced to the
General Staff that the Eighth Army Air Force would attack marshalling yards in Dresden on the morning of 13th February. But,
as we have seen, although the American crews were briefed for this
mission, the weather conditions had, apparently, forced the cancella-
tion of the operation.

> As is seen from this communication [a Soviet historian wrote to the
> author] the Allies made known to the Soviet Command only their
> intention to bomb the marshalling yards at Dresden. Mass attacks
> on the city area itself were not communicated to the Soviet Army
> General Staff.

Nevertheless, the Soviet Army must have been fully aware of the
implications of a large scale attack by British and American bombers
on marshalling yards, from what they themselves knew of the
Allied raids on a score of other German railway centres. On the
following day, 13th February 1945, Major-General Hill again
announced that, if weather permitted, the Eighth Air Force would
attack the marshalling yards in Dresden and Chemnitz on the
following day. On 14th February the weather was favourable in the
early hours of the morning, and the executive order was issued by
the American Air Force commanders for the attack on Dresden, the
third blow to the city within fourteen hours; an almost simultaneous
attack was to be launched on Chemnitz, 35 miles to the south-west.
The Chemnitz attack would pave the way for a renewed night
offensive by Sir Arthur Harris' bombers on the same night. Thus
Chemnitz was to suffer the fate originally planned for Dresden—
the American attack preceding a British double-blow. It will be
relevant therefore to consider additionally the execution and failure
of the attack on Chemnitz on the night of February 14th, in

148

order to judge how nearly Dresden too escaped the fate of total destruction.

Even before the returning Lancasters of Bomber Command had crossed the English coast, the flying personnel of over 1,350 Flying Fortresses and Liberators, and of all fifteen American fighter groups, were sitting down to the usual pre-operational breakfast of cold powdered eggs and coffee; briefing began at 4.40 on the morning of 14th February, long before dawn broke across the frosty East Anglian countryside. The 1st Air Division was to deliver this third blow to Dresden with a force of some 450 Flying Fortresses; once again, the heaviest bombers, with maximum bomb-carrying capacity, were allocated to Dresden: all others were despatched on secondary tasks, missions to Magdeburg, Wesel—and Chemnitz. Once again, the problem that worried the navigation leaders was how to avoid faulty navigation which might take the Fortresses beyond the Russian lines. For the Dresden operation, they decided to route the bombers out to an Initial Point on the River Elbe, the bombers entering enemy-held territory over Egmond, on the Dutch coast, and making a rendezvous with groups of P-51 Mustangs at a point south of the Zuider Zee. The fighter groups would accompany and escort the bomber formations, flying in their tight boxes of 36–40 heavily armed aircraft, to Quakenbrück, south-west of Bremen; from Quakenbrück, the bomber formations would head south-east for exactly 200 miles in a straight line across Höxter to Probstzella. The Magdeburg Liberator-formations would follow the same route, and divert from a point near Höxter on a heading which would take them equally well to Magdeburg or Berlin. The 450 1st Air Division Fortresses detailed for the Dresden mission accompanied by some 300 more of the 3rd Air Division attacking Chemnitz, would then head north-east to their respective targets. Chemnitz was 110 miles or more from the Russian lines, and the dangers of faulty navigation were not so severe. In the case of Dresden, the lead navigators in the Bombardment Group were instructed to set course for Torgau, fifty miles north of Dresden on the River Elbe. From Torgau, they needed only to head south to the first large city with a river snaking through it; this would be Dresden. They were to attack the railway-station in the Neustadt (New Town) area. The crews do not appear to have been briefed to look for a smoke pall above the city; in fact the Germans were so adept at faking dummy targets by day, that the lead bombardiers of the Bombardment Groups were warned to rely only on their crews' navigation, and not to take the aspect of the target below them into account. The briefing for the crews was unusual in only one respect: the flak defences at Dresden were reported to be 'moderate, to heavy, to unknown'. There was only one other briefing like it: that was for Royan in France, where the flak defences guarding a German stronghold where also reported to be 'unknown'. The bomber call-sign was announced: *Vinegrove*. Should the weather close down severely over the Continent the recall codeword for the Dresden operation was *Carnation*. The fighter escort flights were to be identi-fied by various call-signs—*Colgate*, *Martini*, *Sweepstakes*, *Ripsaw* and *Roselee* were among them.

It is interesting to note that although it was the intention of this triple blow on the Saxon capital to destroy the town and make it impossible for the Germans to fall back on the city as an adminis-trative headquarters, the bombardiers were warned that they were attacking 'railway installations'; General Carl F. Spaatz, the Commanding General of the Eighth Air Force, had hitherto stead-fastly resisted all proposals to attempt to terrorize the Germans into capitulation. On 1st January 1945, General Eaker had advised him against sending heavy bombers to attack transportation targets in small German towns, for there would be many civilian casualties and the German people might be convinced that the Americans were barbarians, just as National Socialist propaganda charged:

We should never allow the history of this war to convict us of throw-ing the strategic bomber at the man in the street.

Nevertheless, if those were the sentiments of early January 1945, the first week of February showed what was likely to be the outcome of any large-scale blind attack, especially on a small target in the centre of a residential area. The 3rd February attack on 'railway and administrative targets' in Berlin, which resulted in the death of some 25,000 of the civilian inhabitants of the city in one afternoon, must surely have been a warning light to the American Air Force of the result of such blind attacks; but General Arnold, Commanding General of the American Army Air Forces, was convalescing from an illness, and the 8th Air Force raid on Dresden followed before the implications of the tragic attack on Berlin had fully sunk in (the B-17 crews attacking the Reich capital had been led to believe that the Sixth Panzer Army was passing through the city to the Russian front). The initial E.T.A. for the Flying Fortress formations over Dresden was given as noon, but as the aircraft flew in self-defensive boxes, and as the B-17's flew in visual contact with each other, the same accuracy was not required of the individual navigators which was required for night bombers trying to stay in a pre-routed stream five miles wide, knowing that if they strayed out of the stream they lost the protection given them by *Window* and were more vulnerable to night fighters.

The Flying Fortress crews were in their aircraft by 6.30 a.m., and were relieved to hear that engine-starting—provisionally set for 6.40 a.m.—had been postponed for an hour. Apparently there was still some uncertainty about the weather over the Continent. The Lancasters were returning over the East Anglian coast and the American airmen must have seen them passing high overhead, as they waited beside their aircraft for the signal to take off. Finally at 8.00 a.m. the Very-lights were fired; the Fortresses rolled down the runway and set course for the radar 'splashers' over which they would meet other squadrons, other Bombardment Groups, and where they would finally join up with the whole 1st Air Division making its way to the Dutch coast. The formations were escorted by Spitfires as far as the coast-out point. At the Zuider Zee, Mustang fighter groups were duly waiting for the bombers, and the whole force set out to cross Germany. On the way into Dresden some of the Bombardment Groups became scattered on condensation trails; there were cloud layers not only above them, but also below them: ten-tenths cloud was still covering the whole of the Continent: it was unlikely that conditions would permit visual bombing of the target. At Kassel, the bomber formations were greeted with a large flak barrage, but few were hit.

The 20th Fighter Group was escorting the first two Bombardment Groups of the 1st Air Division to Dresden; the remaining escort duties were undertaken by the 364th, 356th and 479th Fighter Groups. It will suffice for the purposes of this narrative to describe the 20th Fighter Group's role in the operation. For this mission, Number 260 in the Group's history, the Group was subdivided into two groups, denoted 'A' and 'B'. Both 'A' and 'B' Group fighters—seventy-two P-51s in all—were due to rendezvous with the Bombardment Groups at the Zuider Zee rendezvous soon after 10.45 a.m. The 'B' Group fighters were not permitted to move from their visual contact with the bomber boxes, but were to ward off any attempts by Luftwaffe day fighters to break up the formations. 'A' Group pilots were briefed that as soon as the bombers' attack on Dresden was over, they were to dive to roof-top level and strafe what were euphemistically referred to as 'targets of opportunity'. Columns of soldiers being marched into or out of the wrecked city were to be machine-gunned, lorries attacked by cannon-fire, and locomotives and other transportation targets destroyed by rockets. Both groups of P-51s would withdraw from the bomber formations at 2.25 p.m., at a point near Frankfurt, where escort duty would be taken over by P-47 Thunderbolts.

.   .   .   .   .

The bomber formations picked up the Initial Point of the bombing run at Torgau successfully and followed the river down to Dresden. The first bombs began to fall on the city, still burning furiously from the previous night's attack, at 12.12 p.m. For eleven minutes the salvoes of bombs whistled down through almost complete cloud cover on to the northern section of the city, Dresden New Town.

> The clouds came up high, not far below us [reports one of the bombardiers], but they broke up from ten-tenths, and over Dresden there was about nine-tenths cloud. There was no flak for us at the target. Bombs away at 12.22. . . .

Simultaneously with the end of the American attack at 12.23 p.m., the thirty-seven P-51s of the 20th Fighter Group's 'A' Group raced low across the city together with the 'A' Groups of the other three fighter groups operating over Dresden. Most of the pilots appear from eyewitness accounts to have decided the safest attacking runs could be made along the Elbe river banks. Other's attacked transport on the roads leading out of the city, crowded with columns of people. One 'A' Group P-51 of the 55th Fighter Squadron flew so low that it crashed into a wagon and exploded. The other fighter pilots were, however, disappointed by the lack of opportunities for combat, especially the crews of the 'B' Group aircraft, although, again, none of them regretted the absence from the target area of the dreaded German jet-fighter, the Me. 262. Only three Me. 262s were reported during the Dresden operation making passes at the bomber formations in the Strassburg area, without firing; one of the jets was claimed damaged.

Curiously enough, although the 'A' Group fighters were briefed to attack targets of opportunity, once again the overcrowded fighter airfield at Dresden-Klotzsche was not attacked. The Luftwaffe flying personnel were all evacuated from the airfield (V./NJG. 5 being a night fighter squadron, there was no part the airmen could play in daylight operations) and had to witness the American attack on Dresden from the fields to the north of the city; all were once again certain that the rocket-firing fighters would be attacking the airfield, where enormous damage could have been done to the fighters and transport planes parked there.

For at least one of the Bombardment Groups, however, the operation on Dresden went astray. The 398th Bombardment Group lost its way flying through the cloud layers at its predetermined altitude, and when the B-17s emerged above the cloud layers the lead navigator was not too happy about the formation's position. They should have picked up Torgau and headed south-east to the first big city with a river (the Flying Fortress' lead navigators were relying on *APS.15* radar for their navigation). Curiously enough, the High Squadron of the formation was attacked by German fighters; it struck some of the airmen as peculiar that German fighters should so calmly have attacked such a massively escorted bomber formation. But in fact the American fighter escort had long evaporated. The formation had been subjected to S-turns to lose time for an on-time arrival over the target. The Dead Reckoning navigation of the navigation leader was apparently not as good as it should have been. The formation navigation leader picked up and 'identified' Torgau, and turned on a bearing which would take the bombers to Dresden.

Some time passed before the navigator of one of the Fortresses, 'Stinker Jr.', flying Deputy Group Leader, radioed the Group Commander and suggested that in fact they had picked up Freiberg instead of Torgau; he was overruled and reminded about the rules for radio silence over Germany. From time to time the bombardiers reported that they could see a river underneath. The 'mickey-man' operating the *APS.15* radar equipment began to read off the sighting angles on his screen between the aircraft and the city ahead (one bombardier would act as leader; the other bombardiers would all press their releases when they saw the bombs of the first plane fall out of the racks). Six sighting angles were read off and set on the lead bombardier's sighting angle index on the Norden bombsight. There was indeed a river snaking through the city ahead. The bombardier could see no detail of the city to warrant his taking over on a visual run and a blind attack was made by radar. As they were coming away again, the navigator in 'Stinker Jr.' again broke radio silence and insisted that they had in fact not bombed Dresden; the Group's lead navigator checked with the rest of the navigators and their views also conflicted with his. In fact the forty bombers of the 398th Bombardment Group had delivered quite a heavy attack on Prague. This was a bitter blow to the pilot of 'Stinker Jr.'. He was a Czech citizen, born and bred in the city, who had fled to America

when the National Socialists occupied his country. But most of the
other B-17s had found Dresden, and 316 of them had made
'effective sorties against the marshalling yards'. This is the figure
given in the Eighth Air Force Target Summary; the official American
history, *The Army Air Forces in World War II*, quotes a figure of 311
B-17s. Another 771 (American, 'long') tons of bombs had been
dropped on Dresden.

Many of the Flying Fortresses ran into serious fuel problems on
the flight back to England. Many landed on airfields in Belgium
and France; some of the fighter pilots landing in England would
suffer the experience of running out of fuel before they could taxi
their P-51s to the parking aprons.

At the end of it all, a dazed German High Command took stock
in its secret Situation Report: 'For the first time a daylight attack
was delivered by all available American heavies in the West on
Dresden; firestorms were caused by this attack and those of the
previous night. The Central Station has been knocked out. There
are now 500,000 homeless in a city of 650,000 inhabitants—a
figure swollen enormously by refugees. Only 146 of our dayfighters
[took off] in Dresden's defence; they were savagely beaten down
by 700 American fighters. We shot down two bombers, but 20 of
our own fighters are missing'. But already the favourable weather
which had made the R.A.F. Bomber Command night attacks
possible had sadly deteriorated.

    .   .   .   .   .

The only partial success of the Chemnitz attack was to set the
pattern for the rest of the offensive on the eastern population centres.
The judgment that such a series of blows might have won the
sudden capitulation of the German people is perhaps best substantiated by the observation of ex-*Reichsminister* Albert Speer, the
former German Armament Minister: during his July 1945 interrogation he remarked that:

> In every case in which the R.A.F. *suddenly* increased the weight of its
> attacks, as for example . . . in the attacks on Dresden, the effect not only
> upon the population of the town attacked but also upon the whole
> of the rest of the Reich was terrifying, even if only temporarily so.

The attack on Dresden had indeed attained all that could possibly
have been desired of it: over sixteen hundred acres of the city had
been devastated in one night, compared with the rather under six

hundred acres destroyed in London during the whole war. Bomber crews returning with the Flying Fortresses from their 8½-hour flight reported that 'huge fires were still burning in the city after last night's attack by R.A.F. Bomber Command, with a layer of smoke over the whole city'. The tired Bomber Command crews, who had stumbled into their beds soon after nine in the morning, were roused before 3.00 p.m. in the afternoon and told to expect a big operation that night. As they walked across to the briefing huts they could see the lines of fuel tankers filling up the Lancasters again, and could tell from the minimal bomb-loads being winched up into the bomb racks that it was to be a long distance raid again.

This time less attempt was made to veil the real nature of the target city. Curiously, although Chemnitz as a city possessed many obviously military and legitimate targets—the tank works, the large textile and uniform-making factories, and one of the largest loco-motive repair depots in the Reich, in at least two widely separated squadrons of two Bomber Groups an almost identical wording of the briefing was used by the Intelligence officers. Thus No. 1 Group crews were informed:

> Tonight your target is to be Chemnitz. We are going there to attack the refugees who are gathering there, especially after last night's attack on Dresden.

No. 3 Group crews were briefed:

> Chemnitz is a town some thirty miles west of Dresden, and a much smaller target. Your reasons for going there tonight are to finish off any refugees who may have escaped from Dresden. You'll be carrying the same bombloads, and if tonight's attack is as successful as the last, you will not be paying many more visits to the Russian front.

The wording is from the diary kept by one of the bomb aimers who was present at one of the No. 3 Group briefings.

Once again Sir Arthur Harris had divided the attacking force into two waves; but this time, as the German fighter controllers in the 'battle opera house' at Döberitz would probably be aware of the significance of this concentrated offensive on the eastern cities, Harris had prepared a much more complicated strategy of feints and spoof attacks to divert the night fighters. A force of Lancasters was to attack the Deutsche Petroleum AG refinery at Rositz, not far from Leipzig; this attack was to be carried out by 244 of No. 5 Group's Lancasters. In the first wave of the Chemnitz attack 329 heavy bombers, including 120 Halifaxes and Lancasters from No. 6 Group, were to set the city on fire; three hours later, 388 bombers, including, unlike the Dresden attack, the No. 4 Group Halifaxes, and 150 Lancasters from No. 3 Group, were to attack the burning city. Diversionary sweeps were to be conducted by a minelaying force in the Baltic, while the Light Night Striking Force provided by Air Vice-Marshal Bennett attacked Berlin. Nevertheless for all the complex strategy behind the attack, and for all the scale of the offensive mounted, the attack on Chemnitz was a failure.

The weather forecast from the Bomber Command meteorological section had predicted that Chemnitz would not be obscured by cloud, but an amendment had been later issued indicating a risk of thin broken alto-cumulus or alto-stratus cloud, or both, and thin stratus cloud at low altitudes; unlike the very accurate weather forecast that had been issued for the attack on Dresden the night before, this forecast was grossly mistaken.

One Australian Lancaster pilot reported that when he was 120 miles from Chemnitz the sky began to cloud over, and over Chemnitz itself there was ten-tenths cloud piling up to 15,000 feet which prevented visual identification of the aiming point. The city was totally covered by cloud when the first force arrived, and the Pathfinders were forced to rely entirely on sky marking. The flares disappeared into the clouds almost as soon as they had been dropped. The Master Bomber during the second blow, a Canadian, was clearly worried as to where to direct the bombers; he repeatedly called over the radio telephone for more flares; few were forthcoming. He seemed indecisive, unlike his counterpart the night before, and had difficulty in locating the target at all. In addition the bomber formations were seriously pestered by the German night fighters, which seemed not to have been misled by the elaborate feints: fighter flares were laid all the way from the frontier to the target and back. But the difficulties under which the young pilots of the German *Nachtjagd* were labouring, their equipment jammed by No. 100 (Radio Counter Measures) Group, are described by this illuminating extract from a night-fighter pilot's diary:

14th February, 1945: Just as expected: scrambled this evening. This time the B-crews were scrambled too, and in good time. Target: Chemnitz, a major air-raid. Our operations were under an unlucky star right from the start: *EiV* [*Eigenverständigungs-Anlage*, the recognition system in the aircraft] broke down, no radio beacon picked up, *FuG.16* VHF-receiver jammed, [picking up] flak-predictors, *Window* echoes, and enemy fighter-approach radar [*Fishpond*]. Radio communication with Prague suddenly evaporated, so had to fly south-west. Could not find a landing ground, fired *ES* [*Erkennungssignale*, emergency recognition cartridges] last hope: maintenance and repair airfield, at [Windisch-] Laibach, very small. Nevertheless, a clean landing. Another fifteen minutes and we would have had to jump.

The efforts of the Luftwaffe to ward off Sir Arthur Harris' lunges into the heart of Germany can be no better mirrored than in the notes of this young fighter-pilot, desperately struggling to engage a technically far superior air force.

The results of the fire-storm that had started in Dresden were apparent to the aircrew of the No. 5 Group force attacking Rositz: as they passed by fifty miles from Dresden, the fires were still burning (Dresden burned, as one British prisoner of war in the city noted day by day in his diary, for seven days and eight nights). Some 730,000 incendiaries were dropped on Chemnitz; but the raid was a failure, in comparison with that on Dresden. All historical evaluations of this attack are in agreement that the city was not damaged severely, either by the daylight attack of the American Flying Fortresses or by the British double-blow: the Canadian Bomber Group history reports:

> There was no marked concentration of bombing and the numerous fires which left a glow on the clouds were scattered over a large area.

The Chemnitz railway system was scarcely hit at all; this is not to admit that in fact the railway system through Dresden received a chronic drubbing; in fact, as we shall see, the German General charged with the emergency reconstruction of railways in blitzed cities was able to open up a double track through the length of the city within three days. In Chemnitz, however, the damage to the railway system was even less. A number of incidents were reported across the city, but in no one part of the city was there anything approaching a fire-storm.

Once again this demonstrates clearly how the random methods of blind bombing through overcast or on sky markers failed to achieve the scale of devastation attained by No. 5 Group's sector attack method. Perhaps if Sir Arthur Harris had required No. 5 Group to start the Chemnitz attack as well—they had after all proved their worth in the Dresden double-blow—a fire-storm might have been started of sufficient violence to provide crews of the second attack with a bright enough glow to aim around. There is, however, no explanation on record of why he delegated the task to the No. 8 Group Pathfinders, unless one may be permitted to suspect that it was the result partially of a desire to please the Pathfinder Commander—who was naturally happy when the honour of leading mass attacks was accorded to his force—and

partially to Harris' conviction at this stage of the war, when the
Rumanian and other Eastern oilfields had been finally overrun
and the transportation attacks were introducing a degree of throm-
bosis into the German railway networks, that the attack on the oil
plant at Rositz was worthy of the precision attention of No. 5
Group while the attack on Chemnitz was not. This latter was a
motive which certainly inspired the American bomber commander
to return, after Chemnitz, to an immediate resumption of the oil
offensive, as we shall see.

.   .   .   .   .

The former German Armaments Minister, discussing the 1943
attacks on Hamburg, delivered at a stage when German morale
had possibly never been higher, admitted in his July 1945 interrogation that:

> I . . . reported to the Führer that a continuation of these attacks
> might bring about a rapid end to the war.

In the Battle of Hamburg, lasting for over a week, some 48,000 of
the port's civilian inhabitants had been killed, mostly on the fire-
storm night of 27th July 1943. But the British double-blow on
Dresden, and to a lesser extent the American daylight attacks, had
cost 135,000 of the city's inhabitants their lives: for the first time
in the history of the war, an air raid had wrecked a target so disas-
trously that there were not enough able-bodied survivors left to
bury the dead. The attempt to repeat the catastrophe at Chemnitz,
however, had been defeated, not entirely by the adverse weather;
the opportunity of crippling German civilian morale by two
'Dresdens' within 48 hours had been lost—or squandered. Had the
two attacks succeeded in their purpose, had they indeed forced the
precipitate capitulation of the German people, then probably there
would have been no outcry; if the immediate surrender of the enemy
had been the result, as in the later cases of Hiroshima and Nagasaki,
where the first two atomic devices used operationally produced
death-rolls each rather smaller than that in Dresden, then there
would have been few recriminations.

PART FOUR

THE AFTERMATH

CHAPTER I

ASH WEDNESDAY

As the dawn of Ash Wednesday, February 14th, broke over Central Germany the wind was still blowing strongly from the north-west. In Dresden the arrival of the dawn was hardly noticed: the city was still obscured by the three-mile-high column of yellow-brown smoke and fumes which characterised the aftermath of a fire-storm. Perhaps this different colour of the fire-storm smoke pall was a measure of the extraordinary flotsam of charred and shrivelled fragments of buildings, trees and debris from the luckless city, which had been caught in the grasp of the artificial tornado and was still being sucked up into the sky.

As the masses of smoke drifted down the River Elbe towards Czechoslovakia, the people in the towns and cities over which it passed must have looked up to the sky and have guessed that here were the results of no ordinary raid, that the pillar of smoke drifting across the countryside was in fact the last mortal remains of a city which twelve hours earlier had sheltered a million people and their property. As the smoke pall was driven ever further from the still burning city, the air cooled; as the air cooled, the damp clouds heavy with dust and smoke began to break; the rains fell along the whole length of the Elbe Valley. Not only rain descended from the sky: the countryside to the leeward of Dresden was drenched with a steady shower of wet and sooty ash: British prisoners of war working in the large parcels sorting dump at Stalag IVB over twenty-five miles south-east of Dresden noticed that the smoke pall lasted three days and that particles of smouldering clothing and charred paper were still floating down over the camp for many days after that. The owner of a house in Mockethal, some fifteen miles from Dresden, found his garden littered with prescriptions and pill boxes from a chemist's shop: the labels showed them to have come from the heart of the Dresden Inner City. Papers and documents from the gutted Land-register Office in the Inner City showered down in the village of Lohmen, near Pirna, some eighteen miles away; schoolchildren had to spend several days scouring the countryside for them.

These were the manifestations of the last and most terrible fire-storm in the history of the R.A.F.'s area offensive against German cities. The fire-storm, which appears to have arisen about forty-five minutes after zero hour of the first attack and which subsided only gradually, had itself caused the deaths of thousands of frail and old people who otherwise would have been able to fight their way out of the encircling ring of fires.

. . . . .

The Battle of Hamburg in July 1943 had brought Germany's first-ever fire-storm: eight square miles of the city had burnt as one single bonfire. So horrific was the phenomenon that the Police President had ordered a scientific investigation of the causes of the fire-storm, so that other cities might be warned:

> An estimate of the force of this fire-storm could be obtained only by analysing it soberly as a meteorological phenomenon: as a result of the sudden linking of a number of fires, the air above was heated to such an extent that a violent updraught occurred which, in turn, caused the surrounding fresh air to be sucked in from all sides to the centre of the fire area. This tremendous suction caused movements of air of far greater force than normal winds.
> In meteorology the differences of temperature involved are of the order of 20° to 30°C. In this fire-storm they were of the order of 600°, 800° or even 1,000°C. This explained the colossal force of the fire-storm winds.

The Police President's gloomy forecast was that no kind of A.R.P. precautions could ever contain a fire-storm once it had emerged: the fire-storm was clearly a man-made monster which no man would ever tame.

In Dresden, the fire-storm appears, by examination of the area more than seventy-five per cent destroyed to have engulfed some eight square miles; the city authorities now put the area as high as eleven square miles.

Nevertheless the fire-storm was undoubtedly the most devastating that had ever been experienced in Germany. All the signs observed in Hamburg were repeated in Dresden multiplied in scale many times. Giant trees were uprooted or snapped in half. Crowds of people fleeing for safety had suddenly been seized by the tornado and hurled along whole streets into the seat of the fires; roof gables and furniture that had been stacked on the streets after the first raid were plucked up by the violent winds and tossed into the centre of the burning Inner City.

The fire-storm reached the peak of its strength in the three-hour interval between the raids, just the period during which those sheltering in the cellars and vaulted corridors of the Inner City should have been fleeing to the surrounding suburbs.

A railwayman sheltering near the Post-platz observed how a woman with a perambulator was hurled down the street into the flames. Other people, running for their lives along the railway embankments which were the only escape routes not blocked by rubble, reported how railway trucks on exposed portions of the lines were blown over by the gale. Even the open spaces of the large squares and great parks were no protection against this unnatural hurricane.

.   .   .   .   .

Once the fire-storm had emerged, there was nothing that the fire-fighting forces could do to contain or control it. In all the great German fire-storm raids the swift and unhindered growth of the fires had been ensured by an early disruption of telephone communications between A.R.P. Control Rooms and external reinforcements. In Germany, as in England, the fire brigades had been re-organised during the war on national, para-military lines, one feature of which was the constant mobile reserve of fire-fighting regiments held outside danger zones.

Most of the major cities had at this stage of the war been equipped with alternative telephone communications and with radio links between important control posts. But invariably these were unreliable when it came to the test, and the A.R.P. authorities had to fall back on the standard Post Office telephone network. Much therefore depended on how long this system functioned before it finally succumbed. In the Battle of Hamburg the telephone communications had very soon broken down on the night of the first raid and, when the fire-storm came three nights later, the service had not been completely repaired; added to this, as we have seen (*The Precedents*), the burning down of the Police Praesidium, with the A.R.P. Control Room, had for a while seriously hampered adequate fire-fighting measures. In Kassel, the telephone exchange had been hit twenty minutes after the start of the attack and the motor-cycle messenger service had proved inadequate for this emergency: for this reason, fire brigades arriving in Kassel from nearby cities waited for several hours without any definite orders for action.

Now, in Dresden, the almost immediate destruction of telephone communications was to seal the fate of the city. Dresden, with a native fire-brigade of less than one thousand men and with few fire appliances under direct Dresden control, was dependent on immediate assistance arriving from outside the city. But, soon after the first bombs had fallen in Dresden, the electricity supply of the telephone exchange failed. To add to this, the emergency power supply in the building had been irreparably crushed by a collapsing wall.

Both the main power station and all the administrative buildings lay well within the sector marked out for attack. From this Warning Post, the reports had to be transmitted to the Air Zone Command (*Luftgaukommando*) IV Headquarters in General Wever-strasse, and the Command had then to report direct to the Führer-HQ in Berlin. Now that was impossible. It would neither be possible to inform Berlin of the air raids, nor to forward reports from the Saxon Observation posts to the Fighter Command Divisional Headquarters at Döberitz near Berlin. Only from the cities near Dresden were reinforcements forthcoming immediately after the first raids; the glow beyond the horizon told its own story. By 1.00 a.m. local fire brigades were arriving in Dresden from all over Saxony, and penetrating the city's outskirts. The electric sirens could not sound the warning for the second raid.

'The fire-fighting forces and passive defences of the city,' the Allied air commanders could report drily, 'were overwhelmed by the double blow.'

Exact statistics are not available for all fire-fighting forces in action in the city. One example should give a clear indication of the fate of most of them: the fire-brigade dispatched to Dresden by Bad Schandau, ten miles from Dresden, arrived soon after 1.00 a.m. From the men of this brigade there was not one survivor. All were overwhelmed by the second raid.

At 1.05 a.m. the city's A.R.P. engineer, Georg Feydt, reported to the A.R.P. control room, a concrete bunker several storeys below the Albertinum building, across the road from the now burning Police Praesidium. The bunker was packed with Party and A.R.P. officers, small though it was—barely six feet by nine; Gauleiter Mutschmann was there as well. They were still trying to build up a picture of the destruction, trying to discover the main seat of the fire-storm. But, just as the destruction of telegraph wires and the breakdown of the exchanges prevented appeals for help from being dispatched at once, so it also threw into confusion their communications with fire-watchers and local A.R.P. control posts.

Within a few minutes of the start of the second raid, the Albertinum was surrounded by blazing buildings, and the massive sandstone edifice was in danger of being gutted itself. The Gauleiter and his whole staff then made a dash for safety through the blazing streets and collapsing Inner City into the open areas outside; that same night, according to an official account, all reported for duty at the emergency control room built in Lockwitzgrund; Lockwitz was a village some five miles south-east of Dresden where the N.S.D.A.P. had prepared an auxiliary Gau headquarters for just such an emergency as this.

.   .   .   .   .

As was the case everywhere else in Germany, the city's A.R.P. organisation was incorporated in the National Socialist Party structure, with the City's Police President in the *ex officio* role of A.R.P. Leader. Everybody had a role to play, down not only to the Hitler Youth, but also to the *Deutsches Jungvolk*, an organisation comparable with the Wolf Cubs.

In February 1945 I was fifteen years old, and during the period of total war my duty was as an air raid messenger [records one such *Deutsches Jungvolk* boy].

13th February was the day of our great Shrove Tuesday Carnival and I spent the evening at the Circus Sarassani, which has a permanent building in Dresden New Town. During the last number of the programme, a hilarious performance of donkey-riding by the clowns, the Full Alarm was sounded over the loudspeakers. The audience, amid the jokes of the clowns, was instructed to make its way to the vaulted basement of the Circus building. Because of my Messenger's Pass I was permitted to leave the building.

The city was lit as bright as day already by the first white flares of the Illuminator Lancasters, and like most of the native Dresdeners the young boy did not even guess what these lights meant.

At the time I was deeply impressed by the flares. Dresden New Town was not hit at all during the first raid, so I ran home immediately. There was nothing to be done there, so according to orders, I reported for duty as a Messenger at the Party Headquarters in the Local Group *Hansa* of the N.S.D.A.P. in Grossenhainer-strasse. The Local Group Leader, in his S.A. ('brownshirt') uniform, issued damage-reports to me and other youngsters to take to the Civil Defence Control Room in the centre of the Inner City. We were given blue steel helmets, gasmasks and bicycles, and set off.

The Castle, the Residence Church, and the Opera were already burning fiercely and the bridges across the Elbe were strewn with

spent or still burning incendiaries. The streets were flooded with
water from burst mains. The gallant but hardly properly equipped
A.R.P. messengers had only penetrated as far as Post-platz square
when the second raid began. They could only take refuge in a
hospital basement near the Post-platz. The messages were still in
their hands, but they would never be delivered.

Thus the A.R.P. organisation in the centre of the city was kept in
total ignorance of the locations and development of the fires, as one
after another their telegraphic, telephonic, radio and finally their
human lines of communication were severed.

.   .   .   .   .

During the post-war years the legend has grown around this
unlucky city, encouraged by the present occupation authorities,
not only that Dresden was undefended by guns or fighter aircraft,
but that no kind of A.R.P. precautions had been taken.

To a certain extent this was true: it was not considered necessary
to build huge concrete and steel public air-raid bunkers of the kind
which had saved the lives of hundreds of thousands of people in
other fire-storm cities. In Hamburg, even the hospitals had been
provided with special bunkers—by 1st June 1943 there had been
four operating-theatres and three maternity-homes built into bunkers.
In Dresden neither of the biggest hospitals, Friedrichstadt and
Johannstadt, had such amenities. Little attempt had been made to
construct alternative sources of water or electric power for the pumping stations in the event of a major collapse of the water mains or
the breakdown of the electricity stations. But, on the other hand, it
was not expected that Dresden would be bombed. When it was
announced late in 1944 that as part of the 'expanded *Führer-programm*'
several thousand Reichsmarks were to be expended on A.R.P.
measures, the city's population had only laughed carelessly. To be
sure, from the beginning of the war onwards the A.R.P. Police
(*Luftschutzpolizei*) had worked in two shifts on the construction of a
subterranean escape tunnel network, had erected large static-water
tanks in the Altmarkt square, Seidnitzer-platz, and Sidonien-
strasse, and had even begun building underground water-tanks.
'Train-loads of concrete were used on this scheme, not just lorry
loads,' emphasises the city's A.R.P. Engineer of the time; the
measures were directed by senior architects of the City's School
of Architecture.

Without doubt the citizens of Dresden were better protected against
air raids than those of many comparable British towns, who thought

themselves safe with their Morrison or Anderson shelters, contrivances which, in a fire-storm, would have been perfect death-traps.

Later on, as Dresden had filled with refugees from East and West, and as the rumble of guns on the Eastern front could sometimes be heard, the city's authorities had nervously adopted further limited measures of protection for its population. Schoolchildren had been put to work digging out zig-zag lines of splinter-proof trenches in Bismark and Wiener Platz (on either side of the Central Station), Barbarossa-platz and in most of the parks and green strips in the city; a complex system of *Mauerdurchbrüche* had been built, specially constructed weak spots in the partition walls separating the cellars of adjacent houses. In emergency, if the houses caught fire during localised air-raids, the inhabitants could then break through to the next-door cellar, and escape through that; if, however, that house was also on fire, the people could smash down one cellar wall after another, until finally they reached a house from which they could escape.

These measures had been adequate for the small attacks which other cities, and even Dresden, had suffered up to February 1945. Nobody, however, could have foreseen the sea of fire and flame which was to engulf the Saxon capital. The cellars and basements of each Victorian house were sheltering some eighty or ninety people when the attack began, with more and more people clambering down the steps from the street. When the first attack died down, the rush to escape began. Again and again the same circumstances prevailed: refugees from the eastern marchlands who had never before heard a siren's wail or the explosion of bombs, now found themselves trapped at the heart of the biggest conflagration in history; they could not escape on to the streets—they were swept by forty- and fifty-foot-long jets of flame. They could only surge from one cellar to the next, smashing through the thin partition breaches, until finally they reached the open air—or the end of the street.

This contingency had in fact been foreseen by the Hamburg Police President, Major-General Kehrl, when he advocated the construction of such an underground system of escape routes: after referring to the 'terrifying' number of people killed in basements in the fire-storm areas, he had warned that where rows of houses were interrupted by cross-streets, the houses on opposite sides of the street should be connected by tunnels. His warnings, however, had not been heeded in Dresden and a system which might have averted a major tragedy when completed, in fact itself led to the deaths of large numbers of people not hitherto endangered by carbon monoxide or smoke fumes, as we shall now see.

.   .   .   .   .

Most people hoped that the fires would die down, and that they would then be able to emerge, unscathed and with their property intact. Thus the people were still waiting in their cellars and underground tunnels at 1.30 a.m. when, without warning, the second raid began. The commander of a *Reichsarbeitsdienst* transport company which had hastened in convoy to the rescue from a village outside the city described it:

> The detonations shook the cellar walls. The sound of the explosions mingled with a new, strange sound, which seemed to come closer and closer, the sound of a thundering waterfall; it was the sound of the mighty tornado howling into the Inner City.

> When the raid had ebbed [reported another R.A.D. officer similarly trapped with his men], I confirmed for myself that we were surrounded on all sides by fire: enormous flames were sweeping across the streets. I learned from the others that further down the street there was an open square, with the Circus Sarassani building. I ordered my men to break through the breaches from house to house, and so we finally stormed out into the open air. In the middle of the square was the circus building; I believe there had been a special Carnival night performance. The building was burning fiercely, and was collapsing even as we watched. In a nearby street I saw a terrified group of dappled circus horses with brightly coloured trappings standing in a circle close to each other.

These magnificent Arab horses did not themselves have long to live; during the second R.A.F. attack, forty-eight of the horses from the Circus Sarassani were killed. In the days following the raids, their carcasses were to be dragged down to the Elbe Embankment's northern shores, Königsufer, between Albert-bridge and Augustus-bridge, where on 16th February a grim scene was witnessed with the arrival of a flock of vultures which had escaped from the City's Zoo.

In many cases during the night raids, people, finding that dense suffocating fumes from above were rolling down into the unventilated basements, broke down the wall breaches. Thus the smoke had access to the next-door cellars as well. This was a dilemma which would have puzzled even the citizens of Hamburg or Cologne, hardened as they were by long experience of Allied air attacks. To the million inhabitants and more of Dresden on the night of 13th

February, lulled into a false sense of security, and totally unversed in Civil Defence practice—a description which might now once more be applied to every major British city—the dilemma became a nightmare, a nightmare to which all too many of the people were prepared finally to resign themselves.

A cavalry captain, on his way to his unit on the Eastern front, recounts in detail the fate that befell the people who were with him in this second attack; between sixty and eighty of them, mostly elderly people and children, were to lose their lives as a result of infiltrating fumes. His temporary billet was in Kaulbach-strasse, a street in the heart of the area which became a fire-storm centre in the second raid:

> Somebody, foolishly, broke down the wall-breach from the next-door cellar; that house was burning fiercely, and the sound of crackling flames and a dense smoke poured in. Something had to be done. I informed the people in my cellar that we would all suffocate in the cellar if we did not get out into the open; I told all the people to soak their coats in the regulation fire-buckets, placed in the cellar. Only a few agreed, as the women were very unwilling to ruin their valuable fur coats like this; they were the first things they had taken with them. I ordered them all to gather behind me on the staircase, and when I shouted 'Now!' they were to run out onto the street. My appeals to them did not have any effect, so I finally shouted the order, and myself ran up into the street. Only a few followed me.

A man with the courage of this cavalry captain, decorated, incidentally, with one of Germany's higher military awards, might risk his life in this way and escape to tell the tale. The majority of the people in the city were not young or brave; many understandably preferred dying peacefully in their homes to running for their lives through the fires. These cellar breaches were themselves the doom of the cellar inhabitants.

.   .   .   .   .

Underneath the Post-platz square there was one extensive tunnel system of the type described. But this too proved of little avail when it came to the test; while these tunnels did indeed connect up the main administrative buildings round the square, and while other streets nearby were also provided with these advanced tunnel networks, the scale of the fire-storm was such that they proved virtually useless. The ventilation in the Ostra-allee tunnel broke down, causing many casualties. As the whole of the Inner City was on fire, all exits from the tunnel network were blocked.

The Post Office Savings Bank had been hit by an air mine, and from the basements of nearby private houses a stream of people poured out of the underground connecting tunnels [described a switchboard operator from the Central Telegraph Office]. I remember one old woman who had lost her leg. Some of the other girls suggested making for the streets and running home. A staircase led from the Telephone Exchange basement to a glass-roofed courtyard; the Exchange had been built round this quadrangle. Their idea was to escape through the courtyard's main gate onto Postplatz. I did not like the idea; all at once, just as the girls—twelve or thirteen of them—had run across the courtyard and were struggling to open the main gate, the red-glowing glass roof crashed down, burying them all underneath it. The whole Exchange was by now on fire.

Thus trapped in the heart of the Inner City, they could only wait for the fire-storm to ebb and hope that their supplies of air in the basement would hold out until then.

Had the half-hearted A.R.P. measures in Dresden been completed, had there been adequate provision of properly ventilated bunkers, as in other German cities then and now, then the catastrophe which befell Dresden during the fourteen hours of the triple blow could have been averted. In view of the National Socialist leaders' belief that Dresden would never be bombed, these shortcomings may appear excusable; nevertheless over a hundred thousand of the city's civilian population were now to pay for their leaders' lack of fore-sight with their lives.

CHAPTER II

THE VICTIMS

THE American bombers of the third blow had still not arrived
when the first columns of rescue and salvage workers had
begun pouring into Dresden from all over Central Germany;
local A.R.P. leaders had at last found means of broadcasting an
appeal, and motorised convoys with emergency food supplies,
medical aid, and several battalions of TN-Engineers (the *Technische
Nothilfe*) were heading for the capital of Saxony. From as far afield
as Berlin and Linz in Upper Austria squads of able-bodied men were
being hastily impressed to take part in fire-fighting and rescue work
in Dresden. In addition, A.R.P. police and Fire-Protection police
(*Luftschutz* and *Feuerschutzpolizei*) were sent into action.

Meanwhile the *Hilfszug* 'Herman Göring', a motorised convoy
of mobile kitchens and first-aid lorries, had arrived on Nord-platz
in Dresden New Town. A second convoy, *Hilfszug* 'Goebbels',
was making its way to Dresden-Seidnitz. Although there were in
each convoy only about twenty lorries, the supplies were desperately
needed for the city. By 16th February, *Hilfszüge* were arriving in
Dresden from every region of the *Land* of Saxony to provide hot and
cold meals for the homeless families and rescue workers. 'Nobody
will have to worry about food,' the N.S.D.A.P.'s Dresden newspaper
Der Freiheitskampf declared proudly, if optimistically, on 17th
February.

The Party organisation was able to ensure, together with the
German Red Cross, that the tens of thousands of mothers in the
population knew where to obtain milk and baby-food; at the main
stations in Dresden National Socialist relief centres run by the
Party's *Bund Deutscher Mädchen* and *Frauenschaften*—the German
equivalents of Girl Guides and W.V.S.—were speedily set up.

'It was,' said one bombed-out woman with a ten-day-old baby, 'a
real act of kindness on the part of the Party that we could get
baby-food and warm drinks for the children, and bread for the
grown-ups'.

Doubtless these small acts of kindness by the Party were designed to bolster sagging morale in other cities wrecked by Bomber Command; Dresden, however, was damaged more than warm drinks and baby-food could effectively repair.

Arriving too was General Erich Hampe, director of emergency repair operations to railway systems in blitzed cities. He had travelled through the night from Berlin with an aide:

> I could not immediately reach the Central Station [he reported], because the way into the city was completely blocked. The first living thing I saw on entering the city was a great llama. He had apparently escaped from the zoo. Everything in the Inner City was destroyed, but my concern was only for the Central Station and the railway system. None of the leading railway officials was at hand. I had to send for a leading *Reichsbahn* official from Berlin to help sort out the tangle and to discuss measures to be taken to get the traffic flowing again.

The first stage of the railway repair work was to clear the debris from the station halls and fill in bomb craters along the railway embankments; this work was done by soldiers from the barracks, prisoners of war and forced labourers. The second stage, the construction of emergency lines, was the duty of Hampe's special troops (*Technische Spezialtruppen*); in Dresden he had two battalions of these engineer-troops, each 1,500 strong, mostly elderly engineers beyond military age.

. . . . .

The carnage at the Central Station in the Dresden-Altstadt, to the south of the Elbe, was the worst that General Hampe had ever seen. Two days before, the last official refugee train from the Eastern Front had arrived in the city, its passengers crowded into primitive wagons and even goods trucks. Still the refugees had continued to arrive in the city, however, thronging the regular passenger trains from the East. The endless, organised refugee columns, each with its own *Führer*, had been directed one after another to the designated 'reception areas': to the Grosser Garten, where many thousands had now died; to the Exhibition Site where hundreds had been burnt to death by blazing oil flowing from the wrecked Wehrmacht transport dump there; and, those who had been hoping to travel further westward, to the public squares on either side of the Central Station. Few refugees who had been queueing at the station on the evening of Shrove Tuesday had escaped with their lives, however: only one train which was at the station when the sirens sounded had escaped to the West—the express to Augsburg and Munich.

In the vaulted basement underneath the Central Station there were five roomy gangways in which there had been room for some 2,000 people. However, there were neither blast-proof doors nor ventilation plants fitted into them. In fact, the city authorities had provided for the temporary housing of several thousand refugees from Silesia and East Prussia, together with their baggage, in these underground passages below the station, where they were cared for by the Red Cross, R.A.D.w.J. (Female Reich Labour Service), *Frauenschaften*, and N.S.V. (National Socialist Welfare Service). In any other city in the Reich, the combination of so many people and so much inflammable material in such a vulnerable and potentially dangerous locality as the Central Station would have appeared suicidal; but once again this lapse was understandable, in the face of Dresden's vaunted immunity from attack on the one hand and the pressure for any usable living space—it was after all mid-winter—on the other.

'Even the stairs to the high-level platforms had been made impassable by the piles of baggage heaped up on them,' described the *Führer* of one refugee column arriving in the Central Station on the night of the attack. The platforms themselves had been over-flowing with people, the crowds surging backwards and forwards as each empty train arrived.

Outside, in Bismarck and Wiener Platz, the station squares, there had been further endless queues of waiting people.

In the middle of this chaos and confusion the Full Alarm had sounded at 9.41 p.m. on 13th February, echoing suddenly and clearly across the city from Klotzsche in the north to Räcknitz in the south, from western Friedrichstadt to the suburbs in the east. Every light in the Central Station had gone out, leaving the station lit only by the signal lamps at the end of the platform hall. Then they too had been doused. The people, however, had been apathetic, refusing to admit the possibility of an air-raid. Many refugees had been waiting for several days in the queues for trains, and were unwilling to forfeit their places just because of what might well be Dresden's 172nd false alarm. Two trains had just arrived from Königsbrück, full of evacuated *Deutsches Jungvolk* children from K.L.V. evacuee camps in the provinces now being overrun by the Red Army.

In spite of the crowds and confusion inside the station hall, by the time that the bombs had begun falling every train had been shunted into the open air. The loudspeakers had instructed everybody to go down to the vaults under the platforms. At first few had obeyed; then, as the bombs began to fall, a stampede had begun.

The Central Station lay outside the sector marked out for the first attack and little damage had been done by the time the first raid had passed. It was then that the railway officials had made what was to prove a fatal mistake. The disruption of communications between Dresden, Berlin and the Observation Corps outposts had left the city's A.R.P. leaders completely ignorant of the air situation. Believing Dresden had seen the last of the Royal Air Force for one night, the stationmaster had ordered the trains to be shunted back into the station halls again. Within three hours, the station had been working at top pressure again, with the streams of people from the burning Inner City adding to the confusion. The platforms were once again busy with Red Cross and N.S.V. workers, refugees, evacuees and soldiers, when totally without warning the second attack had begun. This time the station had been in the heart of the area under attack.

The two trains full of evacuee children between twelve and fourteen years old had been left standing on the open yards outside the station, near the Falken-brücke bridge. After the first attack had passed over the station without incident, the evacuee camp leader, an elderly Party official of some fifty-five years, had unwisely explained to the curious children that the white 'Christmas-tree' flares marked out the area for the bombers to destroy. With the unheralded return of the bombers he must have cursed himself for his tactlessness; although he had hastily ordered the children to draw their blinds, the youngsters noticed clearly that the parachute flares now marked out a broad rectangle in the centre of which lay the station itself.

Hundreds of incendiary bombs had rained through the fragile glass roof of the station. The piles of baggage and cases heaped up inside the station hall had burst into flames. Other incendiaries penetrated the lift-shafts of the baggage-tunnels where many people had taken refuge, filling the tunnels with poisonous fumes and devouring the precious air.

The tunnels and gangways under the platforms had not been equipped as air-raid shelters, and possessed no kind of ventilation gear. One young mother had arrived in a passenger train from Silesia just as the first raid started. Her husband had written to her from the Dresden barracks that there was an agreement that the city would not be bombed because 'the Allies want it for their post-war

German capital'; she had come with her two infant children to Dresden and safety:

> Only one thing saved me: I had pushed through into a boiler room, underneath one of the platforms. In the thin ceiling was a hole made by a dud incendiary. Through this hole we were able to get sufficient air to breath now and again. Everybody else seemed to be leaning against us. Several hours passed. Then I heard someone shouting and an Army officer helped me out through a long passage. We passed through the basement: there were several thousand people there, all lying very still.

On the square there were thousands of people standing shoulder to shoulder, not panicking, but mute and still. Above them the fires stormed. At the station entrances were mounds of dead children, and others were already being piled up, as they were brought out of the station.

> There must have been a childrens' train at the station. More and more dead were stacked up, in layers, on top of each other, and covered with blankets. I took away one of these blankets for one of my babies, who were not dead, but alive and terribly cold. In the morning some elderly S.A.-men came and one of them helped me and my family to get through the town to safety.

Among the victims were children in Carnival costumes, who might perhaps have been waiting at the station to meet parents from the East.

While only the fortuitous piercing of the ceiling had saved this handful of people in the station boiler-room, several thousands had not been so fortunate. Of some 2,000 refugees from the East who had been actually billeted in the only tunnel in which any reinforcing measures had been taken, only one hundred had been burnt to death by direct incendi￹ary action; but an additional five hundred had been suffocated by the fumes, the station's A.R.P. Director reported.

> I had left all the baby clothes and medicines in my bags underneath the platforms [continues the account of the refugee woman from Silesia]. It was at first quite impossible to obtain any baby clothes, so I ventured to visit Dresden and the station again. The station cellars had been cordoned off by S.S. and police units. There was danger of typhus, they said. Nevertheless, I was permitted to enter the main cellar accompanied by a one-armed *Reichsbahn* official. He warned me

that there was nobody alive down there, everybody was quite dead. What I saw was a nightmare, lit as it was only by the dim light of the railwayman's lantern. The whole of the basement was covered with several layers of people, all very dead.

Once again, the majority of people in the Central Station had fallen victim not to the 'hundreds of high-explosive 4,000- and 8,000-pounders' so much as to the 650,000 incendiaries dropped on the city. Most of the casualties had been caused by inhalation of hot gases, and by infiltrating carbon monoxide and smoke poisoning; to a lesser extent lack of oxygen had added to the death-roll. 'What we noticed when we escaped were not so much dead bodies as people who had apparently fallen asleep, slumped against the station walls,' recalls a Panzer grenadier officer cadet, who had had to change trains at Dresden *en route* to Berlin. Of eighty-six cadets with him less than thirty survived the night to arrive for their leave in the Reich capital.

However, while the incendiaries indeed proved their worth both as anti-personnel weapons and in starting a general conflagration in the city itself, they were hardly the best weapons for an attack on the city as a 'main communications and railway centre'.

In view of the Allied Governments' insistence that the triple blow was delivered to disrupt the traffic through Dresden and that the attack was highly successful in this respect, some estimate should be reached for the time during which the main lines through the city were unserviceable.

· · · · ·

With the arrival of General Hampe and his two battalions of engineers in Dresden, salvage and repair work to the railway system commenced at once. Curiously enough, as is amply borne out both by eye-witnesses and by study of post-raid reconnaissance photographs, the very large Dresden-Friedrichstadt marshalling yards had been scarcely damaged. The photographs showed twenty-four goods, passenger and hospital trains standing in the marshalling yards after the raids, while all around the buildings were burning fiercely, very large areas being visibly on fire. Of the three engine-roundhouses in the yards, one had been hit by incendiaries at one end. In the goods yards could be seen over four hundred wagons and carriages, still perfectly ordered, waiting on the sidings and weighbridges, with scarcely a gap in their ranks. The Marien-brücke railway bridge across the river was undamaged.

If they had really wanted to disrupt the traffic through the city [General Hampe observed], they need only have concentrated on this one bridge; it would have taken many weeks to replace, during which time all railway traffic would have had to make long detours.

Working night and day, General Hampe and his *Technische Spezialtruppen* were able to open up a double line of railway track for normal working within only three days of the triple blow.

> The importance of Dresden as a railway centre [Hampe declares], which was considerable, was not diminished by more than three days as a result of these three air raids.

This observation must seem surprising when viewed in the light of the Allies' claims that the attack on Dresden's traffic installations had been successful; the official American history of the U.S.A.A.F.'s operations in the European theatre, while referring suspiciously to how the R.A.F.'s post-raid report 'went to unusual length to explain how the city had grown into a great industrial centre and was there-fore an important target', has this to say:

> If casualties were exceptionally high and damage to residential areas great, it was also evident that [Dresden's] industrial and transportation establishments had been blotted out.

The East German history of the destruction and reconstruction of Dresden states:

> The railway lines were not particularly seriously damaged; an emergency service was able to repair them so swiftly that no severe dislocation of traffic resulted.

Many non-communist sources also support this claim. It will be remembered that the Master Bomber of the second R.A.F. night attack had reported during his post-raid interrogation that the marshalling yards 'appeared to have escaped major damage'; while there was no mention of this unfortunate preservation of the Dresden railway system in subsequent public Air Ministry pro-nouncements, it is clear that the intelligence was not withheld from the Allied bomber commands themselves: thus Mission Report No. 266 of the American 390th Bombardment Group, in describing an attack made on 2nd March on the city, relates:

The crews were diverted by weather from an oil assignment [on Ruhland]. The great Dresden marshalling yards, one of the few north-to-south channels into Czechoslovakia which have not been bombed severely, were the PFF target.

After referring acidly to the devastation wrought on the city's cultural treasures, the East German history continues that:

The debris on the permanent ways at the Central Station was cleared away within only a few hours, and the trains diverted to temporary tracks.

Regular trains were again running through Dresden New Town by 15th February.

West German post-war accounts of the destruction in Dresden also draw attention to the escape of the Dresden railway system. The responsible Munich newspaper *Süddeutsche Zeitung* wrote on 22nd February 1953:

The explanation [of the American State Department] that Dresden was bombed on Soviet instructions to hinder the movement of troop reinforcements through Dresden, is a patent contradiction of the facts. The railway between Dresden and the Czech frontier [the one in question] is built between a mountain chain and the River Elbe. To destroy these lines would have been simple for the marksman of the Royal Air Force.

No strategist could honestly assume that German troops would in fact be marching in massed formations through the centre of the city to the Eastern Front.

On the contrary [the newspaper's editorial continued], one is amazed at the extraordinary precision with which the residential sections of the city were destroyed, but not the important installations. Dresden Central Station was full of mounds of corpses, but the railway lines had been only slightly damaged and after a short period were in service again.

Chapter III

ABTEILUNG TOTE

E<small>ARLY</small> on the morning of 14th February thousands of British prisoners were marched into the city; although the whole Inner City was now burning fiercely the men were still directed to their former work place, destroyed schools in Wettiner-strasse, the area hit by the small American raid of October 1944. At 11.00 a.m., however, the prisoners were marched back into their camps: rescue work in the Inner City was still out of the question, with furnace heat in the narrow streets, and none of the cellars cool enough to enter. This early return saved many lives, for had they been in the city at noon, they too would have been caught by the American attacks.

Thus the fires were able to burn uncontrolled for fourteen hours and more, and few efforts were made to carve passages through to those still surviving, who were trapped in the roomy underground catacombs of the city. In Brunswick, it will be remembered, the swift decision to use the 'water-alley' technique had saved the lives of several thousand trapped in the city's *Hochbunker* in the heart of the fire-storm area, even before the raid was over.

Only at 4.00 p.m., three and a half hours after the American raid had passed, were the first large-scale rescue operations in Dresden set in motion. Companies of soldiers from King Albert Barracks in Dresden New Town were roll-called and loaded onto lorries with storm-equipment, gas masks, steel helmets, water bottles, digging tools, and food for one day. On the eastern banks of the Elbe the columns of lorries were halted; the bridges had been mined four days previously and the charges might be detonated by any new vibrations.

As the soldiers were marched in single file across Augustus-bridge, many must have paused and gazed at the scarred Dresden skyline. Most of the familiar Dresden landmarks had vanished, many of the church and cathedral spires had collapsed in the raids; the Castle was still blazing and the dusk was darkened by the masses of smoke still moving slowly up into the sky. Miraculously, however,

Dresden's most famous landmark, the 300-foot dome of Georg Bähr's Frauenkirche cathedral, was still standing, the grey smoke pall drifting round the gold cross and lantern on its summit. The Frauenkirche had survived many wars: it was from this very dome that the young Goethe had in 1768 surveyed the devastation wrought during the long bombardment by the artillery of King Frederick II of Prussia in the Seven Years War. Canaletto's pictures of the ruins in Dresden then bear a striking resemblance to the destruction after 1945. If the Frauenkirche was still standing, then somehow the destruction of Dresden was incomplete.

> . . . . .

By this time, however, the civilian population was completely stunned by the weight of the blow which had hit Dresden. Just a few hours before, Dresden had been a fairy-tale city of spires and cobbled streets, where it had been possible to admire the crowded shop-windows in the main streets, where the evening hours had not brought the gloom of total black-out, where the windows were still unbroken and the curtains had not been removed, a city where the evening streets had been full of people thronging home from the Circus, Opera or the scores of cinemas and theatres which, even in these days of 'total war', had still been playing. Now total war had put an end to all that. Now the columns of soldiers were marching into the centre of a Dresden strangely quiet and very empty.

The ferocity of the U.S.St.A.F. daylight raid of 14th February had finally brought the people to their knees. The sky had been overcast and the bombs dropped by the Flying Fortresses were widely scattered.

But it was not the bombs which finally demoralised the people: compared with the night's bombardment by two and four-ton 'blockbusters', the American 500-pound General Purpose bombs must have seemed very tame; it was the Mustang fighters, which suddenly appeared low over the city, firing on everything that moved, and machine-gunning the columns of lorries heading for the city. One section of the Mustangs concentrated on the river banks, where masses of bombed-out people had gathered. Another section attacked targets in the Grosser Garten area.

Civilian reaction to these fighter-strafing attacks, which were apparently designed to complete the task outlined in the air commanders' Directives as 'causing confusion in the civilian evacuation from the East', was immediate and universal; they realized that they were absolutely helpless.

Abteilung Tote

American fighters strafed Tiergarten-strasse, the road bordering the Grosser Garten on the southern side. Here the remnants of the famous Kreuzkirche children's choir had taken refuge. Casualties on record here include the Choir Inspector, seriously wounded, and one of the choir-boys killed. British prisoners who had been released from their burning camps were among those to suffer the discomfort of machine-gunning attacks on the river banks and have confirmed the shattering effect on morale. Wherever columns of tramping people were marching in or out of the city they were pounced on by the fighters, and machine-gunned or raked with cannon fire.

It is certain that many casualties were caused by this low-level strafing of the city, which later became a permanent feature of American attacks.

. . . . .

Understandably, there was an immediate and urgent need for hospital accommodation. But the hospital situation was desperate: not only had Dresden been relied on as a centre for convalescing and wounded servicemen from all fronts, but nearly all the temporary hospitals had been hit, and out of Dresden's nineteen major permanent hospitals, sixteen had been damaged and three totally destroyed. The Vitzthum High School, for example, served as a hospital with 500 fully occupied beds; only two hundred invalids could be evacuated in the half-hour between the air-raid warning and the attack: the rest all perished.

Other temporary arrangements were made for caring for limited numbers of wounded and sick civilians from Dresden. A vast euthanasia-hospital for mentally incurables, the *Haus Sonnenstein* at Pirna, was turned over to meet their needs; part of the bunker being blasted by an S.S. unit into the solid rock-face near the Mordgrund-bridge, was placed at the disposal of the Red Cross for setting up a temporary hospital and shelter for the homeless; the sixty-foot-thick roof made the bunker absolutely bomb-proof.

Of the two largest hospitals in the city, Friedrichstadt and Johannstadt, the former was still partially inhabitable, while the latter, in the east of the city, containing also the city's biggest maternity home, the *Frauenklinik-Johannstadt*, was completely wrecked.

When the bombers had appeared over the city the clinics had still not been completely cleared; the warning period was too short. A block-buster had hit 'B' Block. Two labour wards, an operating-theatre, the maternity wards, the gynaecological surgery and the sterilisation equipment in the three departments had been destroyed.

Immediate attempts had been made to transport the patients from 'B' Block into 'A' Block; a wing of 'A' Block had begun to burn, however, and the invalids there had had to be evacuated too. When daylight had come 'A' Block was burning so strongly that fire-fighting was out of the question; 'B' Block had been destroyed by five high-explosive bombs; 'C' Block had been devastated down to the ground floor, and burnt right out; even 'D' Block showed heavy damage. Only 'E' Block had escaped lightly, although its roof was on fire. The bombs of the American daylight attack had not hit the *Frauenklinik*, but one solitary Mustang fighter had machine-gunned 'C', 'D' and 'E' Blocks.

An indication of the amount of damage done to Dresden's hospitals is the scale of the casualties. In the *Frauenklinik* in Johannstadt, where the damage is best documented, some two hundred people had been killed, for example. Of these, however, only 138 could be identified. In the hospital at least the usual pattern of the fire-storm aftermath was being repeated: in Kassel 31·2 per cent of the victims could not be identified; in the Johannstadt *Frauenklinik*, for which the casualties were analysed in detail, 31 per cent of the casualties were unidentifiable. Of the remainder, 95 were patients, 11 were nurses, 21 were student midwives, nurses and orderlies, 2 were French rescue workers, and nine were men of the German rescue gang; among the total of 95 identified patients were 45 expectant mothers.

For the rest of the war this hospital was out of commission. Arrangements were made for the city's surviving expectant mothers to be transferred to the undamaged wing of the Friedrichstadt general hospital, where several wards had been cleared for this purpose.

A multitude of medical cases requiring the most urgent attention had to be cleared, as well as the obvious problem of surgical care for the thousands of injured. Inevitably the process was slow, and many sick and injured died before they could be properly attended to. Gradually the already enormous death-roll crept higher, and still no organised attempt at rescuing those trapped beneath fallen masonry had begun.

. . . . .

It was not until the late afternoon of Ash Wednesday, 14th February, that even the troops stationed in the city's barracks were put to work on rescue operations: for army units stationed further away from the city the delay was even longer. At Königsbrück, where army units were assembling for action on the Eastern front, the situation in Dresden had still not been realised two days after the attacks. Not the least of the difficulties was that the seat of the fire-storm, and therefore the damage to life and limb, in the city was on the left bank of the Elbe, while Königsbrück and most other troop concentrations were on the right bank. But the left bank of the Elbe was designated as the 'home front', while everything east of the river was assigned to the 'rearward army district'. Any initiative for such troop movements had to come from the appropriate authorities. Only on 16th February did the necessary marching orders arrive.

In the case of the Allied prisoners of war based on Dresden, of whom there were over twenty thousand at the time of the attack, the instructions to participate in rescue work came even later.

Although there were over 230 Allied prisoners, for example, in one working detachment, No. 1326 in Dresden-Übigau, as a result of their narrow escape of 14th February, no further working parties were organised until 21st February, when 150 of the prisoners were ordered by Army District Command IV to march in gangs of 70, 50 and 30 into the city to assist in salvage operations. For a whole week the men were confined to camp.

A prisoner in another camp remarked bitterly that although the area all around them had been badly damaged in the triple blow, their German guards forced them to march right across the city each morning to a site in eastern Dresden; the intention was evidently to 'rub their noses' in the horrors their fellow-countrymen had caused, and to aid the almost completely unsuccessful recruitment of prisoners to join a 'Free British Corps' to fight the Russians on the Eastern front.

Most of the British prisoners worked with a will at rescue and salvage operations. This was indeed an anomalous situation. Many were later to pay for their willingness with their lives, when, after weeks of living on diminishing rations, their rescue operations brought them within reach of intact food stores in wrecked shops and hotels. Thus an American from a camp in Dresden-Plauen was found with a tin of food in his uniform during a routine search; a young French-Canadian soldier was caught smuggling a looted gammon of ham into the camp in Dresden-Übigau. Both were shot by firing-squads. Both Germans and non-Germans were treated the same way. A German labourer was found to have secreted between 150 and 180 wedding rings in his pockets in Grunaerstrasse;

he, too, was executed on the spot. In Dresden a state of emergency had been declared since February 17th.

> On the orders of the Gauleiter [announced *Der Freiheitskampf* grimly that same day] a number of plunderers and looters were shot yesterday on the spot, immediately after their capture. Where plunderers are discovered, they must be handed over at once to Party officials or their representatives; Gauleiter Mutschmann has no intention of allowing any kind of softness in this, his so cruelly tested Gau. This is a matter for the whole community: he who commits a crime against the community is worthy only of death.

Not only looters were being executed in Dresden, adding to the enormous death-roll of the triple blow. It was ascertained that 'unscrupulous elements' were increasingly spreading rumours which were both uninformed and unkind.

> The rumour-monger serves the interests only of the enemy, and must expect immediate death. The Gauleiter has decreed that all rumour-mongers are to be shot out of hand; this has already happened in certain cases.

.   .   .   .   .

For several days after the triple blow, the streets of the city were strewn with thousands of victims still lying where they had been overcome. In many cases limbs had been torn away; other victims had peaceful expressions on their faces and looked as though they had just fallen asleep. Only the greenish pallor of their skins betrayed that they were no longer alive.

After their two-day delay, the troops were now worked feverishly digging for survivors; the soldiers had to work for twenty-four hours straight off, with very little food; all sort of organisation had collapsed, and rescue troops could not expect a meal until they were relieved by further troops.

> The work was very tough [relates one soldier detailed for Dresden rescue operations]. It took four men to carry away each wounded survivor. Other soldiers before us had already started by removing the rubble and opening up the cellars. Sometimes twenty, sometimes more people had sought shelter from the bombs. The fire had robbed them of their oxygen supply and the heat must have tortured them terribly. We were lucky to find here and there one or two still surviving. This went on for hours. All over the ground lay these corpses, shrivelled in the intense heat to about three feet long.

He and his company were later set to work rescuing survivors trapped in the gutted Opera, where there had been a special performance on the night of the attack; this Semper building had seen the premieres of Wagner's *Rienzi*, *The Flying Dutchman*, *Tannhäuser* and, more recently, of Richard Strauss' *Der Rosenkavalier*. Now it would present nothing more to the world of culture. Like the Circus Sarrasani it had collapsed, leaving only a hollow, gutted shell, and many people buried under the ruins.

As the columns of soldiers were marched back across the river they could see that now the dome of the Frauenkirche too had collapsed. Stored in the basement of the cathedral were extensive film archives of the German Air Ministry and—just when the Cathedral's fire-fighters thought they had controlled the flames—the heat generated in the basement had caused the celluloid to ignite with explosive violence. The dome collapsed at 10.15 a.m. on Thursday morning, 15th February. Now the destruction of the city's architecture, too, was complete.

.   .   .   .   .

The Police Praesidium had been made uninhabitable by the triple blow, and as a result the headquarters of the Security Police and the S.D. Party organisation were transferred with the Headquarters of the S.S. and Police Director to the half-complete rock bunker blasted into the cliff face at Dresden's Mordgrundbrücke bridge.

On 19th February *Der Freiheitskampf* published the first announcement requesting people searching for missing relatives to contact a newly organised *Vermissten-Suchstelle*—a Missing Persons Inquiry Office—in the still-intact Ministry of the Interior building on the Königsufer embankment of the Elbe; it was the first step towards reuniting the thousands of families split up by the triple blow.

At the same time, a more ominous organisation was set up, compiling the registry of the missing people who would never be found again. In each of the seven Dresden administrative boroughs, a *Vermissten-Nachweis*—Bureau of Missing Persons—was established. The Bureaux for the boroughs of Weisser Hirsch and Dresden-Central were in the local Town Halls; for the boroughs of Blasewitz, Strehlen, and Cotta they were in the local elementary schools; the Trachau Bureau was in Dobelner-strasse, and that in Leuben was at No. 15 Neuberin-strasse.

For inquiries about victims with no permanent residence in Dresden, including refugees, soldiers and forced labourers, the appropriate Bureau was the last one, in Dresden-Leuben; here a Central Bureau of Missing Persons—*Vermissten-Nachweis-Zentrale*—was established to collate the information from all the others.

On the morning of 15th February, Hanns Voigt, an assistant master at one of the schools in the city, which had been closed down on 4th February like so many of the Dresden schools for conversion into a Luftwaffe hospital, was ordered to report to the new V.N.Z. office in Dresden-Leuben, which had been established in a former children's day nursery in Neuberin-strasse, some seven miles to the south-east of the city. This part of the city could expect to be spared further air-raid damage, and had the advantage of being on the left bank of the river: prevailing opinion in Dresden anticipated a speedy Russian invasion. The Russians were after all only some seventy miles away by now.

Voigt was ordered to establish and organise an *Abteilung Tote* for the V.N.Z.—a Dead Persons Department which would take over the records and effects of all people known to have died, and later of the thousands of victims to be recovered from the ruins of the city.

For two weeks, with characteristic German thoroughness, he collected assistants and formulated a plan for what was to prove the biggest task of identification and registration in history. On 1st March Voigt was able to report to the V.N.Z. that his Department was fully operational, with a total complement of clerks and officials numbering over seventy; a further 300 were employed in the V.N.Z. The *Abteilung Tote* would be responsible for identification of the victims and for arriving at some final estimate of the death roll. On 6th March the Department was recognised by the Reich and incorporated in the V.N.Z. The careful, bureaucratic thoroughness with which we have come to associate the German people, was well demonstrated by the structure and activities of this macabre institution. Dresden was divided for the purposes of identification procedure into seven operational districts, each with its own central S.H.D. office: the S.H.D. was the *Sicherheits und Hilfsdienst*, the service most commonly in action in blitzed cities. The recovery of the corpses was supervised by four squads of the Repair Service (*Instandsetzungsdienst*) and its four companies of medical orderlies, by two battalions of soldiers, and the squads of the Emergency Technical Service (*Technische Nothilfe*). A command post for the *I.-Dienst* was organised in the concrete bunker underneath the Albertinum building, as was the command post of the *Technische Nothilfe*.

The organisation of the rescue work, the identification and the counting was closely co-ordinated. Officials were at hand to supervise identification work on the spot, the bodies being lined up for one or two days on the space cleared on the pavements for this purpose. All valuables, including jewelry, papers, letters, rings and other identifying material, were placed in separate paper envelopes. These envelopes bore the essential information: the place and date of finding, the sex and, if known, the person's name, in addition to a serial number. Each victim had affixed to it a coloured card with the same serial number on it. At the same time, each head was counted by officers, and these daily tallies, together with the lorry-loads of valuables, were collected by the S.H.D. leaders of the seven district offices. Each night the V.N.Z. assembled all the envelopes and registered the names and serial numbers in their indexes, to enable the data to be processed during the following weeks.

> The recovery work was the hardest task [the *I.-Dienst* Director in Dresden explained]. The gases which had collected in the hot basements were a very grave danger to our rescue gangs, as there were not enough gas-masks to go round.

For the first week the units of *I.-Dienst*, police, R.A.D., and S.H.D. companies were forced to work without rubber gloves—the whole stock of rubber gloves had been lost in the fires. Experience in other fire-storm areas had demonstrated how recovery-workers were frequently exposed to disease and *post-mortem* virus. Nevertheless, for the first week the men and women working on corpse recovery had to work with bare hands or improvised protectors. With a lack of efficiency that was hardly German, rubber glove supplies began thereafter to build up in great surplus until soon they were even being sold to the public. Rubber boots were also urgently needed: normally dry cellars and basements became otherwise impassable, with moisture emerging from the serous corpses.

In this respect Dresden was as ill-prepared as Kassel had been for the fire-storm: in the A.R.P. District 'Kassel' the supplies had not been enough either, and extra stocks had had to be delivered by aircraft. Nor were these the only supplies lacking then in Kassel. 'To combat the very strong stench of decay which arose after some days, all forces taking part in the recovery work were provided with cognac and cigarettes'; even eau-de-cologne and special soap rations had been available at the time of the Kassel raids. Some salvage squads had worked with gas-masks on, with alcohol-soaked wadding inserted in the filter-frame.

In Dresden the lessons learned from other air raids about the personal needs of salvage squads had been put into practice, and it was fortunate that only the rubber-glove stocks had been destroyed: the large stores of schnapps in the deep vaults both of the Hygiene Museum and of the Albertinum remained undamaged. The task of carrying the corpses out of the cellars, often the most degrading work, was delegated to auxiliary labour forces: the forced labourers, Ukrainian and Rumanian troop units from the barracks, and prisoners of war.

Some parts of the Inner City were so hot that the cellars could not be entered for many weeks; this was especially the case where, contrary to regulations, large stocks of coal had been hoarded in the cellars and had caught fire. One street in the Inner City was impassable for six weeks. As in Hamburg, the usual fire-storm aftermath of melted preserving-jars, pots and pans, and even completely incinerated bricks and tiles were discovered in some cellars in the centre of the Inner City. These too were indicative of the 1,000°-plus temperatures prevailing in the fire-storm area.

During the first weeks the city police were entrusted with loading the victims onto the wagons and organising attempts to count them. A police officer was sent each day to collect thirty bottles of cognac per gang from the stores. Allied prisoners, held collectively responsible for the raids, were not included in either cognac or cigarette issues.

The women recovery-workers, mostly from the Reich Work Service (*Reichsarbeitsdienst*), not being permitted to drink alcohol, were given treacle and twenty cigarettes a day to calm their nerves. The first task given to the recovery-workers was to clear the victims off the streets.

> One shape I will never forget [a Dresden pensioner wrote to his mother five days after the raids] was the remains of what had apparently been a mother and child. They had shrivelled and charred into one piece, and had been stuck rigidly to the asphalt. They had just been prised up. The child must have been underneath the mother, because you could still clearly see its shape, with its mother's arms clasped around it.

Nobody would ever be able to identify either again.

Clearly a gargantuan task would face the identification authorities. Another witness, one of the soldiers engaged in recovery work, wrote:

Abteilung Tote

All the way across the city we could see the victims lying face down, literally glued to the tarmac, which had softened and melted in the enormous heat.

The city's A.R.P. Engineer, Georg Feydt, counted between 180 and 200 bodies lying in Ring-strasse alone.

A comrade asked me to help him find his wife in Muschinski-strasse [described another soldier from the New Town barracks]. The house was burnt out when we reached it. He shouted and shouted, hoping that people in the cellar might hear him. There was no answer. He refused to give up the search, and continued poking around in the cellars of neighbouring houses, even prising up charred torsos from the melted asphalt to see if one of them was his wife's.

However, even by inspecting their shoes, the soldier was unable to identify one as his wife: his inability positively to recognise his own wife was characteristic of the problems facing the V.N.Z.

.   .   .   .   .

Never would I have thought that death could come to so many people in so many different ways [said Director Voigt of the V.N.Z. *Abteilung Tote* in Dresden]. Never had I expected to see people interred in that state: burnt, cremated, torn and crushed to death; sometimes the victims looked like ordinary people apparently peacefully sleeping; the faces of others were racked with pain, the bodies stripped almost naked by the tornado; there were wretched refugees from the East clad only in rags, and people from the Opera in all their finery; here the victim was a shapeless slab, there a layer of ashes shovelled into a zinc tub. Across the city, along the streets wafted the unmistakeable stench of decaying flesh.

Some people had met extremely unpleasant ends when central-heating systems had burst and basements had flooded with scalding water. In most cases, however, death had been both peaceful and slow. Probably over seventy per cent of the casualties were caused by lack of oxygen or by carbon monoxide poisoning.

CHAPTER IV

ANATOMY OF A TRAGEDY

Nᴏᴛ the least disturbing aspect of the shock-wave from the triple blow on Dresden was the effect it appears to have had on the higher *echelons* of the N.S.D.A.P. officials and German Government; for a month, in growing volume, Dr. Goebbels had been preaching the story of the Morgenthau-Plan, the half-fact, half-fantasy plan for post-war Germany, which the enemy were supposed to be discussing at Yalta. Now, suddenly and dramatically, the nightmare which they in their own disordered minds had created, appeared to be coming true. Overnight, as the first figures current in Berlin showed, 'between two and three hundred thousand people' had been massacred in a great German city. The Inspector of German Fire Services wrote after the war in his memoirs:

> The conflagration in Dresden nourished the suspicion that the Western Allies were concerned only with the liquidation of the German *Volk*. For one last time, Dresden brought the Germans together under the swastika-banner and drove them into the arms of their propaganda service, which now more credibly than before could lay the accent on fear: fear of merciless air-raids, fear of the ratified Morgenthau-Plan, fear of extinction.

Other senior German officers held opposing views on morale after the triple blow: 'When this catastrophe became known to the whole of Germany, morale disintegrated everywhere,' a Colonel, in perhaps significantly the *Luftwaffe*, is quoted as admitting in his Interrogation. To those in Dresden who had survived the first attack, however, it must indeed have seemed that all they had been warned of concerning the Allies' Morgenthau-Plan was materialising only too quickly.

. . . . . .

On the Altmarkt-square in Dresden, under the victory-memorial erected after the Franco-Prussian war, large static water tanks about 90 feet square had been built. Several hundred people had tried to save themselves and extinguish their burning clothes by climbing into the water tanks; but, although the tanks' walls were about two-and-a-half feet above the ground, in fact the water was over eight feet deep. The sloping walls of the concrete tanks made it impossible to climb out again. Those who could swim were dragged under by those who could not. When the rescue gangs cleared their way through to the Altmarkt-square next afternoon, the tanks were half empty—the water had evaporated in the heat. The people in the tanks were all dead, very dead.

The commander of a Speer-Organisation Transport Company based on Dresden was faced with a terrible sight when he and his men finally struggled through to Lindenau-platz, a square to the south of the Central Station, where their Headquarters were.

Lindenau-platz measured about 100 yards by 150 yards. In the centre there were lawns, with a few trees. In the middle of the square lay an old man, with two dead horses. Hundreds of corpses, completely naked, were scattered round him. The tram-shelter was burnt out; but the most extraordinary thing was the way the people were lying naked all round it. Next to the tram-shelter was a public lavatory of corrugated iron. At the entrance to this was a woman, about thirty years old, completely nude, lying face-down on a fur-coat; not far away lay her identity card, which showed her to be from Berlin. A few yards further on lay two young boys aged about eight and ten clinging tightly to each other; their faces were buried in the ground. They too were stark naked. Their legs were stiff and twisted into the air. In a Litfass-pillar [a cylindrical advertising pillar] which had been overturned, there were two corpses, also naked. There were about twenty or thirty of us who saw this scene. As far as we could make out, the people had stayed in their basements too long; when they were finally driven out, they were suffocated by lack of oxygen.

In this case it is unlikely that carbon-monoxide poisoning was the cause of death: *rigor mortis* would not have set in as described.

Some areas of Dresden had been so severely hit that it was unlikely that any people had escaped with their lives. One of these areas was around Seidnitzer-platz. In this square there was also a static water tank, some fifty feet square, but not as deep as the ones in the Altmarkt. It was a grotesque sight. Between 200 and 250 people were still sitting there on the edges of the tank, just where they had been on the night of the raid. There was a gap, here and there, where someone had rolled forward into the tank. But all, again, were dead.

On the corner of Seidnitzer-strasse and the square there had been the local hostel for R.A.D. girls, and next to it a temporary hospital for legless soldiers. At the moment when the Full Alarm sirens had sounded on 13th February the R.A.D. girls and the soldiers had been watching a Carnival performance of a puppet show in the hospital basement. In the hospital where the surviving R.A.D. girls had to undertake rescue work later, they found that between forty and fifty of the patients and two doctors had succumbed to the fires; only two doctors and one nurse escaped. The attack had fallen on the city before the soldiers could be evacuated.

'I had never realised that corpses would shrivel so small in intense heat; I had seen nothing like it, even in Darmstadt, before,' says the *Führerin* of the R.A.D. unit, who had herself survived the fire-storm in Darmstadt.

Along the southern edge of the Grosser Garten ran the rambling zoological gardens, housing one of the most famous menageries in Central Germany. The bombs that had struck the zoo had already released a considerable number of the animals from shattered cages. The Hagenbeck Zoo in Hamburg had been specially reinforced against air-raid escapes of wild animals: cages had been double-barred and the zoo premises had been encircled by trenches and traps. In Dresden most of the cages were damaged and, to prevent a mass break-out, servicemen were called in to shoot all the remaining animals in the early morning hours after the raids.

Even ten days after the raids, the human victims had still not been removed from the green lawns of the Grosser Garten. A Swiss resident described how two weeks after the raids he set out across the devastated area to visit a friend in Dresden-Gruna. His journey took him along the broad boulevard of Stübel-allee, where *Reichsstatthalter* Mutschmann, Gauleiter of Saxony, had his villa; the road was hard, not only because of the craters and rubble, but also because of the sickening sight of heaps of victims stacked up everywhere. He was later to describe his experiences during the Dresden tragedy in a three-day account of the Allied bomber force's triple blow in one of Switzerland's leading newspapers, commencing on 22nd March, after he had smuggled the notes out of Germany. His account shocked not only the Swiss: less than six days later the Foreign Office made representations to the Prime Minister presumably about the effect that bombing operations on this scale were having on world opinion. This neutral witness had written:

The sight was so appalling that without a second glance I decided not to pick my way among these corpses. For this reason I turned back and headed for the Grosser Garten. But here it was even more appalling: walking through the grounds, I could see torn-off arms and legs, mutilated torsos, and heads which had been wrenched off their bodies and rolled away. In places the corpses were still lying so densely that I had to clear a path through them in order not to tread on arms and legs.

For the R.A.D. the Dresden raids were especially tragic. Girls were required to work for one year in the organisation, and six further months (by Führer-decree of July 1941) in the Auxiliary War Service (*Kriegshilfsdienst*) working in the Post-office organisation, bus and tram services, and hospitals. *Bezirk* VII, 'Dresden', which directed all female R.A.D.w.J. labour in Saxony (the male R.A.D. units were subject to the authority of *Arbeitsgau* XV, 'Dresden'), had received many requests from parents to let their daughters serve their final six months' K.H.D. in Dresden, which was universally regarded as Germany's 'safest air-raid shelter', rather than in Central and Western Germany. Now the casualties among this section of the German labour front were all the heavier: as one of the girls' unit leaders (*Maidenführerin*) estimates, during the Dresden triple blow some 850 K.H.D. girls alone had been killed. In König-Johann-strasse the corpses were laid out in lines for relatives and neighbours to identify. One group was of a dozen K.H.D. tram-conductresses, young girls in uniform. To one of them a card had been pinned: PLEASE LET ME HAVE THE BODY; I WISH TO BURY MY DAUGHTER MYSELF. Already the survivors of the raids were hearing of the crude mass burials of the victims outside the city.

When it came to salvage duties the R.A.D. and K.H.D. girls were as hardy as the toughest Ukrainian soldiers and forced labourers. They did not blench when it came to entering the basements, even in the middle of the night—during the early days rescue work was continued round-the-clock—and hauling out the bodies onto the pavements. All the victims were searched for personal papers which would throw light on their identity; if the identity could be proved beyond doubt, it was written onto a yellow serial-numbered card, which was fastened with a skewer to the corpse. In addition to this, the girls were required to open up the clothing of unidentified victims and cut samples from the blouses and underclothes, parts of which were pinned to the bodies, the remainder inserted in the envelopes of personal effects. Unidentified bodies were serial-numbered with red cards to avoid confusion.

For the R.A.D. girls, however, the most heart-rending task was that of processing their own colleagues. In the big hostel in Weisse Gasse, for example, a narrow street hard by the Altmarkt, the basement was crowded with ninety girls; all of them had died.

> The girls sat there, as though stopped in the middle of a conversation [describes the leader of the squad which first reached the hostel's basement]. They looked so natural, even though they were dead, that it was hard to believe they were indeed not alive.

The Allied prisoners entered into rescue operations with enthusiasm, developing their own listening gear, driving gas pipes into the cellars to provide air supplies for any survivors and listen for signs of life, and engaging in the most hazardous rescue operations. In many cases, however, there were scenes of violence as the population vented its bitterness on the helpless prisoners; they were admittedly properly handled by their guards, while taking part in rescue and salvage operations, but on occasions the German civilians lost their tempers: they did not object to Germans being rescued alive by Allied prisoners, but it irked them that their enemies had to handle their dead.

Director Voigt of the V.N.Z. *Abteilung Tote* wished at this stage to be present at as many cellar-openings as possible, to see conditions for himself. Some ten days after the triple blow he was summoned by the squad-leader of an S.H.D. unit to a house near Pirnaischerplatz. A gang of Rumanian soldiers was refusing to go into one of the basements; they had freed the steps leading to it, but clearly something out of the ordinary had happened inside. The workers stood sullenly round the basement entrance, as the civilian Director, wishing to set an example, marched down the steps to the cellar, an acetylene lamp in his hand. He was reassured by the lack of the usual smell of decay. The bottom steps were slippery. The cellar floor was covered by an eleven or twelve-inch deep liquid mixture of blood, flesh and bone; a small high-explosive bomb had penetrated four floors of the building and exploded in the basement. The Director instructed the S.H.D. leader not to attempt recovery of any victims, but to spread chlorinated lime over the inside of the basement, and leave it to dry out. An interview with the *Hausmeister* of the block yielded the information that 'there would have been 200 to 300 people down there on the night; there were always that many during other air-raid alerts'.

In Seidnitzer-strasse equally gruesome scenes presented themselves to the recovery workers. Even some toughened soldiers could not stand the strain of the work after long: two men, working on the recovery of bodies from basements here, refused to carry on with the work. They were ordered by their squad-leaders to return to work, but again declined to comply. Both were executed on the spot by a Party official. The bodies were loaded immediately onto the horse-drawn carts, together with the putrescent bodies of the air-raid victims.

Very large heaps of corpses rapidly collected on the streets outside the numerous cinemas and pubs in the city, where the people in their hundreds had been on the Carnival evening of the attack. At the time of the beginning of the triple blow on Dresden, the cinemas and theatres had still been playing.

The first sight that Director Voigt had of the Central Station showed mounds of corpses being stacked on the railway lines, in heaps ten to twenty yards square and ten feet high. The dead soldiers who had been passing through the city or on leave at the time of the raid were being hauled out of the ruins for several days, and stacked with pitch-forks onto wagons standing in the squares outside, their heads ordered one way and their feet the other. The first estimate, released on the day that he was inspecting casualties there, gave the number of dead at the station alone as between seven and ten thousand.

As in many other instances, the figures for the area destroyed differ widely; there are two estimates for the damaged area in Dresden. The findings of the British Bombing Survey Unit, based on an aerial survey, were that 1,681 acres of the 'built-up (Target) area' had been destroyed. In 1949, however, the Dresden *Stadt-planungsamt* published its own detailed survey of the damage caused from which the following figures are derived: 3,140 acres were more than 75 per cent destroyed; a further 1,040 acres were more than 25 per cent destroyed. As this central area was not the area which was to suffer from the later heavy raids by the U.S.St.A.F. of 2nd March and 17th April 1945, it is difficult to understand the disparity but this may have arisen from the different methods of assessment used by the British and the Germans.

. . . . .

The further the salvage operations were pressed into the centre of the worst-hit areas, the more hopeless seemed the ideal of perfect registration of the victims. Finally the salvage squads were restricted by the sheer size of the task to removing wedding-rings and to obtaining cloth-samples of all garments worn by each victim. In Dresden-Leuben, Director Voigt, of the *Abteilung Tote*, had within a few weeks perfected an indexing system simple enough to be operated easily by his limited staff, yet comprehensive enough to afford every inquirer a positive chance of learning the fate of relatives.

On 19th April, the *Oberbürgermeister* of Dresden announced that as his Central Bureau of Missing Persons was now the most comprehensive source of information about victims, casualties and survivors, the inquiry office formerly operated by the C.I.D. in the Ministry of the Interior building would be closed down at once; the C.I.D.'s information and collection of salvaged property, together with the personal effects still pouring in from the recovery-gangs, would be redirected to the Central Bureau, and thence to the *Abteilung Tote* under Hanns Voigt.

One after another he built up and perfected four filing systems, each based on different data. The first indexing system contained several thousand clothing-cards (*Kleiderkarten*); onto these cards were pasted inch-square samples of all clothing found on unidentified bodies, together with details of the locality, date of finding, place of burial, and the universal serial number. The clothing-cards were filed according to the streets and house numbers, and kept available for searchers in filing cabinets in a hut at the end of the office's garden, because of the smell of decay. 'Up to the capitulation we had almost 12,000 of these cards completed,' submits the Director.

The second indexing system provided filing-cards, again organised street by street, on which were listed miscellaneous personal effects of unidentified victims found in houses, or in the street outside. The third index was a simple alphabetical register of bodies identified by identity-cards or personal papers on their bodies. This list was, however, one of the shortest, and was finally closed on 29th April 1945.

The fourth, and last, index was perhaps the saddest of all: a list of wedding rings recovered. They had been cut from the bodies with bolt-croppers, to provide further identification: German custom required the initials of the wearer to be engraved on the inside of the ring; often the complete name or names were engraved with the date of engagement and wedding. By May 6th there were between ten and twenty thousand of these rings stored in two-gallon buckets at the Ministry of the Interior on Königsfer. All these rings did not necessarily belong to women; German custom was for men to wear wedding rings as well.

Nevertheless, with these four indexes the *Abteilung Tote* was able to clear up the identity of some 40,000 of the dead. Another figure, not too widely differing, is provided by the Chief Civil Defence engineer in the city; he has written:

> The official number of identified dead was announced as 39,773 up to the morning of May 6th, 1945.

These figures represent an absolute minimum deathroll in Dresden.

However, as a result of the premature intervention of officials from Berlin, the identification work was several times halted, and even by-passed. Early in March, an S.S. *Kommando* from Reichsamt Berlin arrived in Dresden and presented itself at the V.N.Z. office in Dresden-Leuben; the identification work being conducted by the *Abteilung Tote* was delaying burial of the victims, and the danger of epidemics in the city was being increased. Identification work was in future to be partially transferred to the burial grounds.

The Dresden Burial Office opened up three new branches, as it was unable to cope unaided with the enormous call on its services.

Every effort was made to ensure that the maximum number of victims could be buried properly, even if only in mass graves. On the Heide-friedhof up to the end of the war, the last mortal remains of 28,746 victims had been buried. This figure for one of the Dresden burial grounds is accurate only in so far as it represents the number of heads literally counted by the recovery squads. However, as the Chief Gardener of the cemetery has pointed out:

> The mutilated and charred corpses whose heads had been burnt off or crushed could be counted just as little as those who had been cremated alive in the fire-storm, and of whom nothing remained but a scattered heap of ashes.

The burial troops, for the most part airmen summoned from the Radar-training and Flying School at Dresden-Klotzsche, were instructed that the victims of the triple blow were to be buried without coffins or shrouds. Mass graves were dug out by excavators and bulldozers. The first victims to arrive were granted a space of 90 cms each, about three feet.

Of the fifteen city hearses, fourteen had been destroyed in the air-raids. The farmers and peasants from the surrounding villages were ordered to drive their teams of horses into Dresden for the task. At the same time an uninterrupted stream of individual people arrived, bringing their own dead to be buried. Some victims were brought on coal-lorries, some by tram. Nobody was offended if the dead were wrapped in newsprint or brown paper tied with string. R.A.D.w.J. units at one stage were supplied with the paper-bag stock of a cement works to pack the crumbling torsos into.

The S.S. and Police units had been despatched with their police lorries from Berlin to carry the casualties to the burial grounds. Police officers ordered the tipping up of a whole lorry-load of corpses into a mass-grave; after they had departed, the burial-troops had to sort the tangled mass of corpses out again, in order that at least some kind of order could be preserved in this wild empire of chaos. The recovery squads had been fixing yellow cards to the identifiable bodies, and red ones to all others. They were buried in separate sections of the cemetery.

It became obvious that the three feet allowance for each victim was too much, and soon the bodies were placed shoulder to shoulder in the mass graves. With the arrival of the authorities from Berlin, the orders were amended so that the corpses were buried three layers deep. The vast Heide-friedhof offered apparently unlimited space for the corpses of all the victims of the Allied air-raids on the city, even had they been twice as many. But while space would permit a decent burial for all the victims, the warmer weather would not. As the weeks passed, and still the work was not completed, a stench of decay pervaded the city.

· · · · ·

The Army erected barricades around the centre of the old city, the cordoned-off area being a square bounded by streets about three blocks to either side of the Altmarkt. The recovery squads received a change of orders. The bodies were not all to be taken to the burial grounds outside the city any longer, but to be sent to the Altmarkt, in the heart of the area cordoned off by the Army. Burial in the Heide-friedhof involved the transport of long columns of corpse-laden wagons through Dresden New Town, which in spite of the military barracks and industrial areas had hardly received a single bomb; the authorities did not wish the population to see this depressing spectacle.

Identification of the victims was becoming chaotic. Large mounds of unidentified corpses were accumulating at the cemeteries. Some cemeteries were able to achieve miracles: at the Johannis-friedhof, in Dresden-Tolkewitz, for example, the Police-unit leader was able to complete identification of nearly all of the victims. But in other burial grounds the corpses began to pile up beside the mass graves and complications arose; S.S. officials who returned and saw one mound of some 3,000 victims on the Heide-friedhof ordered their immediate burial without identification; the bodies were bull-dozed into the mass graves.

The early March weeks were cold and bleak, but in the middle of the month the weather changed and an inordinately warm early spring sun beat down on the dead Inner City. The ruined buildings dried out, but hundreds of the crushed and blocked basements had still not been cleared by the end of April. Unusually large rats were seen scurrying about among the ruins, their coats streaked with the slaked lime spread inside the ruined houses. Soldiers working late at night in the cordoned-off dead zone reported seeing rhesus monkeys, horses and even a lion hiding in the shadows of the buildings where they had been living and feeding since their cages had been destroyed two months before. But already the Altmarkt was witnessing more fearful scenes than once-caged animals prowling in the darkness.

Chapter V

THEY SHALL REAP THE WHIRLWIND

As the winter was replaced by the warmer months of spring, the tempo of daily life in Dresden quickened. Whereas previously the recovery and disposal of victims had been spread over two or three days, now a new urgency hastened the steps of the salvage gangs: the real danger of a typhus epidemic.

People searched for many days for missing relatives so that they could be spared the indignity of mass burial in a common grave; but now while they departed to search for wheelbarrows or carts to remove the victims to a cemetery to bury them themselves, all too often the S.H.D. gangs had dragged the bodies away, and they were already lying neatly stacked on a jolting cart under a pile of thirty other decaying bodies, making its way in procession along the Grossenhainer-strasse to the pine and eucalyptus forests north of the city. Who was right? The relatives who wanted a decent burial for the victims, or the S.H.D. gangs whose duty was to avoid epidemics and try to arrange speedy identification work on the cemeteries? Many of those who saw the endless caravans of horse-drawn carts and lorries trundling northwards out of the city must have silently vowed that they would never let their relatives be carried to their graves like that.

> On Markgraf-Heinrich-strasse three men spoke to me [recalls an evacuee from Cologne who was in the city]. They were carrying between them a black overcoat on which lay a body. One of them asked me: What kind of building used that one to be? I told him: That used to be a school, but then it was a military hospital. All he could say was: I have to bury my wife: I might as well do it here. Later on, I saw them hollowing out a shallow grave. There weren't any coffins, and the man seemed to be a stranger in the city.

Some people would not realise, the harassed Director of the *Abteilung Tote* complained, that they did not have a personal right to the bodies of their relatives. In some cases the relatives dug up the corpses from the mass graves, and took them away to family

tombs. Thus the legal and statistical position was hopelessly confused. One man provides another instance of the prevailing desire
not to let the recovery squads get hold of near relatives:

> In order to spare their parents a mass-burial, my sister-in-law first
> of all took her father out of the city on a wheelbarrow to bury him, and
> then returned for her mother. But in the meantime a recovery gang had
> taken her away; thus, most of the people who died were spirited away,
> and their death certificates read, like her two parents: DECEASED IN
> DRESDEN, 13th FEBRUARY, 1945.

Such was the effect of the triple blow on Dresden in terms of
human suffering. Analysed in statistical detail, the blow was no
less impressive. In so far as the attacks on Dresden and on Chemnitz
had been designed to destroy the residential areas of the city and
make it impossible for the German Army to billet soldiers in the
town, the Dresden raids might indeed accurately be described as a
shattering success. In November 1945 the city's Planning Office
published detailed statistics of the damage done to the city—not
only by the R.A.F. Bomber Command attacks but by all the attacks,
including the later U.S.St.A.F. attacks as well. This statistics
are reproduced in an appendix at the end of this book. Of the
35,470 residential buildings in the Dresden area, only 7,421 houses
were undamaged or not destroyed. Expressed in terms of homes and
flats, of the 220,000 living-units, over 90,000 were destroyed or made
totally uninhabitable by the attacks. Expressed in terms of square
feet, 51,150,000 square feet of living space were completely destroyed
and 48,850,000 square feet had been moderately damaged. Expressed in the dry terms in which German air-raid statisticians
excel, while by comparison there were to each citizen of Munich
8·5 cubic yards of rubble, in Stuttgart there were 11·1 cubic yards,
in Berlin there were 16·5 and in Cologne 41, in Dresden, for each
of the citizens (including those who had died), there were 56 cubic
yards of rubble, more than eleven lorry-loads of rubble per inhabitant.

The damage to the industrial section of the city might at first
have appeared mortal: of the twelve vital public utility services
and power installations in the city, only one was completely undamaged; but by 15th February most of Dresden Neustadt was
supplied with electric power again, and as the swift resumption of
outlying tram services indicates, most of the suburbs were with
electricity again within one week of the raids. By 19th February
electric tram services had been resumed between the Industrial

Estate, Weixdorf and Hellerau; between Weissig and the Mord-grund-brücke bridge, soon to be extended into the devastated city itself; between Mickten and Coswig; between Cossebaude and Cotta; and between Niedersedlitz and Kreischka. To compensate for the total destruction of the tram service across the Inner City, an improvised shuttle service of Elbe river-steamers was operated between Pieschen and Laubegast, between Blasewitz and the Old City, between Dresden and Bad Schandau and Pirna; these services were timed to connect with local tram services in the suburbs.

In the Inner City the damage was, however, insurmountable: over 500 kilometres of sewers and canals had been destroyed, and 1,750 bomb craters would have to be filled before the streets would be passable; 92 kilometres of tram wires had been torn down. A total of 185 trams and trailers had been completely wrecked, 303 more damaged in varying degree. This latter statistic is illuminating: the tramcars could be considered to have been evenly distributed across the city at the time of the attacks; yet while in the whole Battle of Hamburg 600 tramcars had been damaged in a week of massive air-raids, in Dresden 488 had been damaged in a single night.

Industrial recovery in Dresden, nevertheless, was swift, as Speer indicated in his post-war interrogations; the industrial areas had been scarcely damaged in comparison with the rest of the city and among the major industrial plants in Dresden, only the Zeiss-Ikon optical works in Dresden-Striesen was seriously damaged; the works, in the area bounded by Schandauer-strasse, Kipsdorfer-strasse, and Glashütter-strasse, was just under three miles east of the city centre, and on the fringe of the area of total devastation; it is believed that they were not able to resume production before May 1945.

The two Sachsenwerk plants manufacturing electronic components in Dresden-Niedersedlitz (five miles south-east of the city centre) and Radeberg (nine miles to the north-east) were not hit by explosive bombs; the Niedersedlitz plant was hit by a few stray incendiaries which were effectively tackled by the works fire-watchers, and suffered otherwise only glass damage. On the morning after the triple blow, few of the staff of this plant reported for work, and there was at first no electric power or gas supply; the employees of the Sachsenwerk plants however suffered surprisingly few casualties: although all records relating to the plant were destroyed before the end of the war, senior staff have reported that certainly fewer than three hundred of the five thousand employees failed to arrive for work within a week and were assumed to have been killed; of the

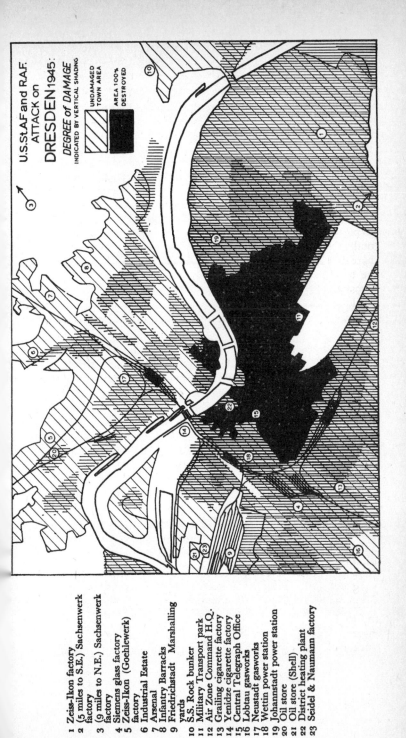

U.S. St.A.F. and R.A.F.
ATTACK on
DRESDEN 1945:

DEGREE of DAMAGE
INDICATED BY VERTICAL SHADING

UNDAMAGED
TOWN AREA

AREA 100%
DESTROYED

1 Zeiss-Ikon factory
2 (5 miles to S.E.) Sachsenwerk
   factory
3 (9 miles to N.E.) Sachsenwerk
   factory
4 Siemens glass factory
5 Zeiss-Ikon (Goehlewerk)
   factory
6 Industrial Estate
7 Arsenal
8 Infantry Barracks
9 Friedrichstadt Marshalling
   yards
10 S.S. Rock bunker
11 Military Transport park
12 Air Zone Command H.Q.
13 Grailing cigarette factory
14 Yenidze cigarette factory
15 Central Telegraph Office
16 Löbtau gasworks
17 Neustadt gasworks
18 Wettin power station
19 Johannstadt power station
20 Oil store
21 Oil store (Shell)
22 District heating plant
23 Seidel & Naumann factory

eighty employees in the machine tool department, for example, all without exception reported for work within that time.

The explanation of this apparently remarkable resilience is in fact simple: on the one hand, few of the Niedersedlitz plant's workers lived in the town area, the majority having been recruited from over eighty surrounding villages; on the other hand, the areas of total devastation in Dresden embraced the middle-class suburbs, but left the working-class areas of Neustadt, Striesen, Löbtau, Friedrichstadt, Mickten and Pieschen more or less undamaged.

Similarly, the Zeiss-Ikon Goehlewerk fuse-factory in Grossenhainer-strasse, Dresden-Neustadt, probably the only factory built in Dresden with the possibility of an air-raid in mind, was undamaged, as was the Industrial Estate on the site of the former Arsenal in Dresden-Neustadt; all of these plants and factories suffered of course from the immediate indirect effects of an air-raid: loss of power supplies, demoralisation and depletion of labour forces, and shortage of transport. But in no case except that of the Striesen Zeiss-Ikon works was the physical damage to plant overwhelming.

Less than two weeks after the delivery of the triple blow, police authorities in Dresden decided on a measure more dreadful in its ruthlessness than any that had been employed at any other stage of the Allied area offensive. The victims which were still being recovered in hundreds and thousands each week from the Inner City's ruined streets and cellars would not be transported to the mass burial-ground in the pine and eucalyptus forests north of Dresden any longer. The dangers of epidemics and the spread of typhus by these long wagon-caravans of decaying bodies were too great. The whole of the centre of the city around the Altmarkt had already been cordoned off. Relatives who stumbled across the still-impassable streets into the Inner City were waved away by police and Party officials. The Dresden National Socialist newspaper *Freiheitskampf*, reporting the summary execution of a group of German civilians found looting a ruined building, warned that the Inner City was out of bounds to civilians without passes:

> The Police President of Dresden, as District A.R.P. Director, decrees: 'Especial circumstances constrain me to point out that entering areas outside the paths already re-opened to the public is strictly forbidden. People encountered elsewhere, who cannot satisfactorily explain their purpose and prove their identity, will be regarded as looters and treated accordingly, even if nothing suspicious is found on their persons.'

Army, police and *Volkssturm* patrols had been issued with these instructions: people who wished to go digging for their own property were earnestly enjoined to report first to the appropriate police station for a guide.

The peasants' wagon-loads of corpses, each hauled by two horses, were now driven to the frontiers of this cordoned-off area by S.H.D. and forced labourers, and there handed over to *Wehrmacht* drivers and officers. The wagons were driven into the centre of the Altmarkt, and there their loads were tipped onto the cobbled paving of the square. Scores of police officials were at work here, making last efforts to identify the people; they had been sworn to secrecy about what was happening. The unbent girders of the Renner department store had been winched out of the ruins of the building and were now laid across crudely collected piles of sandstone blocks. A series of massive 25-foot-long grills had been erected. Under these steel girders and bars were poked bundles of wood and straw. On top of the grills were heaped the corpses of four or five hundred victims, with layers of straw between each load. The soldiers, many of them Ukrainian Vlassov troops, trampled up and down on top of the decaying heaps, straightening the victims, trying to make room for more, and carefully building the stacks. Many of the dead children sandwiched into these terrible pyres were still wearing shreds of the colourful Carnival clothes they had donned on Shrove Tuesday, two weeks before.

A senior officer cleared the square of all unnecessary soldiers, and set a match to the fire-wood heap under the grills. Within five minutes the pyres were burning fiercely. 'The thin and elderly victims took longer to catch fire than the fat or young ones,' related an eye-witness. In the late hours of the evening, after the last of the bodies had been completely incinerated, the soldiers were called back to shovel the ashes into the still-waiting horse-drawn carts; with a fitting touch of reverence the Party officials saw to it that the ashes were collected and taken to the cemeteries to be buried too. It took several small carts and ten large lorries with trailers to carry the ashes to the Heide-friedhof cemetery. Here the ashes of 9,000 of the victims who had thus been openly cremated were buried in a pit 25 feet long and 16 feet wide. In spite of their attempts to keep secret the fate of the victims who had been swallowed up in the ruined emptiness of the Inner City, the story did emerge. Some citizens risking their lives made their way to the Altmarkt to check the truth behind the rumour. On 25th February one man even succeeded in taking a score of photographs, many of them in colour, of the terrible scene; he was not as lucky as many others and was arrested almost at once by police officials; instead of executing him on the spot, as they had threatened, however, they took him instead before the S.S.-*Brigadeführer* who was in charge of the Police Praesidium, newly transferred to the S.S.-Bunker blasted into the rock face at the Mordgrundbrücke. The *Brigadeführer* ordered the photographer's release and thus the pictures of what might otherwise have been a hardly credible scene have survived to this day.

In Dresden, history was repeating itself in a cruel and grimly ironic way: the Dresden City Chronicle of 1349 recorded how in that year the Margrave of Meissen, Frederick II, had burnt his enemies at the stake in Dresden in 1349. Then it was the Jews, accused of having introduced the plague to Dresden; then, too, the burning was in the Altmarkt square; and, by a cruel coincidence, then too the blow had fallen on Shrove Tuesday Carnival day.

In fact this was not the first time that the suggestion had been mooted that air-raid victims should be secretly burned in open squares to speed the clearance work. The Hamburg Police President's report on the fire-storm also describes how:

> To prevent epidemics and for reasons of morale it was decided to burn the bodies at the spot where they had been found in the fire-storm area. But after deliberation it was established that there was no danger of epidemic, so burial was resumed in common graves.

     •   •   •   •   •

Attacks on Berlin, on the Ruhr cities and other industrial centres the German leaders were prepared to accept as necessary and inevitable. But the 'barbarians' who had mounted the attacks on Dresden with such fearful consequences encouraged some of the most powerful invective of the Party leaders.

> It is the work of lunatics [Dr. Goebbels, the Reich Propaganda Minister, is reported to have said]. It is the work of one particular lunatic who recognises that he lacks the ability to build mighty temples and so is determined to show the world that at least he is an expert in their destruction.

Dr. Goebbels had even gone so far as to suggest that as a reprisal for Dresden, the German Air Force should now employ poison gas in attacks on British cities. The Germans had at that stage developed a gas which could penetrate standard British gas-masks. The Propaganda Minister appears, however, to have been overruled.

However, just as, quite early on, the Allies had learned the value of propaganda campaigns based on the indiscriminate Luftwaffe raids, so Dr. Goebbels too was now beginning to realise the positive value of the Allied area offensive. When Coventry had been bombed, the newspapers were permitted to give great prominence to stories of the massacre in the centre of the city; in the same year great publicity had been accorded to the statement of the Dutch Government-in-exile that in the May 1940 attack on Rotterdam '30,000 civilians had been brutally killed'. In fact post-war inquiries in Rotterdam show the true figure to have been rather less than 1,000. Nevertheless, the British and American public, in ignorance of the real scale of casualties caused by enemy attacks, were rightly incensed at this apparent brutality and were not really satisfied until R.A.F. Bomber Command and the U.S. Eighth Air Force were delivering attacks on the scale of those described earlier in this book; thus the propaganda campaign was able to channel public sympathy into an offensive which analysed now, '*sine ira et studio*', as Dr. Goebbels had once put it, most citizens would be quick to disown.

Now, if a trifle belatedly, in the weeks after the American and British destruction of Dresden, Dr. Goebbels was also discovering the use to which bombing propaganda could be put. At the beginning of the fourth week in March he set in motion a cleverly designed campaign of whispers calculated to galvanize the German people into a last horrified stand against their invaders. For this purpose he appears deliberately to have started a rumour about the death-roll in Dresden, wildly exceeding any figure within the realms of possibility.

On 23rd March a 'top secret Order of the Day' was leaked to certain Berlin officials who could be relied on not to keep their tongues still:

In order to counter the wild rumours circulating at present, this short extract from the final report of the Dresden Police President on the Allied raids on Dresden of 13th to 15th February, 1945, is reproduced: 'Up to the evening of 20th March, 1945, altogether 202,040 bodies, primarily women and children, were recovered. It is expected that the final death-roll will exceed 250,000. Of the dead, only some thirty per cent could be identified. As the removal of the corpses could not be undertaken quickly enough, 68,650 of the bodies were incinerated; as the rumours far exceed reality, these figures can be used publicly.'

It was characteristic of the highly advanced National Socialist propaganda experts that they did not try to spread this figure through public press announcements, but by means of this apparently indignant denial of an exaggerated rumour. All responsible authorities place the Dresden death-roll considerably below this figure. Neither the Dresden Police President nor his Report on the air raids survived the end of the war, the President dying by his own hand, and the report never having been referred to outside this spurious 'Order of the Day'.

.   .   .   .   .

On 6th May Hanns Voigt of the *Abteilung Tote* was summoned to the Criminal Police H.Q. in the Ministry of the Interior and instructed to take command of the stores of valuables and wedding rings; the high-ranking National Socialists in the city were apparently covering their traces and heading westwards, but were keen nevertheless to ensure that the valuables did not fall into enemy hands. Seven or eight large buckets of wedding rings, mostly gold, had been collected from all over the city. He himself declined to accept responsibility for so many valuables, worth over a million pounds. Thus they were still waiting on the right bank of the river when the Russians arrived in the city two days later, on 8th May. It was the last day of the war: it could indeed be said that the destruction of the Saxon capital had not speeded its fall by one day.

Red Army officials moved into the Ministry buildings, and the complete collection of valuables, including the wedding rings, fell into their hands; removed, too, was the priceless collection of paintings, including the Sistine Madonna, which had survived the last months of the war in a railway tunnel; for eleven years the paintings were to stay in Moscow, before their return to the East German Government in 1956.

The 300 clerks and more working in the V.N.Z. organisation's seven offices throughout Dresden were evicted from their offices, and all identification work ceased. Director Voigt was instructed to remove the records to new quarters in Dresden-Leuben Town Hall. He was allowed to keep three clerks in the Dresden-Leuben office to work under him on the existing filing card systems: inevitably all attempts to continue registering new victims ceased, and the work of the office devolved upon further processing of the 80,000 to 90,000 index cards collected for known and unknown victims during the months after the triple blow.

The Red Army had taken over the former offices of the *Abteilung Tote* in Neuberin-strasse, as another V.N.Z. official reported, and had turned loose a score of pigs in the shed housing the clothing cards which were the last hope for identifying some eleven thousand more victims; a few days later the cards were burnt because of their offensive smell.

Communication with the seven separate districts was severed. During an interview with the V.N.Z. Director, the Soviet occupation authorities, true to their insistence that the Allied air forces were not an effective weapon of war, refused to accept the estimate of 135,000 dead reached by the V.N.Z. *Abteilung Tote* Director and, according to Voigt, 'calmly struck off the first digit'.

By chance, as was described in an earlier section, the last officially organised refugee trains from the provinces to the east of Dresden had been unloaded only on the day before the first of the three Allied air attacks: the first of the refugee trains planned to run to the west was not to leave until some days later. For this reason, just on the night of the triple blow, the city's population was the biggest it had ever been, and would ever be again. This factor, coupled with the most violent fire-storm in history, resulted inevitably in a death-roll bigger than that for Hamburg.

As in Hamburg, the Dresden fire-storm had embraced the most densely populated area of the city; of the 28,410 homes in the city centre (Dresden IV, including districts 1, 2, 5 and 6) the November 1945 survey showed 24,866 homes totally destroyed; a Dresden inhabitant returning to the city after the raids was informed at the V.N.Z. office that of 864 inhabitants in Seidnitzer-strasse registered with the police on the night of the attack only eight were known to have survived; at No. 22 Seidnitzer-strasse, his former home, he was told that of twenty-eight inhabitants, only one had survived; of No. 24, next-door, he was informed that all forty-two inhabitants had been killed. This one example is more than sufficient to show the crushing effectiveness of the triple blow on Dresden.

It is known that in Hamburg, in the heart of the fire-storm area, about one-third of all the population had been killed. In the district of Hammerbrook the proportion of fatalities during the fire-storm had been as high as 361·5 per thousand inhabitants. If a death-roll on this scale could have been possible in a city like Hamburg, where the most elaborate air-raid precautions had been taken, it seems not unreasonable to assume at least the same proportion and very probably a higher proportion of fatalities during the triple blow on Dresden, where an inexperienced populace was completely un- provided with public air-raid shelters or *Hochbunker*, where the fire-brigades were powerless to help, where the non-existent defences enabled a concentration of bombing far superior in time and in space to that in the Battle of Hamburg, and where, above all, the triple blow did not take a week of anxious, alert days and nights as in Hamburg, but suddenly descended on the city and was all over within fourteen hours.

In Hamburg those who were most likely to lose their nerve, those who by getting in the way of the fire-fighters or panicking might have themselves increased the death-roll, had long been evacuated; but Dresden, far from being evacuated, was at the time overflowing with evacuees from other German cities.

Immediately after the raids there was the usual tendency wildly to exaggerate the number of casualties. In Berlin official sources at that time were putting the figure between 180,000 and 220,000: it is known that even leading officers in the Propaganda Ministry had been told that the figure was between two and three hundred thousand. A few days later, however, the figure was more moderately estimated by the authority responsible for relief measures in blitzed cities as 'between 120,000 and 150,000 people lost'. This figure, given only very shortly after the raids, is close to the conservative estimate of the death-roll provided by Hanns Voigt of the *Abteilung Tote*; with a large degree of certainty one can take Voigt's figure of 135,000 as the best estimate within the limits set by the Berlin authority's figure. Even the fire attack on Tokyo on the night of 9th–10th March, delivered by the Superfortresses of the United States 21st Bombardment Command, did not exceed the Dresden death-roll, although in Tokyo a conventional bombing attack again produced a death-roll in excess of that at Hiroshima— 83,793 people killed according to Tokyo's official reports, compared with 71,379 at Hiroshima. Tokyo was not, of course, as poorly defended as Dresden, and neither town had Dresden's refugee population on the night of their destruction.

PART FIVE

NEITHER PRAISE NOR BLAME

CHAPTER I

THE REACTION OF THE WORLD

S OON before 9.00 a.m. on 14th February, even as the new formations of Flying Fortresses were already heading out to Dresden,
the first full length bulletin announcing the execution of the
R.A.F. attacks of the preceding night was released by the Air
Ministry.

In a statement describing the target city in unusual detail, the
Air Ministry stressed the vital importance of Dresden to the enemy:
as the centre of a railway network and as a great industrial town it
had become of the greatest value for controlling the German
defences against Marshal Koniev's armies. The telephone services
and the means of communication were almost as essential to the
German Army as the railways and roads which met in Dresden;
Dresden's buildings had been desperately needed for troops and
administrative offices evacuated from other towns, the bulletin
added. With rather less accuracy, the statement pointed out that
'among other war factories, Dresden had large munitions workshops
in the old Arsenal, and a great number of light engineering works
engaged in war production of all kinds'. There were important
factories making electric motors, precision and optical instruments,
and chemicals; the city was comparable in size with Manchester.
In issuing this bulletin the Air Ministry was giving an assessment
of the strategic importance of the city, and of its industrial installations, for which Bomber Command's Intelligence staff had found no
support in the days preceding the attacks; R.A.F. Bomber Command was more modest in its claims for the city which it had so
successfully attacked: in its secret *Weekly Digest* No. 148, which was
not intended to have the same wide circulation as the Air Ministry
bulletins, the Command was satisfied with citing Dresden as a city
which had developed into a target of first class importance, and of
high priority as a communications centre and control point in the
defence of the Eastern frontier of Germany.

In the 6.00 p.m. news bulletin the first news was released to the public about the Dresden raids by the British Broadcasting Corporation. The raid was described as one of the more powerful blows promised by the Allied leaders at Yalta.

> Our pilots report that as there was little flak they were able to make careful and straight runs over the targets without bothering much about the defences; a terrific concentration of fires was started in the centre of the city.

Perhaps significantly, the open admission in this first news bulletin that East German raids had been promised to the Russians was omitted from the main 9.00 p.m. news bulletin; the raid on Dresden, which was referred to as 'a great industrial city' comparable with Sheffield, was now termed an example of the 'further close co-operation between the Allies'. When the full extent of the Dresden tragedy became widely known throughout the world, and especially after the Prime Minister had penned his apparent reproach to the Allied Bomber Commands for the triple blow, as we shall see, both the temptation and the tendency were to imply that the Russians had requested the raid. The communist regimes did not in the post-war period miss the opportunity of generating anti-Western propaganda in East Germany and Central Germany from the Dresden tragedy and it became an annual event, every 13th February, for church bells to be rung throughout these countries from 10.10 p.m. until 10.30 p.m.—the duration of R.A.F. Bomber Command's first attack on Dresden; to the embarrassment of the Western Allies, this custom even spread to West Germany, and it was in an attempt to kill this campaign that the American State Department announced on 11th February 1953, to forestall further demonstrations, that the 'destructive war-time bombing of Dresden was done in response to Soviet requests for increased aerial support, and was cleared in advance with the Soviet authorities'. While, as we have seen earlier, this announcement did not fundamentally contradict the facts, the hope was plain that either in time or in translation this statement would be quoted as proof of a Russian demand for an attack on Dresden, and not just acquiescence; if this was indeed the hope, the Americans were not disappointed, for by February 1955, the tenth anniversary of the raids, even responsible newspapers like the *Manchester Guardian* were readily recalling the bombing of Dresden which had been 'carried out by British and American planes as a result of the Soviet request to attack this important communications centre'.

· · · · ·

In Germany itself, the first published report on the Dresden affair appeared on 15th February 1945 in the German High Command communiqué which reported tersely:

> *14th February, 1945.* Last night the British directed their terror-raids at Dresden.

In the German national newspapers there was no further direct mention of the raids or their consequences until after the beginning of March. German foreign language broadcasts were not so reticent, however, and a shrill storm of propaganda invective against Britain and America was unleashed into the ether.

The B.B.C. Monitoring Service had published throughout the war a daily Confidential Report on both Allied and Axis broadcasts, amounting to some seventy or eighty duplicated pages a day; on 15th February, the main Monitoring Digest prefacing the Report was unusual in that it surveyed one topic only, the reaction not only of Germany but also of the neutral and Allied countries to the first news of the Dresden raids; from all the German-controlled stations, it was apparent at once that Dr. Goebbels' Ministry was pulling out all the stops of its propaganda organ, using every means of exploiting the Dresden tragedy to the full.

At 3.00 p.m. that day B.B.C. monitors picked up a transmission in an Arabic tongue from a station calling itself *Free Africa*, which was obviously a clandestine German station:

> It was reported from London that the number of refugees in Dresden had increased enormously; at the same time the British news service reported that Allied aircraft had launched the biggest attack in history on Dresden. Such reports need no comment; it is obvious that these heavy raids were directed against the millions of refugees, and not against military targets.

This served to provide a very clear picture of 'so-called Allied humanity', the broadcaster suggested, 'but patience; tomorrow is not far away!' At 3.57 p.m. the official German foreign information telegraph service commented bitterly on the B.B.C.'s description of Dresden as a major communications centre:

> Dresden's factories mainly manufactured toothpaste and baby-powder [the foreign information service insisted]. Nevertheless, they were bombed. As in all large towns the Dresden goods stations lie on the outskirts of the town; only the passenger station is in the centre. But troops and war materials are not transported from passenger stations, only from goods stations.

The attack on the centre of Dresden could therefore not be justified from a military point of view.

> The Americans [the cable continued] who claim to possess the best bombsights in the world, have elsewhere proved that they can hit precise targets whenever they please. It would therefore have been possible to have spared the residential districts of Dresden, and the historic town centre. The use of incendiaries proves that the architectural treasures and residential districts were being deliberately attacked. It is pointless to drop incendiaries on railway installations; they have never been used to destroy railway installations in this war.

With a touch of telling sarcasm, the bulletin concluded that the Allies were claiming to stand on the threshold of victory, yet they had found it necessary to reduce Dresden and Chemnitz to ashes. The inclusion of Chemnitz was a characteristic tactic of German propagandists: although, as was described above, the Chemnitz attack was largely a failure, Dr. Goebbels as Propaganda Minister had long recognised that if the enemy heard from the Germans' own broadcasts that a target was destroyed, there would not be the same pressure to deliver a second attack; Chemnitz, with its big tank-engine works, was a target which needed a long respite.

The neutral countries were equally horrified at the stories reaching them from their own correspondents inside Germany; some made attempts to see that the German people, too, were not kept uninformed about events in Central Germany and also to inform the occupied territories. At 10.15 p.m. on 15th February a Swedish news bulletin transmitted to Occupied Denmark, in Danish, proclaimed that between 20,000 and 35,000 people were already known to have lost their lives: 'Yesterday morning 6,000 victims were dug out.' Fifteen minutes later the *New British Broadcasting Station*, like *Free Africa* a German-controlled station, beamed to England a curious piece of propaganda about the raids, which, again, the B.B.C. Monitoring Service considered it necessary to report in its entirety to the British Government:

> The night before last I was sitting with a colleague who understands a bit of German, and we were listening to a special radio programme in Germany which is supposed to let the German population know which part of the *Reich* our bombers are attacking [the bogus Englishman began]. The Jerry who was speaking kept on breaking into the music with his guttural *Achtung, Achtung!* Then my friend would translate what he was saying. I must say it felt damned queer sitting there and hearing about the way our waves of bombers were going in to

unload their cargoes of death and destruction on Dresden. One minute I found myself thinking: Well, against air war like this, the Jerry won't be able to carry on for long. But then the very next moment I found myself thinking: Who the devil is going to get anything out of it? We contribute the bombs and the machines and the crews who don't return from these raids. The Dresdeners themselves don't get anything out of it, naturally. The only ones who look like getting anything are the Russians—they get Dresden at our expense.

I wasn't unduly worried about human considerations [the voice concluded, broadly]. After all, we must win the war. But I don't see any reason why we should go and kill people for the benefit of the Russians alone. Do you?

Next day, the German-controlled Scandinavian Telegraph Bureau reported that Dresden was now 'one great field of ruins', and added that all communications between Dresden and the rest of Germany had been broken; the number of the dead was reported to be 70,000. Now even the Moscow newspapers were reporting the raids.

.   .   *   .   .

Unwilling to incur further censure of world opinion, already deeply moved by accounts flooding the world's telegraph wires of the fate of the Eastern population centres, the American bomber commander had prudently dispatched his aircraft on Thursday 15th February to attack oil targets at Ruhland and Magdeburg as primary targets; 1,100 Eighth Bomber Command bombers undertook to 'bring the oil offensive up to date'. Fate was once again unkind to Dresden and Chemnitz; visibility over the primary targets was poor, and the bombers were diverted to attack secondary targets—the only primary target still clear for attack being the Brabag oil refinery at Rothensee near Magdeburg. Some 210 Fortresses were, however, diverted from Ruhland to Dresden where at about 12.30 p.m. a further 461 tons of bombs were dropped, on instruments, on the city area. Other Bombardment Groups, notably those of the 1st Air Division, had been briefed for missions with Dresden as a secondary target for attack, but their whole operations were scrubbed before take-off. The bombs which were dropped on the Dresden area were not particularly noticed by the populace and must have seemed paltry after what the city had already suffered. The 3rd Air Division, it might be observed, was briefed to attack Kottbus 'city', a detail which has since gone down in the American official history as Kottbus 'marshalling yards'; a thousand tons of bombs were dropped. The attack was reported,

significantly, as being 'in full view of the advancing Red Army'. To
critics in England who might be tempted to reiterate the observation
that these raids were serving only the Russians, the answer was
officially given thus:

> The Eastern and Western Fronts are now sufficiently close for blows
> aimed at German cities between them to have an effect on both fronts
> simultaneously, and the targets were selected for that purpose.

The allied air commanders at Supreme Headquarters in France
must have realised that world opinion was being slowly but certainly
impressed by the flood of German invective unleashed by the
massacres in Berlin and now Dresden; yet it was just at this time,
on the afternoon of 16th February, when the German propaganda
campaign was noisily approaching its climax, that the air commanders entrusted an R.A.F. Air Commodore seconded to S.H.A.E.F.
as A.C.S.2 (Intelligence) officer, to address a press conference.

> On air activities generally, with particular reference to those of the
> enemy. This is all an Intelligence Officer is qualified to do. I had no
> brief whatsoever to discuss the policy on which our bomber operations
> were based. Such policy was decided upon by the British and U.S.
> Air Staffs in London and Washington after approval at Government
> level, and would not be passed on to Intelligence staffs at my level,
> and in the post I held, unless it became necessary to the execution of
> my work.

According to the American Official History, the new Allied plan
that he outlined was to 'bomb large population centres and then
to attempt to prevent relief supplies from reaching and refugees from
leaving them—all part of a general programme to bring about the
collapse of the German economy'.

In the course of a reply to a question put to him by one correspondent, the Air Commodore recalls having apparently referred to
German allegations of 'terror-raids'—he was currently engaged in
Intelligence on German operations—and, once spoken, the word
remained in the mind of the correspondent of the Associated Press.
Within an hour, the A.P. correspondent's dispatch was being put
out from Paris Radio and being cabled to America for inclusion in
the next morning's newspapers:

> Allied air chiefs have made the long-awaited decision to adopt
> deliberate terror-bombings of German population centres as a ruthless
> expedient of hastening Hitler's doom. More raids such as those recently

carried out by heavy bombers of the Allied air forces on residential sections of Berlin, Dresden, Chemnitz and Kottbus are in store for the Germans, for the avowed purpose of heaping more confusion on Nazi road and rail traffic, and to sap German morale. The all-out air war on Germany became obvious with the unprecedented daylight assault on the refugee-crowded capital, with civilians fleeing from the Red tide in the East.

Thus, for one extraordinary moment, what might be termed the 'mask' of the Allied bomber commands appeared to have slipped. The dispatch—which was of course a highly tendentious version of the Air Commodore's more moderate wording—was broadcast throughout liberated France and printed across America as front-page news: not only R.A.F. Bomber Command—whose own air offensive had long been viewed with suspicion in the United States—but also their own U.S. Strategic Air Forces were now delivering terror-raids on German civilians. At the time that the news broke in America, many people had only just finished listening incredulously to a radio message beamed across the Atlantic by German transmitters in which the big Berlin raid of 3rd February by the American bombers was condemned:

> General Spaatz knew that it was taxing the ingenuity of German organisation to cope with the feeding and housing of non-combatant refugees, of whom hundreds of thousands have fled before the organised savagery and terrorism of the communist Red Army invading East Germany. General Spaatz also knew that the available German air forces were concentrated on the Eastern front to combat the Red flood which threatens to destroy Germany and all Europe. These are acts of exceptional cowardice.

It was announced, as a parting shot, that the *Wehrmacht* had awarded General Spaatz the Order of the White Feather for his part in this crime.

Now the vicious propaganda from Berlin was apparently being confirmed officially by an official S.H.A.E.F. announcement; British listeners were fortunately spared this dilemma: the British government, which received news of the S.H.A.E.F. press conference at 7.30 p.m. on the evening of 17th February, imposed a total press veto on publication of the dispatch soon after.

The news was brought to General Dwight D. Eisenhower and General Henry H. Arnold—both were gravely disturbed, not only that the story had received such wide coverage, but also that an American air offensive which was, as they thought, directed only against precision military objectives, was being so manifestly misrepresented. General Arnold cabled Spaatz to check whether in fact there was any significant distinction between blind bombing by radar on military targets in urban areas, and 'terror' bombing, such as the S.H.A.E.F. communiqué—as reported by Associated Press—claimed the Americans were now indulging in. General Carl Spaatz replied, perhaps a shade cryptically, that he had not departed from the historical American policy in Europe—not even in the cases of the 3rd February Berlin raid or the 14th February Dresden raid. This discussion and its subsequent explanation satisfied General Arnold and the controversy was allowed to subside.

General Carl Spaatz had clearly eluded the onus of the responsibility for the Dresden raids and their consequences, but only just in time; his reassurance that the U.S.St.A.F. was attacking only military objectives, as always, pacified both Arnold and Eisenhower.

.   .   .   .   .

The German government, however, aware, in a way that neither the outside world nor indeed the German public could be, of what had really occurred in the Saxon capital, had no intention of relinquishing such a meaty propaganda detail. The very manner in which the report had been issued by S.H.A.E.F. and then—as it was later—hastily stopped, the way in which the British government alone had clamped a total ban on its publication, suggested that there was more to the Associated Press dispatch, which had by now reached Berlin through Sweden, than was superficially evident.

While, up to that point, many Germans had dutifully described Allied raids on German cities, in the standard National Socialist jargon, as 'terror' raids, now there were many who could believe that perhaps that was what they really were. Clearly, if the British government refused to tell the British people what was being done in their name by R.A.F. Bomber Command, then the German government must take the necessary steps to ensure that the truth was not withheld from them. William Joyce, the broadcaster of anti-British propaganda for the German government, was instructed to include in his next 'Views on the News' broadcast to England a speech on Dresden; again the B.B.C. Monitoring Service considered it necessary to report the speech in full to the government.

At 10.30 p.m. on 18th February, the familiar and hateful voice of 'Germany calling' began the task of informing the British people of the Dresden terror-raids; the Germans, alas, could hardly have chosen a less credible broadcaster if they had wanted to influence British public opinion:

> British propagandists are boasting that by attacking such cities as Dresden, the R.A.F. and U.S. air forces are co-operating with the Soviets. They do not remember any occasion on which the Soviet High Command has troubled itself to co-operate with British efforts. Incidentally, Eisenhower's Headquarters have now issued a stupid and impudent denial of the obvious truth that the bombing of German towns has a terrorist motive. Churchill's spokesmen, both in the press and on the radio, have actually gloried in the air attacks on Berlin and Dresden, on the refugees from the East. Various British journalists have written as if the murdering of German refugees were a first-class military achievement. I shall always remember how, alluding to the attack on Dresden, one B.B.C. announcer happily prattled: There is no china in Dresden today. That was, perhaps, meant to be a joke; but in what sort of taste? Far be it from me to strike a sentimental note amidst the grim and dark realities of this phase in a gigantic struggle, which is destined to decide more than the fate of porcelain. . . .

Joyce concluded his broadcast by enumerating the architectural treasures destroyed in Dresden, and also describing the fate of the refugees.

Faced with this massive propaganda barrage from every enemy-controlled radio station in Europe, the only recorded Allied counter-blast was a French contribution through their German-language broadcast from *Radio Bir Hakeim*; broadcasting to Germany it announced that during the air-raid on Dresden, fire-fighting crews had been hastily organised, consisting of Hitler-Youth members and aged men:

> Instead of the fire-fighting implements which they expected and desired, they were given rifles, taken to the station and forced to leave for the front without saying good-bye to their parents.

Quite apart from the painfully obvious detail that the Dresden Station, as well as all lines to the front, were supposed to have been totally destroyed, many people will agree that there were times when the German propaganda broadcasts had a definite edge on those from France and other Allied countries.

The second S.H.A.E.F. communiqué, in which the first report was officially taken back, was issued on Saturday, 17th February. Unfortunately, the briefing officer on this occasion, not the same

Air Commodore as before, described the killing of refugees as being accidental: the bombing of German targets was pursuing the sole aim of destroying towns as transportation or oil centres; the attack on Berlin had been made to destroy communications through the capital; the raid on Dresden had had the same object. It was a pure accident that at the time of the raids Dresden was crowded with refugees. The German reaction was swift and bitter:

> Ever since Air Chief Marshal Harris, the British bomber chief, stated that the main object of the raids was to break the morale of the German civilians, ever since the British Prime Minister painted a grim picture of a Germany where starvation and pestilence would rot out Britain's enemies in the same way as air raids [the German telegraph service commented bitterly on 19th February], there has been no doubt that the S.H.A.E.F. war criminals have cold-bloodedly ordered the extermination of the innocent German public by terror-raids from the air.

As the propaganda campaign against the British and the Americans gathered momentum, as the Swedish, Swiss and other neutral countries began to print horrifying descriptions for the world to read about what the Allies had done to Dresden, the German information service, with its constantly reiterated claim that R.A.F. Bomber Command was delivering pure terror-raids on German civilians, was gaining its most surprising convert in the British government, which indeed had most reason to know the truth about the Bomber Command assault on Dresden.

CHAPTER II

A SERIOUS QUERY

IN spite of the anxiety of the American Secretary for War about public opinion on the Dresden tragedy, a further American daylight attack was launched on 2nd March 1945 by the U.S.St.A.F.'s 3rd Air Division. Over 1,200 bombers, escorted by all fifteen Fighter Groups, took off soon after 6.30 a.m. to attack oil refineries at Magdeburg, Ruhland and Böhlen, and a tank plant at Magdeburg. Once again as the result of weather unfavourable for precise attacks, the marshalling yards at Dresden and Chemnitz were reported as having been attacked as secondary targets. In Dresden the attack was noted as lasting from 10.26 until 11.04 a.m., the bombers flying over the city in five waves, and apparently attacking as many different targets; local observers of the raid suggested that the attack had been intended to destroy the Dresden-to-Pirna railway line, but that the smoke-rocket markers fired by the path-finder aircraft had been displaced by the wind.

The presence of all fifteen fighter groups in this operation was an indication of the extent to which the dreaded German Me. 262 jets were staging a last stand: the Germans had scrambled three large formations of fighters and directed them to Berlin, wrongly expecting an attack on the Reich capital. Finally some 75 of them headed for Dresden and the nearby Ruhland area, where the 3rd Air Division Fortresses were pounced on. At 10.17, with Dresden city still nine minutes' flying time away, the first formations of jets attacked the leading wing of bombers, while slower piston-engined fighters attacked the rear Groups, decoying the escorting American fighters from the front; the 35 jets attacking the head of the formation peeled off and attacked in wings of three jets each, closing in from all positions and levels. By 10.35, when the jets withdrew through lack of fuel, six of the leading Bombardment Group's aircraft had been destroyed. The remaining 406 bombers were recorded as having attacked the 'marshalling yards in Dresden' in the Eighth Air Force Target Summary.

The reports of the individual Bombardment Groups suggest,

however, that as before the marshalling yards were just a euphemism for the city area; thus the 34th Bombardment Group, a radar pathfinder force, which was heavily assailed by the jets, being in the leading wing, found its mean point of impact—M.P.I.—in the 'centre of the city', and the lead bombardier noted that the briefed purpose for the attack (according to his private log) was 'the complete destruction of the town'. Similarly, target photographs taken by the 447th Bombardment Group, while on the one hand displaying a target city less than three-tenths cloud-covered, on the other hand show the carpet of bombs from the Group, on this occasion comprised of two hundred and eighty-eight 500-pound general-purpose explosive bombs and a hundred and forty-four 500-pound incendiary bombs, detonating in the township of Dresden-Übigau, two miles from the nearest railway yards, and the site of a large British prisoner-of-war camp; a large contingent from the camp volunteered to assist in rescue work in the burning houses.

Other Bombardment Groups were equally wide in their aim, if they were indeed aiming for the Dresden-Friedrichstadt marshalling yards. All the patterns of bombs were reported falling in areas widely separated from the yards. The 390th Bombardment Group report of Mission 266 explained that the crews were diverted from their oil assignment to attack the great Dresden yard which had not been bombed severely; the 100th Bombardment Group reported attacking the Dresden 'factory area' as a secondary target, after the failure of an attempt to bomb the Ruhland refinery, with 'good results'.

The damage was widespread across the town, the only noteworthy success being the sinking of the steamer *Leipzig*, which had been adapted as a hospital ship to meet the needs of the thousands of people injured in the Dresden raids of two weeks before; the stick of bombs straddled the steamer, blowing off the stern; the steamer sank slowly, on fire, with few survivors. In another incident a stick of bombs destroyed the camp of Russian labourers in Laubegast.

.   .   .   .   .

The Germans were still exploiting the Dresden raids to the full, though the figure they were publicising for the death-roll was still deliberately under-estimated; although a figure current in closed Berlin circles even only a few days after the raid put the deathroll at over 300,000; although the Berlin authority responsible for welfare in blitzed cities had prepared for a deathroll of 120,000 to 150,000 in Dresden; and although the numbers bulldozed into mass graves in

Dresden had already exceeded some thirty thousand, as late as March 1945 a German propaganda leaflet dropped on Italy still spoke only of 'ten thousand refugee children' who had been killed; on the one side it reproduced a dreadful photograph of two burned and maimed children from the ruins of Dresden—a photograph which one involuntarily compares with the even more terrible photographs later released of the victims of the *Reich* found in German extermination camps—on the other side it awarded the Order of the White Feather to General Doolittle:

> The people of Dresden, including the prisoners of war and the foreign workers, hereby award the Order of the White Feather and the Symbol of the Yellow Heart to Lieutenant-General James Doolittle of the United States Air Force for conspicuous cowardice—and for having turned a sadist.

On 6th March the German propaganda campaign achieved in London a success it could hardly have hoped for before: the occasion was the first full-scale debate on the air offensive since February 1944 when the Bishop of Chichester had raised the whole issue of area bombing of civilian targets in Europe.

This time, when Mr. Richard Stokes took the floor at 2.43 p.m., he had the advantage of a British public more sympathetic towards the question than previously. Although Dr. Bell, the Bishop of Chichester, is known to have received hundreds of letters supporting his stand in the House of Lords, at the time of his speech, in February 1944, he had been debating at the height of the Baby Blitz, and London opinion had been against him.

Now in March 1945, with the end of the war heaving into sight, and with only the V.2 threat hanging over it, the public was more vulnerable to the horrific descriptions of the consequences of these raids now being retailed in the British daily newspapers by correspondents in Geneva and Stockholm. As Mr. Stokes rose to speak, the Secretary of State for Air, Sir Archibald Sinclair, pointedly rose from his seat and left the Chamber; he refused to be drawn back, even when Stokes called attention to his absence. Richard Stokes was therefore obliged to commence his speech, one of the most telling in the political history of the air offensive against Germany, without as it were the most prominent witness for the defence present.

In his speech he returned to the theme he had been representing consistently since 1942; he was not convinced by the Minister's repeated insistence on the precision of Bomber Command's attacks;

he also doubted the advantage of what he announced he would call 'strategic bombing', and commented that it was very noticeable that the Russians did not seem to indulge in 'blanket bombing'. He could see the advantage of their being able to say that it was the Western capitalist states which had perpetrated all these dirty tricks, while the Soviet Air Force had limited its bombing activities to what Mr. Stokes called 'tactical bombing'. In making this observation he was displaying remarkable prescience as the post-war years have demonstrated.

The question was whether at this stage of the war the indiscriminate bombing of large population centres was a wise policy; he read to the House an extract from a report in the *Manchester Guardian*—based on a German telegraphic dispatch—which contained the remark that tens of thousands of Dresdeners were now buried under the ruins of the city, and that even an attempt at the identification of the victims was proving hopeless.

> What happened on that evening of 13th February? [the newspaper asked]. There were a million people in Dresden, including 600,000 bombed-out evacuees and refugees from the East. The raging fires which spread irresistibly in the narrow streets killed a great many for lack of oxygen.

Stokes observed caustically that it was strange that the Russians seemed to be able to take great cities without blasting them to pieces, and added a question which clearly set even the Prime Minister's mind at work:

> What are you going to find, with all the cities blasted to pieces, and with disease rampant? May not the disease, filth and poverty which will arise be almost impossible either to arrest or to overcome? I wonder very much whether it is realised at this stage. When I heard the Minister [Sir Archibald Sinclair] speak of the 'crescendo of destruction', I thought: What a magnificent expression for a Cabinet Minister of Great Britain at this stage of the war.

Stokes called attention to the Associated Press dispatch from the S.H.A.E.F. Headquarters, and indeed read it out in full, thereby putting it on record for posterity; he asked once again the question he had asked so often before: Was terror-bombing now part of official Government policy? If so, then why was the S.H.A.E.F. decision released and then suppressed? And why was it that in spite of the reports having been broadcast from *Radio Paris*, printed throughout America, and even being relayed back to the German people, the British people 'are the only ones who may not know what is done in their name?' It was 'complete hypocrisy' to say one thing and do another. In conclusion Mr. Stokes asserted that the British government would live to rue the day that it had permitted these raids, and that the raids would stand for all time as a 'blot on our escutcheon'. These sentiments were doubly significant in that— expressed in more formal language—they were to reappear in a minute addressed by the Prime Minister to his Chiefs of Staff, warning Bomber Command to reconsider its 'terror' campaign.

Mr. Richard Stokes' speech was completed by 3.7 p.m. on 6th March, but he had to wait until after 7.50 p.m. for a reply from the Government. Commander Brabner, the Joint Under-secretary of State for Air, replied for Sinclair, although the latter had by now resumed his seat. His first action was to point out that although the S.H.A.E.F. report had been received in London on 17th February, it had been denied almost immediately. However, he also stated that he too would like to deny the report, there and then:

> We are not wasting bombers or time on purely terror tactics. It does not do the Hon. Member justice to come here to this House and suggest that there are a lot of Air Marshals or pilots or anyone else sitting in a room trying to think how many German women and children they can kill.

One curious aspect of the S.H.A.E.F. dispatch riddle remained unsolved: When the Associated Press dispatch was circulated and objections were raised in London to its publication, the first reaction from S.H.A.E.F. was that it could not be suppressed, *as it represented official S.H.A.E.F. policy*. To this remark, backed up by the promise of documentary evidence, Sir Archibald Sinclair himself felt obliged to reply: the report certainly was not true, and Mr. Stokes might take that from him.

Thus ended the last war-time debate on Bomber Command's policy; the British government had been able to safeguard its secret from the day that the first area raid had been launched on Mannheim on 16th December 1940, right up to the end of the war.

·   ·   ·   ·   ·

A similar storm had blown up around the Dresden and Berlin raids in Washington, not the violent parliamentary wrangling which had characterised the London controversy, but a more discreet exchange of letters between political and military leaders: On 6th

March General G. C. Marshall was instructed to reply to an inquiry from the American Secretary for War, Mr. Henry Stimson, apprising him both of Dresden's 'importance as a transportation centre' and also of the nature of this Russian 'request' for its neutralisation; whether Marshall's reply was convincing or satisfactory is not recorded; post-war research by the American Air Force historian Joseph W. Angell Jr., has suggested that Dresden was undoubtedly of importance as a military target, although, on the other hand, no documentary evidence has ever been produced as proof of any Soviet request specifying Dresden as a target for attack. General Marshall is understood to have read too much into the original memorandum by Soviet General Antonov at Yalta, which specifically mentioned two Eastern population centres, but not Dresden. In Washington the controversy subsided peacefully, and behind closed doors.

In fact, the Americans later launched their largest independent attack (572 sorties) on 'the marshalling yards' in Dresden on 17th April—a raid which the American Official History does not mention.

In London, however, the private debate did not decline, and indeed when the first reports began to arrive in London from neutral sources, it actually increased. Between 22nd and 24th March one of Zürich's leading newspapers published three articles by a Swiss eye-witness of the Dresden raids; there had been a large Swiss population in the city, and after the raids he had been able to escape to Switzerland and tell his story there. His report was one of the first authentic and full-length descriptions of the aftermath of the attack, and confirmed from an unquestionable source that the city was both shelterless, defenceless and devoid of military targets. It is also known that on 22nd February a representative of the International Red Cross visited Dresden to inquire after the fate of the prisoners of war, and his report may well have contained other information than about the numbers of prisoners among the casualties.

The suggestion in the S.H.A.E.F. dispatch was that the new terror-bombing policy had been formulated by unnamed 'Allied air chiefs', as distinct from their political leaders; this suggestion would prove useful when the time came for responsibility to be accorded in post-war years for an act of war which undoubtedly a section of the European community would be tempted to view in the same light as some of the excesses of the Axis powers.

·   ·   ·   ·   ·

The creation of a scapegoat who could convincingly be blamed for the brutality of the bombing offensive presented few difficulties, now that the prime necessity for the bomber weapon was past. The Official Historians noted:

> The Prime Minister and others in authority seemed to turn away from the subject [of the strategic air offensive], as though it were distasteful to them, and as though they had forgotten their own recent efforts to initiate and maintain the offensive.

On 28th March the Prime Minister signed a minute on the subject of the continued air offensive against German cities, and addressed it to his Chiefs of Staff: he was clearly deeply impressed by reports reaching the Government of the shock waves still coursing through the civilised world about the attacks on the Eastern population centres:

> It seems to me [he wrote] that the moment has come when the question of bombing of German cities simply for the sake of increasing the terror, though under other pretexts, should be reviewed. Otherwise we shall come into control of an utterly ruined land. We shall not, for instance, be able to get housing materials out of Germany for our own needs because some temporary provision would have to be made for the Germans themselves. The destruction of Dresden remains a serious query against the conduct of Allied bombing. I am of the opinion that military objectives must henceforward be more strictly studied in our own interests rather than that of the enemy.
>
> The Foreign Secretary has spoken to me on this subject, and I feel the need for more precise concentration upon military objectives, such as oil and communications behind the immediate battle-zone, rather than on mere acts of terror and wanton destruction, however impressive.

This was indeed a remarkable document. Two possible interpretations were placed upon it at the time by those who learned of its contents: either the minute was hastily penned in the heat and turmoil of great events, and at a time when the Prime Minister was under considerable personal strain, simply recording the lessons learned from the aftermath of Dresden; or it could be construed as a carefully-phrased attempt at burdening for posterity the responsibility for the Dresden raids on to his Chiefs of Staff, and, perhaps more appositely, on to Bomber Command and Sir Arthur Harris. Whatever the Prime Minister's motive for writing this minute— and it seems more charitable to accept the first alternative outlined above than the second—the Prime Minister had now made his own attitude abundantly clear; whereas Mr. Richard Stokes in the House of Commons had spoken of Dresden as an eternal 'blot on the escutcheon' of the British Government, the Prime Minister appeared to accord the blame to the bomber commanders.

. . . . .

It was to the credit of the Chief of the Air Staff that he was unwilling to accept this minute as it was worded, and the Prime Minister was obliged to compose a second one. It may well be that the Prime Minister had failed to appreciate the implication that could be read into the first draft of his minute. Within a few days, Bomber Command's senior officers had also learned of the existence of this minute, although there is some doubt whether Sir Arthur Harris himself was apprised. Sir Robert Saundby, as Harris' Deputy at High Wycombe, had a daily conversation with Sir Norman Bottomley on the scrambler telephone, and it is probable that during one of these informal briefings the Deputy Chief of the Air Staff described the nature of the Prime Minister's minute to Saundby. At any rate, Saundby recalls clearly the surprise and consternation felt by the Air Staff at what they felt to be implied by the Prime Minister: that he had been deliberately misled by his military advisers. What the Air Staff found most surprising, Saundby later related, was the suggestion that Bomber Command had been waging a purely terror offensive on its own initiative, 'though under other pretexts'.

The Official Historians refer to these 'severe words, though not on moral grounds, from the Prime Minister, though it was he himself who contributed much of the incentive to carry it [the Dresden raid] out'.

To the Chiefs of Staff [said Saundby] it looked as though it was an attempt on the Prime Minister's part to pretend that he had never ordered, or even advocated, that sort of thing. It was felt that it was not a fair picture of the Prime Minister to put on record, in view of what he had previously said and done. He was rather given to these impetuous flashes which were all very well in conversation, but not in a written minute. It might have led people to suppose that the Prime Minister himself had been misled by his military advisers to acquiescing in a policy of terror bombing, because they had dressed it up in 'military' garments. At that stage, the Prime Minister was beginning to look beyond the end of the war, however.

It was this possible implication to which the Chiefs of Staff objected. They were entirely in agreement with the main conclusion of the minute.

Having taken this firm stand against the phrasing of this minute of 28th March, the Chiefs of Staff—and the officers at Bomber Command who eventually heard the full story—were doubly surprised, when the Prime Minister withdrew it almost at once.

> We all thought it was a good point in his favour [added Sir Robert Saundby]. He was a big enough man to do it.

In the face of the Air Staff's objection to his first minute, the Prime Minister wrote a second one, more circumspectly worded than the first. It omitted any direct reference either to Dresden on the one hand, or to the advantage of 'terror-bombing' to the enemy on the other.

> It seems to me [the Prime Minister now wrote on 1st April] that the moment has come when the question of the so-called 'area bombing' of German cities should be reviewed from the point of view of our own interests. If we come into control of an entirely ruined land, there will be a great shortage of accommodation for ourselves and our Allies: and we shall be unable to get housing materials out of Germany for our own needs because some temporary provision would have to be made for the Germans themselves. We must see to it that our attacks do not do more harm to ourselves in the long run than they do to the enemy's immediate war effort. Pray let me have your views.

This minute was accepted without reservation by the Air Staff; as Sir Robert Saundby has pointed out, it tallied closely with their own opinions in any case. The prompt reaction of the Prime Minister is of course consistent with the view that his original words were not meant as an attack on anyone and he may have been considerably surprised at the way they were being interpreted.

.   .   .   .

It should here be recalled how on 26th January the Prime Minister had asked the Secretary of State for Air whether Berlin and no doubt other large cities in Eastern Germany should not be considered especially attractive targets; it was as a direct consequence of this minute to Sir Archibald Sinclair—a minute which the Prime Minister did not include in his memoirs—that Sir Arthur Harris was instructed to attend to Dresden, Leipzig and Chemnitz.

The views of the Foreign Secretary on the bombing offensive, as expressed in the second paragraph of the original minute to the Chiefs of Staff, were also a remarkable volte face: three years before, in a letter to the Secretary of State for Air, on 15th April, 1942, Mr. Anthony Eden had expressed a marked support for attacks on

German cities even though they did not contain major targets of importance:

> The psychological effects of bombing have little connexion with the military or economic importance of the target; they are determined solely by the amount of destruction and dislocation caused. . . . I wish to recommend therefore that in the selection of targets in Germany, the claims of smaller towns of under 150,000 inhabitants which are not too heavily defended, should be considered, even though those towns contain only targets of secondary importance.

Sir Arthur Harris claims that he was not informed about the wording of the Prime Minister's first minute, and never once in the post-war years did he call public attention to the part the Prime Minister had himself played in initiating the Dresden raids. Characteristically, even when he was personally informed that the Official History included this evidence of the way that the Prime Minister appeared to disown this type of operation, he refused at first to believe it could be true.

The Prime Minister in his memoirs deals with the tragedy of the Dresden massacre in the following words:

> We made a heavy raid in the latter month [February] on Dresden then a centre of communications of Germany's Eastern front.

No attempt was made to depict the scale of the personal tragedies inflicted on the city, nor the controversial background and consequences to the raid, although his memoirs do highlight his determined stand in persuading General Eisenhower not to plan for American troops to capture Dresden. Sir Arthur Harris was a commander who was neither vindictive nor demonstrative, and even if he had learned the nature of the 28th March minute the Prime Minister intended to address to his Chiefs of Staff, it is unlikely that the C.-in-C. of Bomber Command would have commented on it.

In the eighteen years that have passed since the Dresden affair, the number of times that Sir Arthur Harris has expressed himself in print about the part which he and his gallant force played in winning the war are few indeed; not so reticent have been his critics, of whom there are legions. The post-war Socialist Government, who refused to accept his official *Despatch* on the ground that it contained statistical appendices, especially harboured a deep resentment against a man who had commanded such admiration and respect among his men, and who had inevitably in the course of the war tangled with many of the Socialist Party's leading members—to emerge victorious as only Sir Arthur Harris could.

When the war-time Deputy Prime Minister, Clement Attlee, went on record in 1960 as thinking that Harris was 'never frightfully good', and insisted that 'all that attack on their cities' did not pay as much as if he had made more effective use of his bombs, and he 'might have concentrated more on military targets', Sir Arthur Harris did reply with asperity that:

> The strategy of the bomber force which Earl Attlee criticises was decided by H.M. Government, of which he [Earl Attlee] was for most of the war a leading member. The decision to bomb industrial cities for morale effect was made, and in force, before I became C.-in-C. Bomber Command.

No Commander-in-Chief would have been authorised to make such decisions, however adept he may have proved himself in their execution. Even then, Sir Arthur Harris afterwards admitted his deep regret at having been stung into participating in the public bombing controversy.

In the House of Commons Sir Arthur Harris did not lack his champions. Many former Bomber Command officers and personnel were among the ranks of new M.P.s returned in the 1946 election. One of them during a protracted Debate on 12th March 1946 called public attention to what had been disturbing many men in Bomber Command since the war. He referred at length to the question whether Bomber Command's operations in World War II were militarily and strategically justified, and added:

> This matter is precipitated in my mind by the signal fact that in the terminal honours, at the end of last year, in the New Year's Honours List, the name of the chief architect of Bomber Command, Sir Arthur Harris, was a conspicuous absentee. I know it will be agreed that in the Honours List six months previously, the Commander-in-Chief of Bomber Command received the Order of the G.C.B. But he retired from the Royal Air Force without any public expression of gratitude for the work—not that he had done—but which his Command had done under him. He left the country in a bowler hat for America [en route to South Africa] without having been included in the terminal Honours List. There is a feeling amongst the men who have served in Bomber Command that what appears to be an affront to the Commander-in-Chief of that Command is in fact an affront to the people who served in that Command, and of course to those who suffered casualties. We feel that if our organisation did a good job of work in all respects, as we believe it did, the least that should be done is that an honour should be conferred on its head, comparable to the honours paid to commanding officers of similar units, particularly in the other services.

Sir Arthur Harris, in fact, received a baronetcy in 1953; however, in their concluding survey of the great achievements of Bomber Command, the Official Historians, writing in 1961, commented:

> Naturally the scale of the offensive varied as also did the hazards encountered by the crews, but the whole front line was always involved. Regularly, and sometimes several times within a week, the Commander in Chief committed practically the whole of his front line to the uncertain battle and occasionally he committed almost the entire reserve as well. On each occasion he had to take a calculated risk not only with the enemy defences but also with the weather. On each occasion he might have suffered an irretrievable disaster. The enduring courage, determination and conviction of Sir Arthur Harris, who bore the responsibility for more than three years, deserves to be commemorated. So too does that of his Deputy, Sir Robert Saundby, who shared it with him and his predecessors for nearly five years.

Less than a year after the end of the war with the men of his former Command neither remembered in a national memorial nor offered a Campaign medal for their service in the most bloody and long-drawn-out battle of the war, he announced his decision to leave the United Kingdom to take up a commercial appointment in South Africa where he had spent most of his youth.

On 13th February 1946, the former Commander-in-Chief of R.A.F. Bomber Command sailed from Southampton on the first stage of his journey; that night, throughout Eastern and Central Germany, at 10.10 p.m. the church bells began to peal; for twenty minutes the bells rang out across the territories now occupied by a force as ruthless as any that the Bomber offensive had been launched to destroy; it was the first anniversary of the biggest single massacre in European history, a massacre carried out in the cause of bringing to their knees a people who, corrupted by Nazism, had committed the greatest crimes against humanity in recorded time.

AREA OFFENSIVE APPENDICES

Adviser on Pathology to
Army District IX,
GIESSEN,
November 1st, 1943.

To the Korps-doctor,
Auxiliary Korps H.Q. IX,
Army District IX,
KASSEL.

Report on the post-mortem examinations conducted in Kassel on 30.10.1943.

Five of the corpses selected by the chief Police-doctor in Kassel, *Herr* Senior Staff Police-doctor Fehmel, were dissected at the cemetery. The corpses concerned, of people killed during the terror-raid on Kassel on 22.10.1943, had been recovered from basements after several days. Closer particulars are not known. Two corpses were of male sex and about 18–20 years old; three were of women, of which one was between about 50 and 60 years old, the other two about 30 years old.

There were no external injuries manifest on the corpses, which were in a condition of high-degree putrefaction. A so-called corpse emphysema occasioned by septic bacteriae had affected the skin especially on the head, chest and lower extremities, as well as the inner organs of the individual corpses in varying degree. The skin was partly coloured a uniform red as a result of the haemolysis which had set in, but in extensive areas it was already coloured green. This green colouring is attributed to the action of the ammonium sulphide with the reduced haemoglobin, which had, of course, permeated the skin as a result of the haemolysis which had preceded it. *This green coloration, the analysis of which had been specially stressed at the conferences in Kassel, is as such purely a post-mortem manifestation of corpses, cannot be connected with any particular poisonous chemicals which might have been employed by the enemy during the terror-raid.*

During the post-mortem examinations there were no other grounds to suspect any particular poisonous chemicals used by the enemy, not even in the breathing system. The lungs were noticeably plethoric with little oedema. The body's blood was still fluid; there were small clots of fat in the heart. The blood sample collected from one case and examined by Director Dr. Wrede of the *Hessisches Chemische Untersuchungsamt,* [Chemical Analysis Bureau of

Hessen] in Giessen yielded a high content of carbon monoxide both by spectroscopic and chemical analysis, according to his communication telephoned to me. Thus death in this case, and very probably in the others too, can be attributed to carbon-monoxide poisoning. I should like to mention that in one case a major rupture of the lungs was observed, and there had been a minor effusion of blood in the pleural cavities concerned. It is probable that the said rupture was occasioned by the decompression wave following a heavy explosion, perhaps as a result of a so-called 'air-mine'.

The above mentioned carbon-monoxide poisoning can be explained simply by the burning buildings, set on fire by the large numbers of phosphorus bombs* dropped, a characteristic of the terror-raid on Kassel. In other cases lack of oxygen, heat effects and perhaps also smoke-inhalation played a role. The so-called 'heat-stroke' must have been the cause of death in many cases too, considering the enormous temperatures which were progressively developed in the cellars, and which were even observed when they were entered on 30.10.1943.

By way of conclusion, let me mention the case of a 60-year-old Major of my own military unit, who was dissected on October 30th in Hersfeld. This Major met his end in the basement of his house in Kassel, when his head was trapped between burning floor beams. On section, the skin of the head manifested extensive burns, and, moreover, severe necrosis and incipient superficial eschar formation on the mucous membrane in the windpipe and its branches, together with a confluent lobar pneumonia. Without doubt the necrosis and the eschar were merely the effect of the blazing heat. Finally, the case of the fireman should be touched upon, the case about which Professor Foerster (Marburg) reported to *Herr* Senior Staff Police-doctor Fehmel and which formed the starting point for the examinations and conferences on October 30th. After an attempt at getting in touch with *Herr* Professor Foerster on Saturday failed, I today had a telephone conversation with him from Giessen; Professor Foerster informed me that the fireman did not die of acrolin-poisoning but in his opinion of inhalation of high temperature [gases] which had resulted in the lung changes observed. In the case of this man there was also no green skin-coloration detectable. Thus this case is of no further importance.

Lastly, I repeat that the green skin-coloration of the Kassel corpses was simply a post-mortem corpse manifestation, and no other ground was found either to suspect that any special poisonous chemicals were employed by the enemy.

Signed: Professor HERZOG
Senior Staff Doctor,
Adviser on Pathology to
Army District IX.

* German practice was to describe practically all petrol-benzole-filled fire-bombs as 'phosphorus-bombs' on account of their minute phosphorus ignition capsules.

1. *The Theories.*

    (a) Professor Blackett's theory, stated in his *A Note on Certain Aspects of the Methodology of Operational Research; Examples from the Bombing Offensive,* was expressed thus: 'we should expect 0·2 [Germans] to be killed per ton of bombs dropped'.

    (b) Professor Lindemann's estimate was expressed in his minute of 30th March 1942 to the Prime Minister thus: 'One ton of bombs dropped on a built-up area . . . turns 100–200 people out of house and home.'

2. *The Raids.*

    The seven major raids or series of raids discussed in the book, and for which accurate data on bomb-loads *claimed* dropped (the operative statistic) as well as on numbers of killed and homeless are available are tabulated below. The figures are derived from the city Police President Reports, or where not available from the United States Bombing Survey. For Dresden the figure of homeless has little meaning, as in addition to its normal 650,000 population there were some 300,000 to 400,000 'homeless' refugees in the city before the raids. 75,358 homes were totally destroyed, and 11,500 badly damaged.

3. *The Statistics and the Estimates.*

Date	City	Tonnage claimed	Number homeless	Lindemann estimate	Number killed	Blackett estimate
28.3.42	Lübeck	441	25,000	(60,000)	320	(88)
28.5.43	Wuppertal-Barmen	1,895·3	118,000	(285,000)	2,450	(380)
24.7.43 ⎫ 27.7.43 ⎬ Hamburg 29.7.43 ⎭		⎧2,282⎫ ⎨2,074⎬ ⎩2,240⎭	753,000	(975,000)	43,000+	(1,320)
22.10.43	Kassel	1,823·7	150,000	(270,000)	5,830	(360)
11.9.44	Darmstadt	872	70,000	(130,000)	12,300	(175)
14.10.44	Brunswick	847	80,000	(123,000)	561	(170)
13.2.45	Dresden	2,978	400,000−	(450,000)	135,000	(600)

4. *The Observations.*

On average, Blackett's estimate was 51 times too low; Lindemann's was 1·4 times too high, if the average of his range of '100–200 homeless' per ton is taken; in almost every case the actual number of homeless is within his limits set in his minute.

APPENDIX III: RESULTS OF SURVEY OF BOMB DAMAGE IN DRESDEN, MADE BY CITY PLANNING AUTHORITY ON 11TH NOVEMBER 1945, BY DISTRICTS.

	Trachau	Weisser Hirsch	Cotta	City Centre	Blase-witz	Plauen	Leuben	
Including city areas	13, 14, 15, 16	17, 18, 19	7, 8, 9, 10	1, 2, 5, 6	3, 4, 21, 26	11, 12,	20, 22, 23, 24, 25	
City authority	I	II	III	IV	V	VI	VIII	

								Totals
Residential buildings: Wohngebäude								
Originally	5,382	5,579	4,343	3,420	6,325	4,666	5,755	35,470
Totally destroyed	267	802	1,228	3,308	3,700	954	857	11,116
Seriously damaged	277	220	320	16	371	625	173	2,002
Moderately damaged	251	104	621	28	363	100	143	1,610
Lightly damaged	1,631	3,011	819	68	1,891	1,516	4,385	13,211
Homes: Wohnungen								
Originally	30,157	27,800	39,087	28,410	51,000	22,800	20,746	220,000
Totally destroyed	2,940	4,491	9,000	24,866	25,000	5,930	3,131	75,358
Seriously damaged	1,106	1,232	3,000	242	2,000	3,650	270	11,500
Moderately damaged	1,263	582	2,200	428	1,200	790	643	7,106
Lightly damaged	6,524	16,862	11,700	420	22,000	8,210	15,220	80,936

The figures given are partly obtained by detailed survey, partly obtained by close estimates.

SOURCES

CHAPTER I

The references to the earlier air operations by R.A.F. and Luftwaffe are taken from an Air Ministry Note on the Bombing of Open Towns, 2nd June 1943; the description of the Freiburg raid is based on Anton Hoch's Paper reproduced in *Vierteljahresheft für Zeitgeschichte*, Heft 2, published in 1956 by Institut für Zeitgeschichte, Munich; D.N.B. statement is reproduced in *The Times* of 11th May 1940; the French denial, Air Ministry and Foreign Office statements, and British Government declarations appear in *The Times* and *Manchester Guardian* of 11th May 1940. Dr. Hans-Adolf Jacobsen's paper, Der deutsche Luftangriff auf Rotterdam, was originally published in *Wehrwissenschaftliche Rundschau* (May 1958), Frankfurt/Main; the treatment of Rotterdam in this Essay is based primarily on Jacobsen's work, but also in part on Air Ministry Historical Branch's Paper, published in *Grand Strategy*, H.M.S.O., United Kingdom Military Series, Vol. II, pp. 569 et seq., and on *Report of International Military Tribunal* (Nuremberg), Vol. XI, p. 214, 13th March 1946, and pp. 337 et seq., 15th March 1946. Washington Royal Netherlands Legation statement quoted verbatim from text in *New York Times*, 17th July 1940.

The Times statement commenting on U.S. reports of first Berlin raid was published in their edition of 3rd September 1940; Adolf Hitler's speech quoted from official N.S.D.A.P. published text; details concerning the Battle of Britain and the London Blitz are based on information drawn from the *Chronology of the Second World War*, Royal Institute of International Affairs, and *The Strategic Air Offensive against Germany 1939–1945*, and on figures supplied by the Air Historical Branch. Sir Robert Saundby's views expressed in personal communications with the author; the two 1940 Dresden raids were claimed in Air Ministry Bulletins Nos. 2235 and 1796. The Luftwaffe attack on Coventry is described in detail in *Defence of the United Kingdom*, by Basil Collier (H.M.S.O.) and *Royal Air Force 1939–1945*, Vol. 1.

CHAPTER II

The Butt Report and its background are reported on in *The Prof*, by Professor R. Harrod (London 1959), and *Strategic Air Offensive against Germany 1939–1945*, Vol. I, and Vol. IV. p. 205; Professor Zuckerman's experiments are described in *The Biological Effects of Explosions*, published by H.M.S.O. (London 1953), in *Physiological Effects of Blast*, by P. L. Krohn. D. Whitteridge and S. Zuckerman in *Lancet* 1942, and referred to in *Hansard*, Parliamentary Debates, Vol. 382, Col. 710. Professor Blackett's calculations are reproduced in his Paper, *A Note on Certain Aspects on the Methodology of Operational Research*, published by the British Association in their journal, Vol. V, No. 17, April 1948; Professor Lindemann's Paper is described extensively in *The Strategic Air Offensive against Germany, 1939–1945*, Vol. I, and its consequences in Professor Blackett: *Tizard Memorial Lecture*, 11th February 1960; Chief of Air Staff's inquiry referred to in *Royal Air Force 1939–1945*, Vol. II, p. 124; Casablanca Directive cited in full in *The Strategic Air Offensive against Germany 1939–1945*, Vol. IV, pp. 153–4. Development of H2S is described in *The Bomber's Eye*, by Dudley Saward (London 1959), and German counter-measures in *Sitzungsprotokolle der Arbeitsgemeinschaft Rotterdam* (Zehlendorf, 1943); the description of assistance rendered by captured airman is contained in minutes of meeting on 22nd June 1943; Questions asked about Bombing Restriction Committee appear in *Hansard*, Parliamentary Debates, Vol. 387, Col. 1622, and Vol. 393, Cols. 363–4.

The description of the attack on Wuppertal-Barmen is based on the descriptions published in the Air Ministry Bulletins, in *Royal Air Force 1939–1945*, Vol. II, pp. 290–1, and *The Strategic Air Offensive against Germany, 1939–1945*, Vol. II, pp. 131–2; the discussion of the target map 1 (g) (i) 32 for Wuppertal-Elberfeld is based on communication to the author from Sir Robert Saundby; further information about composition and delivery of the attack was communicated to the author by the Air Historical Branch; German defence timing is described in Major d.R. Dahl's *Erfahrungsbericht über Aufklärung und Gegenmassnahmen zum englischen Oboe-Verfahren*, dated (LGKdo VI, Münster) 30th May 1943. Dr. Goebbels' Wuppertal speech is quoted from printed text in *Völkischer Beobachter* of 19th June 1943.

CHAPTER III

The description of the Battle of Hamburg is based on the report by S.S.-Generalmajor Kehrl, Police President of Hamburg, on the raids of July and August 1943, dated (Hamburg) 1st December 1943; on the published accounts of the execution of the attacks contained in *The Strategic Air Offensive against Germany, 1939–1945*, Vol. II, pp. 138–167, and in *Royal Air Force 1939–1945*, Vol. III, pp. 5–11; on information and charts supplied by Pilot Officer J. Moorcroft. The narrative account of the development of the Corona counter-measure is based on personal communications from Air Vice-Marshal E. B. Addison, Sir Robert Saundby, and Mrs. Barbara Lodge, the W.A.A.F. officer referred to in *The Strategic Air Offensive against Germany, 1939–1945*, Vol. IV, p. 23; the success of the Kassel attack is described from material published in *The Strategic Air Offensive against Germany, 1939–1945*, Vol. II, p. 161, and from the unpublished Police

Sources

President's report, *Erfahrungsbericht zum Luftangriff vom* 22.10.43 *auf den LO. 1. Ordnung Kassel,* dated (Kassel) 7th December 1943. Material relating to the Henschel works is based on the unpublished report by Director R. A. Fleischer, dated (Kassel) 29th October 1943. Further information relating to the composition and delivery of the attack was communicated to the author by Air Historical Branch. The Luftschutzgesetz of 31st August 1943 is quoted from *Reichsgesetzblatt 1943*, p. 506. Dr. Goebbels' remark about the Ruhr was cited by his Press Adviser, Wilfried von Ofen, in his *Mit Goebbels bis zum Ende* (Buenos Aires), entry for 28th June 1943. Sinclair's explanation to Portal is contained in *The Strategic Air Offensive against Germany, 1939–1945*, Vol. III, p. 116. The outline of the Cripps' lecture and its consequences was described in communications from Canon L. J. Collins and Sir Robert Saundby to the author. House of Commons Debate of 1st December 1943 cited from *Hansard*, Parliamentary Report, Vol. 395, Col. 338.

Chapter IV

The V.1's effect on 1,000-pounder production is outlined in *Vision Ahead*, by Air Commodore P. Huskinson, London, 1949; The attack on Munich is based on the description contained in *No. 5 Bomber Group*, by W. J. Lawrence (London, 1951), and on the Police President's report (Unpublished), *Vorläufiger Abschlussbericht über den Luftangriff auf die Hauptstadt der Bewegung vom 25.4.44* (Munich, 25.4.1944). Further material was contained in personal communications to the author from Air Chief Marshal Sir Ralph Cochrane and Group Captain G. L. Cheshire, V.C. The Königsberg attacks were described from material published in Lawrence, op. cit., and *The Strategic Air Offensive against Germany, 1939–1945*, Vol. III, pp. 179–180. The Darmstadt attack was described from material published by Lawrence, op. cit., and from the Police Report as cited in a letter of 26th March 1946 to the American Military Government of Darmstadt; the St. Ludwig's Parish record is cited from *Die Pfarrchronik von St. Ludwig in Darmstadt, 1790–1945* (published in Darmstadt, 1957).

The description of the attack on Brunswick is based on the material published by Lawrence, op. cit., on photographs supplied by Flight Lieut. Steele; fire-fighting and A.R.P measures in the city are described from the published work of Rudolf Preschner, *Der Rote Hahn über Braunschweig* (Brunswick 1955). Other material comes from *Braunschweiger Tageszeitung*, 16th October 1944.

THE HISTORICAL BACKGROUND

Chapter I

The October 1944 request to Soviet government to bomb Dresden was referred to in *The Strategic Air Offensive Against Germany, 1939–1945*, by Webster and Frankland, Vol. III, p. 108, and is borne out in personal

communications with Major General M.B. Burrows, General J. R. Deane,
and Lieutenant Colonel Brinkman; The timing of the 7th October attack
and its execution and composition based on VIIIth Air Force Target
Summary; the results are cited from *Die Zerstoerung und Wiederaufbau von
Dresden,* by Professor Max Seydewitz (Dresden, 1955), with additional
information from various allied prisoners in Dresden; further details
about the effect of the raid, as also the information relating to the industrial
and military installations in the city, are extracted from statements by
Dresden inhabitants.

The Home Office Intelligence Section remark was from a minute
McIvor (Chief of Home Office Intelligence Section) to A. Nicholls, Air
Historical Branch, 12th April 1947. The description of the Dresden flack
dispositions was based largely on statement by Herr Götz Bergander,
Berlin; dates of firing from various private records; further information
from *United States Strategic Bombing Survey Summary Report,* 31st October 1945.

The treatment of the Soviet Army's January offensive is largely
based on *Geschichte des Zeiten Weltkrieges,* by Tippelskirch, p. 562 onwards;
Guderian's appeal to the Führer, and its negative response, is cited in
Tippelskirch, p. 613. The evacuation of the East and the circumstances
leading to the refugee influx into Dresden, together with the description
of the evacuation of Silesia and Pomerania, is based on *Dokumenation der
Vertreibung der Deutschen aus Ost-Mitteleuropa,* Vol. I, published by
Bundesministerium für Flüchtlinge, Vertriebene und Kriegsgeschädigte
(Bonn, 1951). (Other minor points have been extracted from Vols.
II–IV of this historical documentation, available also in English trans-
lation from Federal Ministry of Expellees, Refugees and War Victims,
Bonn.)

The narrative account of the 16th January 1945 air raid on Dresden
is from a statement to the author by Mr. Richard Dugger, former
bombardier of aircraft in 448th Bombardment Group, 2nd Air Division;
statistics are extracted from *VIIIth Air Force Target Summary* and from
published history of the 44th Bombardment Group, 2nd Air Division;
damage caused is described from reference to Seydewitz, op. cit., private
records, and Dresden inhabitants' statements. Death of British private
in raid is described in *Camp Diary of Arbeitskommando 1326,* Dresden; further
reference is from letter to parents of private Norman Lea, 5th February
1945.

Gauleiter Hanke's order forbidding the evacuation of Silesia by able-
bodied men was cited in *Tragedy of Silesia, 1945–1946* (Munich 1952),
p. 53. Bomber Command's information on prisoner-of-war situation was
recalled in personal communication from Sir Arthur Harris to the author;
detailed statistical information was supplied for this work by War Office
Records Department (London) and by Chief Archivist Sherrod East of
World War II Records Division, Washington; details of camps
in transit were based on further War Office communication to the
author, and on Camp Diary of Arbeitskdo, 1326. Refugee work in

Dresden stations was described in diaries of former R.A.D.w. J Maiden-führerin Margarete Führmeister, Mannheim, and Studienrat Hanns Voigt, and in statements of other citizens. The evacuation of Radio Breslau to Dresden was described in detail in three articles in Aktuell (Munich), Nos. 5–7, 1962; evacuation of Breslau Luftgaukommando described by Luftwaffe Major Victor Scheide to author. Closing remark from diary of Corporal S. Gregory.

Chapter II

The discussion of the relation between the Eastern population centre offensive and the *Thunderclap* plan is based on documents published in the Official History of *The Strategic Air Offensive against Germany, 1939–1945*, and in the history of the Army Air Forces in World War II, and on personal communications to the author from Marshal of the R.A.F. Sir Arthur Harris and Air Marshal Sir Robert Saundby. Berlin refugee scenes were described in *The Times*, London, 25th January 1945. Sir Norman Bottomley's instruction to Harris is quoted in full in Webster and Frankland, op. cit., Vol. IV, p. 301 (Appendix 28), as Letter Bottomley to Harris, 27th January 1945.

The discussion of the build-up to the American attack is based on *Army Air Forces in World War II*, Vol. III, p. 722 onwards, and on personal communications to the author from General C. A. Spaatz. British mission in Moscow complication described in personal communication from Lieutenant-General M. B. Burrows. War Office department's representations to C.I.G.S. on Dresden (see p. 37) is based on personal communication from Major (G. S.) D. Ormsby-Gore (Now Sir David Ormsby-Gore); the proposed new directive is quoted in *Army Air Forces in World War II*, Vol. III, p. 725; General Spaatz's comment about how it affected U.S. role is taken from personal communication to the author; Mr. Purbrick's Question about the bombing of Dresden, etc., was quoted from *Hansard*, Parliamentary Report, Vol. 407, Col. 2070.

Silesian refugee statistics were obtained from Documents on the Expulsion, op. cit.; description of Military Police redirection of refugees and soldiers is based on Aktuell, op. cit., and statement to author of one such policeman, Herr Horst Galle, Ruhr.

The description of Bomber Command's reaction to Dresden order is based on personal communications from Air Marshal Saundby; the text of the B.B.C. bulletin referred to was supplied to the author by the British Broadcasting Corporation, London.

The American cable to Hill is described in personal communication to the author from Soviet historian C. Platonov, President of the *Moscow Journal of Military History*, and subsequently confirmed by personal communication from Major-General E. W. Hill; Kuter's reaction to knowledge of new U.S.St.A.F. bombing policy contained in message of 13th February 1945 to General Spaatz, and its consequences are outlined in personal communication to the author from General Spaatz. Air Marshal Oxland's part is described in personal communication from Sir Arthur Harris to the author. The Dresden weather forecast was supplied by Air Ministry's Air Historical Branch 5 to the author.

THE EXECUTION OF THE ATTACK

CHAPTER I

There is a total lack of information in any of the histories already published, regarding the mounting and execution of the triple blow on Dresden; recourse has therefore been taken to the statements made to the author by the senior air officers who delivered the attack, and especially to the clear recollections of the two R.A.F. Master Bombers, Wing Commander Maurice A. Smith and Squadron Leader C. P. C. de Wesselow, who controlled the first and second attacks respectively. Wing Commander Smith especially kept a detailed personal record of his many operations, and this has provided invaluable material for the description of the first (No. 5 Group) attack.

The planning of the Dresden attack as a double blow supported by an American attack is referred to in Sir Arthur Harris' *Bomber Offensive* (New York, 1947), p. 242, and was elaborated in personal communications to the author from Sir Arthur Harris. The inclement weather for long-range flights is referred to in *Royal Canadian Air Force Overseas*, Sixth Year (Toronto, 1946), p. 116, and supported by communication to the author from the Air Historical Branch (Meteorological Records). That the American crews were briefed for the first attack on Dresden on 13th February is confirmed by Mr. Edmund Kennebeck (formerly of 384th Bombardment Group), and by General Carl A. Spaatz. The description of Loran equipment is from Wing Commander Smith, and from his article in *R.A.F. Review*, March 1946. The reason for selecting No. 5 Group for the first attack was elaborated in personal communication from Sir Arthur Harris; the quotation about sirens sounding was from City Archives of Flensburg, Northern Germany. The description of the plan of attack for the No. 5 Group raid is based on statements to the author by Wing Commander Smith, by his navigator Flight Lieutenant Leslie M. Page, by his Marker Leader, Flight Lieutenant William Topper, and by the pilot of the first Flare Force Lancaster, Wing Commander F. Twiggs. Composition of the Main Forces is based on statements printed in *Royal Air Force 1939–1945*, Vol. III, p. 269, on records kept by Flight Lieutenant Edward Cook (No. 3 Group), on details printed in *R.C.A.F. Overseas*, Sixth Year, p. 116, and on information recorded by Wing Commander Smith. Use of H2S Mark IIIF for Dresden reported in *Bomber's Eye* (London 1959), by Wing Commander Saward. The composition of the Pathfinder Force at Dresden was communicated to the author by Air Historical Branch; the operations executed parallel to that on Dresden were elaborated in a personal communication to the author by Air Vice-

Marshal D.C.T. Bennett; diversion attack on Magdeburg described by Wing Commander M. Sewell; preliminary oil attack on Böhlen referred to in *R.C.A.F. History*, already cited. Reactions of A.O.C.'s of No. 8 and No. 1 Groups outlined in personal communications to the authors from Air Vice-Marshal Bennett and Air Vice-Marshal Buckle respectively.

The description of the briefing of the first Master Bomber is based on personal communications from Wing Commander Smith and Air Vice-Marshal H. V. Satterley. The sector allocated to No. 5 Group for attack (as shown in the illustration on p. 119) was marked in white ink on the target map; Air Vice-Marshal Satterley says that this sector was marked out by Bomber Command, not by him.

CHAPTER II

The reference to the necessity to destroy the Mosquitos in the event of a forced landing was communicated to the author by Flight Lieutenant William Topper, Marker Leader. The description of the German Fighter Command Control Bunkers is based on General Adolf Galland's memoirs, *Die Ersten und die Letzten* (1955), and on communications to the author from Major Hans Kuhlisch. The description of V./NJG.5 and the attempts to defend Dresden is based on information supplied by Oberleutnant Hermann Kinder, Bielefeld. The Master Bomber's instructions and other dialogue are reproduced verbatim from the Transcript of Wire-Recorder, Operations Night 13th/14th February 1945, Dresden, which was kept for demonstration purposes after the triple blow, and from the navigator's logsheet in Group Captain Smith's aircraft, on which the timing was also incorporated. The photographs taken by Flight Lieutenant Topper's aircraft bear the official numbers (Coningsby) 2665–2668; the Dresden flak transmitter warnings were noted down by a former Dresden flak soldier, Herr Götz Bergander, Berlin. The public radio warning to the population was reproduced in *Aktuell* (Munich) 1962 No. 3.

CHAPTER III

The Dresden-Klotzsche meteorological records were quoted to the author by the German Central Meteorological Office, in Offenbach. Details of the Main Force briefings were quoted to the author by Messrs Hofmann, Abel, Lindsley and Jones, all former Bomber Command aircrew personnel. Other details were quoted to the author by Messrs Cook, Mahoney, Parry, and other airmen and officers of Bomber Command at the time. That the Air Ministry had spoken of poison gas plants, vital ammunition works, etc., was outlined in a communication from the Air Historical Branch to the author. The timing of the actual attack on Dresden, timed to commence at 1.30 a.m., is based on Operational Record Book of 635 Squadron, and on log book entries of Squadron Leader C. P. C. de Wesselow, Wing Commander H. J. F. Le Good (Deputy Master Bomber), and on the log book entries made by their crew members. The Air Ministry Communiqué which first announced Dresden attack was Air Ministry Bulletin No. 17506.

CHAPTER IV

The description of the Moscow end of the Dresden affair is based on a communication from Soviet historian C. Platonov, President of the *Journal of Military History*, Moscow, and is confirmed in subsequent correspondence with Major-General Edmund W. Hill; the composition of the American attacking force is described in *Army Air Forces in World War II*, Vol. III, p. 733; the routing of the bombers and fighter escorts is based on the account contained in 20th Fighter Group Intelligence Bulletin for 14th February 1945; the mistake made by the 398th Bombardment Group is outlined in communications to the author by bombardier Edward McCormack.

THE AFTERMATH

CHAPTER I

Smouldering clothing report from a statement by allied prisoners including Corporal E. H. Lloyd; Mockethal report came from Herr Hans Schmall, Giessen; Land Register Office report from Herr Hanns Voigt, Bielefeld. All quotations from the Hamburg Police report are extracted from *Geheim: Bericht des Polizeipräsidenten in Hamburg als örtliche Luftschutzleiter uber die schweren Grossangriffe auf Hamburg in Juli/August 1943* (unpublished). Dresden fire-storm area estimated from area more than 75 per cent destroyed in City Planning Office's map of November 1949. Railwayman's report quoted in *Zerstörung und Wiederaufbau von Dresden*, by Prof. Max Seydewitz (Dresden 1955). Railway truck report from personal communication from Herr Hans Kremhöller, Hamburg. Fire-brigade dispositions outlined in personal communication from Major-General Hans Rumpf, German Inspector of Fire Services, and in personal communication from Dresden Fire-Brigade director Ortloph. Fate of Bad Schandau brigade cited by Seydewitz, op. cit. Gauleiter's control operations described by Dipl.-Ingenieur Georg Feydt, in paper published in Ziviler Luftschutz (Koblenz) edition 4/1953.

The description of the Dresden fire-fighting organisation is assisted by report of Herr Günter Arnold, Hamburg, who was a messenger. The discussion of hospital facilities is based on Major-General Kehrl's Hamburg Police Report, op. cit., and on Seydewitz, op. cit. Description of A.R.P. measures in the city based on Feydt, op. cit., Seydewitz, op. cit., and communication from Herr Arnold. R.A.D. Transport Company commander cited was Herr Gerhard Nagel, Lippstadt. Second R.A.D. commander was Herr Heinrich Prediger, Unna. Cavalry captain cited was Dr. jur. Wolf Recktenwald, Bonn.

Ostra-allee tunnel system described by Frau Gertud Nimmow, Visselhövede. Post-office scenes described by Frau Eva Antons, Osnabrück.

CHAPTER II

Information concerning Austrian rescue gangs provided in personal communications from Mr. G. Conway, and from Herr Karl Forstner, Linz. Descriptions of rescue operations based on Feydt, op. cit., Herr Alfred Hempel, Dortmund, and Herr Hanns Voigt, Bielefeld. Quotation on Party welfare organisation taken from communication from Frau Elsa Ködel, Taubbischofsheim. Description of arrival of railway engineers based on personal communication to the author from General Erich Hampe, Bonn. Escape of Augsburg train confirmed by Herr Voigt. Refugee column-Führer was Herr Otto Thon, Krefeld. The evacuee who described the scene inside the children's train was Herr Heinz Buchholz, Köln-Sülz. The woman who escaped from the cellars under the Central Station was Frau Hanne Kessler, Wülfrath; further details from A.R.P. director of Station, Herr Schöne, cited by Seydewitz, op. cit. Description of victims in tunnels from personal communication from Herr Hans Kremhöller, the Panzer-Grenadier officer cadet.

The Friedrichstadt marshalling yards on the morning after the attack are clearly depicted on negative C. 4973 in the Government's picture archives Imperial War Museum. Quotation from the official American history was from *The Army Air Forces in World War II*, Vol. III, p. 731; R.A.F.'s post-raid report referred to was *Bomber Command Weekly Digest 148*, which, as was seen in later chapter, did not stress city's importance in 'unusual length'. Reference to the *Süddeutsche Zeitung* was from edition of 22nd February 1953.

CHAPTER III

Description of strafing-attack casualties among choirboys cited by Seydewitz, op. cit.; further reports of strafing from Herr Nagel, and from Prisoner of War John Heard. Breslau refugee woman's report contained in personal communication from her, Frau Anneliese Heilmeyer, Köln-Braunsfeld. Fate of invalids in Vitzthum school described by Seydewitz, op. cit. Use of Haus Sonnenstein reported by Major V. Scheide, Leverkusen. S.S. Command Centre, described by nurse who set up casualty station there, Frau Marga Staubesand, Köln-Lindenthal. The destruction of the Frauenklinik described in full in Seydewitz, op. cit. Difficulties caused by disposition of army commands on both sides of Elbe described by Dr. jur. Wolf Recktenwald, Bonn. Operation of prisoner-of-war camps in rescue work based on reports of prisoners, especially on diary of 1326 Camp. Free British Corps notes supplied by Mr. Brock. Executions of two prisoners for looting described in *1326 Kdo. Camp Diary*, in Camp correspondence, by Corporal Gregory, and by Mr. Brock. Execution of German looter described by R.A.D.w.J. Maidenführerin Margarete Führmeister, Mannheim.

Organisation of Vermisstenzentrale based entirely on diary of Herr Hanns Voigt, Bielefeld. Rubber-glove stock position outlined in Georg Feydt, op. cit.; comparison with Kassel based on *Erfahrungsbericht zum*

247

Sources

Luftangriff von 22.10.1943 auf den Luftschutzort 1. Ordnung Kassel, by the Kassel Police President. Inner City street which was impassable reported by Herr Voigt; melted utensils reported by Herr Hans Schmall. Shape of mother and child described in letter of Herr C. T. Rademann (now Helmstedt) to his mother, dated 22nd February 1945. Soldier who described victims lying in streets was Herr Rudolf Schramm, of Buchholz, near Hamburg.

Chapter IV

The suggestion that Dr. Goebbels was preoccupied with the Morgenthau plan in his propaganda utterances is borne out by *Völkischer Beobachter* and *Das Reich* throughout February 1945. Quotation of the Inspector of German Fire Services was extracted from Major-General Rumpf's memoirs, *Der Hochrote Hahn* (Darmstadt 1952), p. 135; opposite point of view was taken by Colonel Edgar Petersen on 23rd July 1945; his view was quoted in *The Strategic Air Offensive against Germany 1939–1945*, Vol. III, p. 224. Description of water tanks in Altmarkt comes from Hanns Voigt and others. Description of Lindenau-platz comes from Hans Schmall; description of Seidenitzer-platz from Margarete Führmeister. Shooting of Dresden Zoo animals described by Hans Schmall and Feydt, op. cit. R.A.D.w.J. situation in Dresden before the raids described by Margarete Führmeister, and based on *Aufgabe und Aufbau des Reichsarbeitsdienstes*, Dr. Phil. Wolfgang Scheibe (Leipzig 1942). K.H.D. tram conductresses described in personal communication from Herr Rademann. The figure of 39,773 appeared in Feydt's article, op. cit., for the number of identified dead. Figure for Heidefriedhof cited by Seydewitz, op. cit. Quotation from Obergärtner Zeppenfeld cited by Seydewitz.

Chapter V

Incident in Markgraf-Heinrich-Strasse described by Frau Kate Jaeschke, Koln-Klettenberg. The greater part of the description of the removal of the victims is based on Herr Voigt's diary. The Top Secret order of the day was quoted in Seydewitz, op. cit.

NEITHER PRAISE NOR BLAME

Chapter I

The first full length report on the Dresden raids was issued by the Air Ministry in their Bulletin No. 17493, at 8.46 a.m. on 14th February 1945; the (secret) *Bomber Command Weekly Digest No. 148* is as quoted to author by Air Historical Branch 5. The text of the 6.00 p.m. and 9.00 p.m. news bulletins on 14th February was communicated to the author by the British Broadcasting Corporation, London. The United States State Department statement was cited in *New York Herald Tribune* on 12th

Sources

February 1953; the *Manchester Guardian* statement was contained in its Bonn correspondent's report on 14th February 1955.

The German High Command communiqué was published in *Völkischer Beobachter* on 15th February 1945; there was no further reference to Dresden in this paper until 6th March 1945.

All foreign-language broadcasts about the Dresden raids and other raids on Eastern population centres are in the text extracted from confidential B.B.C. Monitoring Reports (unpublished) No. 2039 to No. 2045 inclusive, covering the period from 14th February to 19th February, inclusive. The Scandinavian Telegraph Bureau report is cited in *Daily Telegraph* of 17th February 1945.

The description of the 15th February air offensive is based on *Army Air Forces in World War II*, Vol. III, pp. 731–2, and the published histories of 100th, 447th, 441st, 34th, 390th, 384th, and 401st Bombardment Groups; the official answer to critics was published as a *Times* editorial on 17th February 1945.

The narrative account of the S.H.A.E.F. press conference and its consequences is based on *Army Air Forces in World War II*, Vol. III, pp. 726–7, and on personal communications from Air Commodore C.M. Grierson to the author; the text of the Associated Press despatch is extracted from the version cited in House of Commons by R. Stokes, *Hansard*, Parliamentary Debates, Vol. 408, Col. 1901.

CHAPTER II

The description of the air offensive of 2nd March 1945 is based on *Army Air Forces in World War II*, Vol. III, p. 739, on private records of former Dresden citizens and account contained in 34th Bombardment Group's published history; particular details were supplied by Lt. Malcolm E. Corum, lead bombardier of the 34th Bombardment Group, 3rd Air Division. Further information was extracted from published histories of 100th, 390th, 401st and 447th Bombardment Groups; also from *Camp Diary of Arbeitskdo. 1326, Dresden-Scharfenbergerstr.* The German propaganda leaflet referred to was leaflet 1325/3 45, about Dresden, entitled: *The White Feather for Gen. Doolittle.*

The Washington controversy is described in *Army Air Force in World War II*, Vol. III, p. 731, citing Memo for Stimson from Marshal, drafted by Loutzenheiser, 6th March 1945. Results of American post-war research into Dresden raids were contained in unpublished paper *Study on the Allied Raids on Dresden*, by Joseph W. Angell Jr., United States Air Force Historical Branch, Washington. Report of International Red Cross was referred to in prisoner-of-war statement to the author by Chief Archivist Sherrod East of World War II Records Division, Washington.

Mr. Churchill's minute of 28th March and 1st April 1945 are cited in full in *The Strategic Air Offensive against Germany 1939–1945*, by Webster and Frankland, Vol. III, pages 112 and 117 respectively. Sir Robert Saundby's views were contained in personal communication, with the author, referred to earlier. The 1942 attitude of Mr. Eden to the strategic air offensive is reproduced in the minute published in Webster and Frankland, op. cit., Vol. III, p. 115. Sir Arthur Harris' reaction to the first news of Churchill's intended minute of 28th March was contained in a personal communication to the author. The ground for the rejection of the Harris Despatch was also a personal communication from Sir Arthur Harris to the author. Earl Attlee's remark was made during an interview reported verbatim in *Sunday Times* on 27th November 1960; Harris' reply was in a letter published in *Sunday Times* on 22nd January 1961. Wing Commander Millington's speech in House of Commons drawing attention to 'affront' to Bomber Command cited from *Hansard*, Parliamentary Debates, Vol. 420.

INDEX

*Note: Items referring exclusively to the Allied attacks
on Dresden are indexed under 'Dresden'*